THE MAN AND HIS TIMES

ABRAHAM LINCOLN'S
EXTRAORDINARY ERA

K. M. KOSTYAL

ABRAHAM LINCOLN PRESIDENTIAL LIBRARY AND MUSEUM

IN ASSOCIATION WITH

NATIONAL GEOGRAPHIC

WASHINGTON D.C.

"I LEAVE YOU, HOPING THAT THE LAMP
OF LIBERTY WILL BURN IN YOUR BOSOMS
UNTIL THERE SHALL NO LONGER
BE A DOUBT THAT ALL MEN ARE
CREATED FREE AND EQUAL."

CONTENTS

Page 1: Lincoln tucked notes, mail, and speeches inside his trademark stovepipe hats.
Page 3: The "Lincoln Gun," a 15-inch Rodman Columbiad, guards Fort Monroe, Virginia.
Page 4: Lincoln appears serious but resolved in this portrait taken on November 8, 1863—just 11 days before he delivered his Gettysburg Address.
The photographer Alexander Gardner took a number of memorable photographs of Lincoln in his last years.

FOREWORD

THE IDEA BEHIND THIS ORIGINAL LOOK AT OUR MOST WRITTEN-ABOUT PRESIDENT IS TO PLACE the events of Abraham Lincoln's life into the context of larger happenings in both the country and the world. As a figure in our historical imagination, Lincoln looms so large that at times we fail to take sufficient account of the forces beyond the United States that had a direct bearing on the struggle for the Union, the outcome of the war, and the emancipation of the slaves.

As *Abraham Lincoln's Extraordinary Era* shows, the tensions between America and Britain that would play an important role during the Civil War began during Lincoln's childhood when the British boarded United States merchant ships to force British soldiers back to England to fight for the Crown. Two decades later, shortly after Lincoln lost his first run for state legislature, Britain abolished slavery throughout its Empire, instilling in the hearts of the English masses a love of freedom that would prove critical three decades later in keeping Britain from recognizing the Confederacy when its economic interests allied her with the cotton-producing South.

In the 1830s, the young naturalist Charles Darwin, born on the same February day in 1809 as Abraham Lincoln, set sail on his famous five-year voyage on the *Beagle* that would culminate in his groundbreaking work, *Origin of the Species*, published the year before Lincoln won the presidency.

In 1837, when Lincoln moved to Springfield, two British inventors successfully transmitted messages along a telegraph line. Six years later, Samuel Morse received a congressional appropriation to lay a telegraph line between Washington, D.C., and Baltimore. Advances in this miraculous new system during the Civil War allowed Lincoln to keep in touch daily with army officials, camps, and forts throughout the entire Union.

In the 1840s, the combination of political upheavals in Europe and the potato famine in Ireland caused millions of Irish and German citizens to emigrate to the United States. The unprecedented flood of immigrants led to the emergence of a nativist movement that would play a significant role in the politics of the 1850s, when Lincoln entered the national political arena.

In 1852, the publication of Harriet Beecher Stowe's *Uncle Tom's Cabin* created a literary sensation, awakening such powerful compassion for slaves and indignation against slavery that many previously unconcerned Americans were transformed into advocates for the antislavery cause.

In 1861, the year that Lincoln assumed the presidency, Tsar Alexander II freed the serfs in Russia. Two years later, Lincoln issued his historic Emancipation Proclamation, instilling in Leo Tolstoy, the greatest writer of the age, a passionate admiration for our 16th president. "Washington was a typical American," he said. "Napoleon was a typical Frenchman, but Lincoln was a humanitarian as broad as the world. He was bigger than his country—bigger than all the Presidents together."

Through this fascinating approach to the Lincoln story, we see Lincoln rise beyond Kentucky and Illinois, beyond Washington and his country, to belong to the ages, as Stanton said upon his death.

—DORIS KEARNS GOODWIN

OPPOSITE: *Mary Lincoln poses with the couple's adored younger sons, Willie (left) and Tad.*

INTRODUCTION

"WRITING—THE ART OF COMMUNICATING THOUGHTS OF THE MIND, THROUGH THE EYE—IS THE great invention of the world," argued Abraham Lincoln in 1859 when explaining the wonders of inventions throughout history. Lincoln held a Western, Judeo-Christian perspective, claiming that his inspiration for the talk came from a cursory review of the book of Genesis. The hardscrabble of a frontier upbringing did not expose Lincoln directly to the larger world. The physical labor required to raise crops and keep his father's farm in good repair took up most of the young Abraham's time. It was only when his parents and siblings slumbered that Lincoln assumed a seat by the glowing embers of the fire to read. Books became a source of self-education for the precocious youth, as well as a source of adventure and escape from the mind-numbing routine of the Indiana frontier. Books and the written word became the chief means by which Lincoln learned about unfamiliar ideas and cultures.

There is no direct line between the books Lincoln read and their influence on his thought. An examination of some of the titles he read as a youth, however, suggests how books shaped his views of the wider world. The two most influential books that continued to be of interest in later life were *Aesop's Fables* and the Bible. The moral lessons of the Greek slave Aesop reinforced the Baptist interpretations of the Bible. The *Arabian Nights* offered sheer escapism, introducing Lincoln to "The Seven Voyages of Sinbad the Sailor" and "Aladdin and his Wonderful Lamp." Lincoln's cousin, Dennis Hanks, recalled telling him the book was "a pack of lies," to which Lincoln reportedly quipped, "Mighty fine lies." John Bunyan's *The Pilgrim's Progress,* Daniel Defoe's *Robinson Crusoe,* and James Riley's *An Authentic Narrative of the Loss of the American Brig Commerce ... with an Account of the Sufferings of Her Surviving Officers and Crew ...* also were popular books that the young Lincoln repeatedly read. Set in mythical or foreign lands, these books emphasized the importance of discipline, perseverance, and moral character—traits that reflected Lincoln's own approach to life. Captain James Riley's account of being shipwrecked off the coast of northwest Africa, the capture of his crew, and their eventual enslavement and escape provide a thrilling adventure story, as well as a moral lesson against the evils of slavery. Riley describes an institution not based on skin color but on mere power of one individual over another. This is a lesson Lincoln took to heart.

At New Salem, Illinois, Lincoln discovered William Shakespeare's plays and the poetry of Robert Burns through his friendship with Jack Kelso. Reflecting the spirit of the fictional character Natty Bumppo, Kelso lived off the land and later left New Salem when it became too crowded. But Kelso was also a literate man who impressed on Lincoln the rich legacy of English poets and playwrights. It was also at New Salem where Lincoln discovered the writings of deists Thomas Paine, Volney, and Voltaire. English common law traditions were integral to the study of law, and Lincoln read and mastered the writings of Blackstone and Chitty. His stint as a surveyor led him to study geometric principles established by the Greek mathematician Euclid. Lincoln would later revisit Euclid when serving in Congress to strengthen his skills of logical reasoning.

OPPOSITE: *In Confederate Atlanta, black people were sold along with china, glass, or any other commodity.*

New Salem offered Lincoln a wider introduction to the world. Life in this frontier village was anything but primitive. Established as a commercial town, its founders and inhabitants were part of a network tying them to global trade. Queensware cups and plates from Staffordshire, England, graced frontier tables. When Lincoln arrived in New Salem in 1831, a thriving trade between New Orleans and St. Louis was already well developed, as steamboats loaded with foreign manufactured goods, spices, and liquor made their way into the western frontier. Lincoln and other Illinois politicians sought to further refine the transportation infrastructure in hopes of expanding the movement of commerce and people.

In Lincoln's Illinois, pockets of French and English settlements remained from Old World ambitions for empire-building. Newer immigrants from Ireland, Germany, Italy, Portugal, Wales, and Sweden arrived to farm, build canals and railroads, and mine the rich coal seams, creating a crazy-quilt of different cultures, religions, and political perspectives. Free and indentured Blacks were also a part of Lincoln's Illinois, including his hometown of Springfield. His barber, William de Fleurville (sometimes "Florville"), was from Haiti. While Lincoln's world remained predominantly influenced by Western European culture, he also realized political sensitivity was required to forge winning coalitions.

Like most Americans of his era, Lincoln was less interested in events transpiring abroad than in the fragile state of domestic affairs. The ongoing American experiment of a democratic republic originated during the Western European Enlightenment. Claiming to throw off the shackles of monarchs and replace it with a mixed system of direct and indirect representation, the Constitution had established a government based on laws and not on the cult of personality. Abolitionists and antislavery advocates understood the contradiction between the aspirations of the Declaration of Independence that declared "all men are created equal" and a Constitution that condoned human bondage. Lincoln was well aware of this contradiction, and he knew that foreign governments viewed it as the most glaring example of American hypocrisy.

The American Civil War provided the ultimate test of both the ideals embodied in the Declaration of Independence and the system of checks and balances set forth in the Constitution. For Lincoln, the preservation of the Union was paramount to preserving the central ideas of the democratic republic. These ideals were necessary both for the survival of Lincoln's vision of America and also to offer an example to the larger world. Early in the war, Secretary of State William Seward suggested that a foreign conflict could reunite Americans to defeat a common enemy. To Lincoln, the absurdity of waging war with a foreign power pointed to the larger problem: The threat to America was not external but rather America's own internal conflict over slavery. Lincoln expressed his view this way: "This is essentially a People's contest . . . a struggle for maintaining in the world, that form, and substance of government, whose leading object is, to elevate the condition of men—to lift artificial weights from all shoulders . . . to afford all, an unfettered start, and a fair chance, in the race of life."

As the war progressed, it became clear that preserving the Union could not occur without emancipation for Blacks. The "new birth of freedom" offered by Lincoln at the dedication of the National Soldiers' Cemetery at Gettysburg, Pennsylvania, hoped to expand the boundaries of freedom to include Blacks in the promise of America. But the new birth of freedom had another message as well: "that government of the people, by the people, and for the people shall not perish from the earth." For Lincoln, the American example was one of the great gifts it had to offer a world of monarchs and military leaders. A year earlier, Lincoln clearly outlined this theme in his annual message to Congress: "Fellow citizens, we cannot escape history … The fiery trial through which we pass will light us down, in honor or dishonor, to the latest generation … In *giving* freedom to the *slave,* we assure freedom to the *free*— honorable alike in what we give, and what we preserve. We shall nobly save, or meanly lose, the last, best hope of earth."

Lincoln understood that he was not fully in control of events or their outcome. But he was part of the historical current and knew he would be judged for what he did or did not do to affect events in his time. It is no surprise that Lincoln's sensitivity to the public pulse, his uncanny timing, and his eloquence in explaining why the outcome of the war mattered to a war-weary nation places him among a small group of celebrated leaders in world history. Extolled by figures ranging from the Russian novelist Leo Tolstoy to the great civil rights leader Dr. Martin Luther King, Jr., Lincoln continues to be a window into America's history, while he casts a larger light, beyond time and geographic space.

—THOMAS F. SCHWARTZ
Illinois State Historian

1858

1858

1860

1861

1863

1863

1864

1865

"HE MUST UNDERSTAND EVERY THING—EVEN TO
THE SMALLEST THING—MINUTELY AND EXACTLY …
AND, WHEN IT WAS FIXED IN HIS MIND TO SUIT
HIM, HE … NEVER LOST THAT FACT."

SARAH BUSH LINCOLN, ABRAHAM'S STEPMOTHER

[CHAPTER ONE]

THE SHORT AND SIMPLE ANNALS OF THE POOR
1809-1830

I WAS BORN FEB. 12, 1809, IN HARDIN COUNTY, KENTUCKY. MY PARENTS WERE BOTH *born in Virginia, of undistinguished families … My paternal grandfather, Abraham Lincoln, emigrated from Rockingham County, Virginia, to Kentucky about 1781 or 2, where, a year or two later, he was killed by indians … when he was laboring to open a farm in the forest. His ancestors, who were quakers, went to Virginia from Berks County, Pennsylvania … My father [Thomas], at the death of his father, was but six years of age, and he grew up, litterally without education."*

So Lincoln began a biographical sketch in 1859, when he was a presidential candidate. The sketch was plainspoken, the bare skeleton of a life. It read almost like an apology—undistinguished heritage, lack of education ("when I came of age I did not know much"), little opportunity ("I was raised to farm work"). But, speaking of his rise as a politician, there is a final proud coda: "What I have done since then is pretty well-known."

In the years to come, Lincoln became one of the immortals of history, his forbearing face and lanky form among the most recognizable—and comforting—likenesses in the world. And the story of his childhood struggles became legendary. He embodied the quintessence of the American dream. If this backwoods boy could save a nation, there was a future full of promise for everyone.

Lincoln's frontier boyhood has been romanticized in art (opposite) and legend. As an adult, Lincoln perpetuated the myth of himself as simple and self-taught. Above, the tattered flag that inspired Francis Scott Key to write the "Star-Spangled Banner."

[15]

NOTABLE DATES

■ **1809:** Abraham Lincoln is born on February 12 in Kentucky to Nancy and Thomas Lincoln.

■ **1810:** The U.S. conducts its third census. The population of 7.2 million includes 1.2 million slaves and 60,000 immigrants.

■ **1811:** The British expand their empire by conquering Java and the West Indies.

■ **1812:** The U.S. declares war on Great Britain for violating its maritime rights.

■ **1815:** Defeated at Waterloo, Napoleon goes into exile on St. Helena.

■ **1816:** The Lincoln family moves from Kentucky to Indiana. Land is available for direct purchase, and slavery is prohibited.

■ **1819:** America acquires Florida from Spain in exchange for recognizing the boundary line that confirms Spanish possession of Texas, New Mexico, and California.

■ **1820:** The Missouri Compromise is passed by Congress, admitting Missouri as a slave state and igniting the slavery conflict.

■ **1821:** Frenchman Jean-François Champollion deciphers the Rosetta Stone, enabling scholars to read Egyptian hieroglyphics.

■ **1824:** Three years after declaring independence from Spain, Mexico becomes a republic.

■ **1825:** The Erie Canal opens, stretching 363 miles to connect the Great Lakes and the Atlantic.

■ **1830:** Scottish geologist Sir Charles Lyell publishes *Principles of Geology*, which paves the way for evolutionary thinking.

An English cartoon entitled "The Fall of Washington—or Maddy in Full Flight" depicts President James Madison and another official fleeing in August 1814 as the British set fire to the capital's few public buildings.

At Lincoln's birth in 1809, America did seem full of promise. Virginian James Madison, the fourth President of the fledgling nation and "Father of the (very recent) Constitution" had been elected to succeed another Virginian, Thomas Jefferson. During Jefferson's two terms in office, he had doubled the country's size with the 1803 Louisiana Purchase—an enormous tract west of the Mississippi River. Industrialization was in the air, and inventor Robert Fulton and his promoter Robert Livingston (the former minister to France who helped negotiate the Louisiana Purchase) had launched the first successful steamboat on the Hudson River. It would change the course of commerce throughout the world.

Meanwhile, new settlers moving onto the American frontier had aroused the hostilities of the Native American inhabitants. In 1809, the year of Lincoln's birth, the Shawnee leader Tecumseh, "Shooting Star," began rallying tribes in the Mississippi Valley to unite against white encroachment. "The Great Spirit gave this great island to his red children," Tecumseh declaimed. "They [the white men] have driven us from the sea to the lakes—we can go no further."

Lincoln's own family was among the settlers pressing west into Indian lands. His Quaker ancestors had moved gradually inland and down the spine of the Alleghenies to the Shenandoah Valley, where his grandfather was born. From a respected but no longer Quaker family in the valley, he had inherited a productive farm, but was willing to give that up for bigger dreams. Spurred on by the promise of his distant relative Daniel Boone—that there were new lands and opportunities in Kentucky (then a part of Virginia)—Lincoln's grandfather had headed west in 1782 with his wife and five children. Like other pioneers, they were willing to brave Indian attacks, bears, panthers, and the wilderness to settle the newest frontier. The constant fight for survival must have set a stamp on each of the Lincoln children.

Thomas Lincoln, who would become the second Abraham's father, was working in the fields alongside his father and two older brothers when Indians attacked. The boys' father was killed, and the oldest brother, Mordecai, ran to the cabin, grabbed a gun, and shot the attacker. What emotional toll these attacks left on Thomas is unknown, but his son, Abraham, would later say that "the story of [my grandfather's] death by the Indians, and of Uncle Mordecai, then fourteen years old, killing one of the Indians, is the legend more strongly than all others imprinted upon my mind and memory."

> "THE SALE ASSURES FOREVER THE POWER OF THE UNITED STATES, AND I HAVE GIVEN ENGLAND A RIVAL WHO, SOONER OR LATER, WILL HUMBLE HER PRIDE."
>
> NAPOLEON, ON THE LOUISIANA PURCHASE

At an early age, the fatherless Thomas had to make his own way. Working as a carpenter, cabinetmaker, and hired laborer, he managed to cobble together enough money to buy land in Hardin County, Kentucky. In 1806, he married Virginia-born Nancy Hanks and the two had a daughter they named Sarah. Thomas was reportedly a good-natured, honest man and a fine storyteller (traits Abraham inherited). Said a neighbor, Thomas "was not a lazy man but a piddler, always doing but doing nothing great." Still, he was reasonably prosperous, and within a few years Thomas was able to buy another wilderness tract about ten miles away. He called it Sinking Spring because it had a healthy spring that originated deep inside a cave. In the one-room log cabin he built near the spring, his second child, Abraham, was born in the winter of 1809.

The boy had no recollection of his birthplace; when he was two years old the family moved again, away from the unproductive Sinking Spring Farm to a tract ten miles north on Knob Creek. This was the earliest childhood home Lincoln remembered.

War with Britain

As the Lincolns settled in to their first year on the new farm, in the East the country was readying for war. In Congress, war hawks were spoiling for a fight with Britain that had been building for a decade. Since the turn of the century, Britain and other European powers had been locked in combat with France, as Napoleon swallowed Europe and parts of the Middle East. His navy had suffered a cataclysmic defeat at British hands in the 1805 Battle of Trafalgar, and Britain

Published a year after the Louisiana Purchase, an 1804 map shows the United States broadening. Extending west from the Mississippi River to the Rocky Mountains, the purchase doubled the size of the U.S. American minister to France Robert Livingstone, who helped negotiate the purchase, called it "the noblest work of our whole lives."

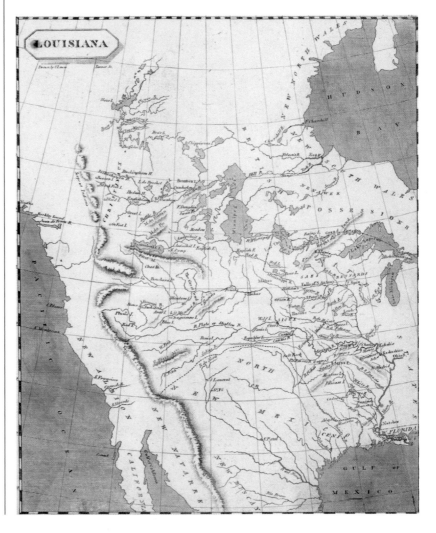

now ruled the high seas. But its overextended navy was considered a "floating hell" that few would voluntarily join. Instead, the British "impressed"—forced into service—seamen, who in turn deserted, many becoming crewmen on American vessels. Boarding U.S. merchant ships on the high seas, the British impressed these men back into service for the crown. In 1807, when the U.S. *Chesapeake* refused to be boarded by the British *Leopard*, the *Leopard* fired on it. To avoid further incidents of this sort, President Jefferson declared an embargo prohibiting American ships from trading with foreign ports. The ill-conceived embargo law plunged the U.S. into financial depression and did little to deflect tensions with Britain.

British Canada was also meddling in America's affairs. Crown agents there were supporting Native Americans—including the powerful Shawnee warrior Tecumseh—in their fight against American settlers. The confederacy of tribes that Tecumseh had formed had been smashed by William Henry Harrison's forces at the 1811 Battle of Tippecanoe in northern Indiana, but the Indian threat along the western and northern frontiers was still a serious concern.

Two young firebrands in Congress, South Carolina representative John Calhoun and Kentucky's Henry Clay, were agitating to annex Canada and expel the British. Native American flare-ups in Florida added to the momentum for war. Florida was in Spanish hands, and Spain was an ally of Britain. Should the U.S. go to war with Britain and prevail, America would have an excuse for claiming the Spanish territory of Florida.

In June 1812, the nation's fourth President, James Madison, bowed to pressure from the war hawks. Appearing before Congress, he declared, "We behold … on the side of Great Britain a state of war against the United States, and on the side of the United States a state of peace toward Great Britain." He asked for a declaration of war, and within three weeks the Senate, by a narrow vote, gave it to him. For two years the outmanned, outsupplied American forces battled the British, who managed to invade Washington and set fire to the Capitol and the President's House.

WORLD PERSPECTIVE

The Louisiana Purchase

The year before Thomas Jefferson was elected President of the U.S., Napoleon Bonaparte engineered a coup d'état that made him ruler of France. While Jefferson focused on creating an educated, enlightened America, Napoleon pursued his dream of a vast French empire; the New World quickly captured his attention. Negotiating a secret treaty with Spain, France took back what it had once owned—the Louisiana Territory, encompassing the Mississippi Valley and the lands west of the river to the headwaters of the river's tributaries in the Rocky Mountains. With New Orleans under French control, Jefferson began to realize that Napoleon had designs on America.

He dispatched American envoy James Monroe to Paris to persuade the French to sell New Orleans and Florida to the U.S.; he could offer up to ten million dollars. In the meantime, Napoleon faced a crisis on the West Indian island of Saint-Domingue (now Haiti) where former slave Toussaint L'ouverture had led a successful uprising. Though Napoleon's forces briefly prevailed against the rebellion, they succumbed to yellow fever. Napoleon had also planned to send his troops to take Louisiana, but his ships had been frozen all winter in a Dutch harbor.

Reconsidering his plans of empire, Napoleon sent his minister Talleyrand to approach the current American minister to his court, Robert Livingston, with a startling question:

An elegantly bound volume contains the original Louisiana Purchase Treaty, signed in Paris on April 30, 1803.

How much would the U.S. pay for the entire Louisiana Territory, which would double the size of the U.S.? Ultimately, the parties agreed to 15 million dollars.

Even before the purchase was proposed, Jefferson had planned to send out an expedition to explore the West. In the spring of 1804, a 32-man corps led by Meriwether Lewis and William Clark set out from St. Louis. Their two-year expedition across the newly acquired Louisiana Purchase and beyond it to the Pacific would remain unrivaled in the annals of American exploration until U.S. astronauts landed on the moon.

In Henry Levy's oil painting (opposite), "Napoleon Bonaparte in the Grand mosque at Cairo," the French general rides in on horseback as Egyptians cower.

"THE PULSE OF THE [VIRGINIA] HOUSE OF DELEGATES WAS FELT ... WITH REGARD TO A GENERAL MANUMISSION [FREEING OF SLAVES] ... IT WAS REJECTED ..."

JAMES MADISON, ON 1785 PETITION

When the Treaty of Ghent officially ended the war in December 1814, neither Britain nor the U.S. could claim victory. Still, the young Republic had proved its mettle.

Life on the Frontier

How much the Lincolns followed the war is unknown. News arrived late to the frontier, and the unending demands of subsistence farming kept people focused on their provincial lives. Like every frontier child, Lincoln was put to work at a young age. He recalled working the "big field" on the Knob Creek farm, growing corn and pumpkins. Twice he was sent to an "A.B.C. school" a couple of miles from the Lincoln cabin. One relative remembered the young boy as exhibiting "no special traits ... except a good kind— somewhat wild nature." Lincoln's own "earliest recollection" was of Knob Creek, which "lay in a valley surrounded by high hills and deep gorges." When it rained, the valley would flood. Lincoln remembered planting pumpkin seeds in a field one Saturday, and on "Sunday morning there came a big rain in the hills ... the water coming through the gorges washed ground, corn, pumpkin seeds and all clear off the field." Lincoln was a young boy at

Rallying his troops, William Henry Harrison (on horseback) urges them on against the Native American Confederation at the Battle of Tippecanoe, in November 1811. Governor of the Indiana Territory at the time, Harrison broke the power of the Native American Confederation and later became President.

the time, but the episode was part of life on a hardscrabble farm.

In 1816, after five years at Knob Creek, the Lincoln family left that farm as well. Ferrying across the Ohio River into Indiana, they moved a hundred miles northwest and settled on another wild tract along Little Pigeon Creek, not far from the Ohio River. Unlike Kentucky, Indiana had been a free state since

The oldest known piece of writing in Lincoln's own hand, the pages from his schoolboy "sum book" include more than numbers. Refer to the quotation on page 29.

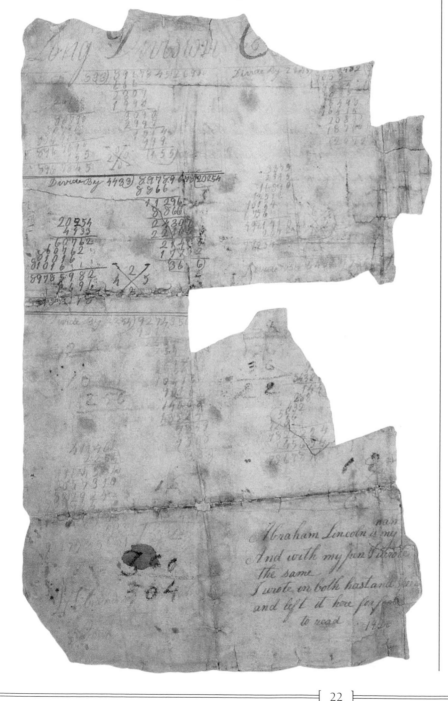

1787, when it and the Illinois Territory were declared so under the Northwest Ordinance. The Second Continental Congress had approved the ordinance as an early, preemptive move on the road to eliminating slavery altogether. Thomas, who disliked slavery, both for religious and economic reasons, probably felt more comfortable in the antislavery climate of Indiana. Also, title to land was easier to establish there than it had been in Kentucky, where claims to all three of his farms had been disputed. "We reached our new home about the time the State came into the Union," Lincoln wrote in his 1859 biographical sketch. "It was a wild region, with many bears and other wild animals …"

The Lincolns' new Pigeon Creek farm was remote, even by the standards of the day, and Thomas had to clear a trail for his family to reach the tract. Then began the backbreaking business of hacking through the forest wilderness and building a simple log cabin. The first winter there the wind seeped between the unchinked logs, and the family lived off whatever game they could hunt. Even the young Abraham kept an eye out for food, and once, when he spotted a flock of wild turkeys outside the cabin, he "shot through a crack and killed one …" Killing game was a way to survive, but it did not suit Lincoln; he never again "pulled a trigger on any larger game."

The family's isolation at Little Pigeon Creek was broken when Nancy Lincoln's aunt and uncle, Elizabeth and Thomas Sparrow, arrived with Elizabeth's 18-year-old nephew, Dennis Hanks. The families had lived near each other at Knob Creek; now the Sparrows built a new farm near the Lincolns' tract. The good-natured Dennis was an anchor in young Abraham's life, and much of what is known about Lincoln's boyhood comes from the recollections of the plainspoken Hanks.

Recalling his own boyhood, Lincoln said that when he was "very young," he "was large of his age, and had an axe put into his hands

The first school Lincoln attended was an old-fashioned log cabin, as was the Lincolns' home near the Knob Creek farm and virtually all the other buildings in the forested upland Kentucky wilderness.

THOMAS LINCOLN, CHURCHGOER AND CRAFTSMAN

A book of minutes from the Pigeon Creek Baptist Church lists Thomas as a vestryman.

Thomas Lincoln made this elegant cherry "plantation desk" for an Indiana doctor.

A cherry daybed also reflects Thomas's skills as a craftsman.

at once; and from that till within his twenty-third year, he was almost constantly handling that most useful instrument." He was also sent to the local mill to have grain ground, and when he was nine, he almost lost his life in a mill accident. A mare he had been goading to hurry up the grinding kicked the boy in the forehead, knocking him unconscious. Locals who saw the kick thought the boy was dead and ran for his father. Abraham survived, of course; some have speculated that his lazy eye was due to his skull fracture.

Two years after the Lincolns' move to Indiana, when Abraham was nine, "milk sickness" spread through the community. Notes one Lincoln biographer, "No immigrant enters a region of Southern Indiana, Illinois, or Western Kentucky … without first making the inquiry if the milk sickness was ever known there." Like other plagues, the sickness first strikes animals, in this case cows, who get "the trembles" and die within

three days. They in turn pass it on in their milk to humans. Its cause, then unknown, is the result of cows eating poisonous snakeroot. Nancy Hanks Lincoln helped nurse stricken neighbors, but by early October, Abraham's "angel mother" also succumbed. Calling her children to her bedside, she told them to "be good and kind to your father—to one another and to the world."

"Mrs. Lincoln … was a woman known for the extraordinary strength of her mind … superior to her husband in every way. She was a brilliant woman of great good sense and morality," one neighbor recalled, then added, "Thomas and his wife were really happy in each others presence, loved one another." Neighbor women would have prepared her body for burial and laid it out in the one-room cabin until Thomas fashioned a coffin; Abraham reportedly made the wooden pegs to fasten the boards together. Nancy Lincoln was laid to rest near the family home, on a wooded bluff beside other neighbors who had succumbed to the disease. Later, when the itinerant Baptist preacher was in the area, a funeral was held at the graveside.

Now the Lincolns were three, Thomas and his two children—12-year-old Sarah and 9-year-old Abraham. The wilderness days were long and hard. Sarah tried to assume

his one-room cabin, now bulging with eight people, including cousin Dennis Hanks.

According to Lincoln, "a joyous, happy boyhood" followed Sarah's arrival. She brought with her a civilizing influence. To the rustic, dirt-floored, windowless cabin, she added order as well as furnishings—a walnut bureau, a table and chairs, knives and forks. To Lincoln, she became his "Mama," the person who supported his intellect and longings and changed his life from that of a motherless ragamuffin to a respectable young boy. "She [was] his best friend in the world," he told a relative, "no man could love a mother more than he loved her."

> "WHEN FIRST MY FATHER
> SETTLED HERE....
> THE PANTHER'S SCREAM,
> FILLED NIGHT WITH FEAR."
> LINCOLN, BOYHOOD POEM

With Sarah's encouragement, Abraham sporadically attended schools, as teachers were available and as he could get away from his chores. But by his own account, "the aggregate of his schooling did not amount to one year." That seems to have been enough to have made him a reader and spurred his intellectual curiosity. Books may have been scarce in his life, but he "was getting hungry" for them, recalled Dennis Hanks. As the hunger grew, apparently Lincoln lost his appetite for the endless hard labor of the farm. "Lincoln was lazy," Hanks reported. "He was always reading—scribbling—writing—ciphering— writing Poetry." The reading and scribbling did not suit Thomas either, and tensions grew between father and son.

By his late teens, Lincoln had also outgrown the provinciality of the Little Pigeon Creek community, where 20 to 30 families lived in cabins scattered through the deep woodland. Lincoln was looking to escape its

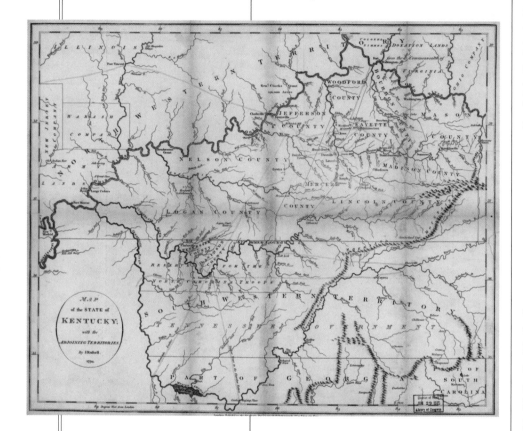

A 1794 map of Kentucky shows the newly created state. Originally a part of Virginia, Kentucky became the 15th state to join the Union in 1792. The Ohio River forming the northern boundary provided access to commerce along the Mississippi River Corridor.

all her mother's duties, but the Lincoln children became increasingly "wild—ragged and dirty." Thomas realized within a year that he needed a wife and partner, and he went in search of one. In Elizabethtown, Kentucky, nearly 15 miles from Knob Creek, he approached a woman he had courted briefly before marrying Nancy Hanks. Like Thomas, Sarah Bush Johnston had lost her spouse and had three children about the age of Lincoln's own. "Miss Johnston, I have no wife and you have no husband," Thomas reported saying, "I came a-purpose to marry you." Sarah accepted and soon arrived with Thomas at narrow possibilities and the hard labor that his aging father had imposed. To Abraham's annoyance, his father sometimes hired him out to other farmers, then pocketed his son's earnings. Abraham, too, took on jobs himself for farmers and businessmen and tried selling firewood to steamers on the nearby Ohio River. He also built a little flatboat and once was asked by two men to row them out into the channel so they could board a

steamship downriver. Each flipped a silver half-dollar to the boy for his troubles, and he "could scarcely believe his eyes … The world seemed wider and fairer before me," he later wrote of this unexpected largesse.

In 1828, at 19, Lincoln was offered his first escape from the region of his boyhood. A local storeowner, James Gentry, asked him to help his own son Allen move a cargo of meat, corn, and flour downriver to New Orleans on

WORLD PERSPECTIVE

South America in Revolt

The revolutionary spirit that brought America its independence came some 30 years later to Latin America. When the 19th century opened, Spain and Portugal claimed dominion over much of Central and South America, even though the Spanish monarchy had collapsed and Napoleon had placed his brother on the throne. These events only exacerbated a simmering discontent in Spanish America. In Mexico, Catholic priest Miguel Hidalgo y Costilla launched a revolt against the Spanish ruling class in 1810. His followers were largely Indians or peasants of mixed race, and within a year they were defeated and Hidalgo executed, but the zeal for revolution did not die with him.

In Venezuela, a man of the privileged class was ready to lead the charge for independence. Simón Bolívar had spent time in Europe and had come to embrace the ideals of republicanism. Fighting with other insurgents to overthrow royalist forces, Bolívar had taken charge of the rebellion by 1813. For years the fighting went on across northern South America, but in 1819 Bolívar—El Libertador (the Liberator), as he came to be called—proclaimed the new Republic of Gran Colombia, encompassing present-day Colombia, Panama, and Venezuela. Within a few years, Ecuador, too, had joined the republic.

As Bolívar's forces battled the Spanish in the north, freedom fighters under Bernard O'Higgins and José de San Martín fought

them in the south, in what is now Argentina and Chile. By 1817, these areas were independent, and within five years current-day Brazil was no longer under the control of Portugal. But Peru, with its rugged interior, stubbornly

¡VIVA LA REPUBLICA!

¡VIVA EL CURA HIDALGO!

UNA PAGINA DE GLORIA.

A Mexican priest and revolutionary, Father Hidalgo is remembered as a leader of the Mexican War for Independence.

remained in the hands of royalists. Finally, San Martín, an Argentine who had spent most of his early life in Spain, approached Bolívar to form an alliance in the fight for

independence. Bolívar exacted a high price for success—that he control Peru.

Throughout the rebellions, America had taken a keen interest in events to the south. Officially neutral, the U.S. had in reality sold ships and supplies to the insurgents. Now, with a dozen new nations in Latin America, limitless opportunities in trade and the sciences opened up, and a new shift in global power seemed possible. By 1823, half of America's embassies were in Latin America, the other half in Europe. The year before, in his annual message to Congress, President James Monroe had announced that "the American continents … are henceforth not to be considered subjects for future colonization by any European powers …" Further, "In the wars of the European powers in matters relating to themselves we have never taken any part, nor does it comport with our policy to do so. It is only when our rights are invaded or seriously menaced that we resent injuries or make preparation for our defense." The implications of the Monroe Doctrine, as it came to be known, changed the complexion of international relations for all time.

Bolívar's hoped-for republicanism would take decades to achieve—and in some places still remains a dream. Before yielding leadership, Bolívar admitted, "Independence is the only blessing we have acquired, at the expense of everything else."

THE BRIEF WAR OF 1812

The fledgling American nation was ill-prepared for the War of 1812. In fact, Congress had barely passed President James Madison's war declaration. With an unseasoned army and navy, America was outclassed by the British.

But the British were war-weary and over-stretched from years of conflict with the French. Initially, Britain did little to wage war against its former colony, except impose an embargo on U.S. mid-Atlantic ports. Despite the fact that the British Navy ruled the high seas, the young American Navy boasted several large frigates that managed to humiliate the Royal Navy on occasion. But on land, the attempted U.S. invasion of Canada early in the war was a resounding failure. By 1814, with the end of the Napoleonic Wars, the crown could fully focus on the American conflict. By late August, the British were within striking distance of the capital, where they later set public buildings ablaze and occupied the city.

The British were less successful in their attempts on Baltimore and New York. But America's stalwart defense did not satisfy war critics, particularly in New England. A movement there to secede from the Union was thwarted only by news of Andrew Jackson's victory in the Battle of New Orleans at the beginning of January 1815. Sadly, that bloody battle could have been avoided—less than two weeks before, the Treaty of Ghent had been signed in Belgium, ending the War of 1812. ■

Britannia and America clasp hands in peace in an allegorical painting (above) depicting the Treaty of Ghent, which officially ended the War of 1812 in late December 1814. Only months before, in late summer, the British had landed a resolute blow to U.S. pride, taking control of Washington, D.C., and setting fire to the partially finished Capitol (left), and the President's House, as well as other government buildings.

A hero of the war, the U.S.S. Constitution *takes on the H.M.S.* Guerriere *in August 1812, capturing it in the first ship-to-ship battle of the war (above). The frigates* Constitution *and* United States *had the firepower, tonnage, and crews to inflict serious damage on His Majesty's ships, making the sea a critical battlefield in the war. Another hero of the war, Andrew Jackson (left, with sword upraised) wrests victory from the British at the Battle of New Orleans, though he was left with facial scars from the combat. Jackson's successes on the battlefield combined to catapult him into the national spotlight, and eventually into the Presidency.*

a flatboat. On December 18, the two pushed off down the Ohio heading west toward the Mississippi. The river was full of commerce-carrying steamships and flatboats, and the young men would have manned their posts at the stern and bow continually during long days. When they moved into the Mississippi, they traded their produce for local cotton, tobacco, sugar. Tied up one night along Louisiana's "sugar coast," they "were attacked by

seven negroes with intent to kill and rob us," Lincoln later recounted. "They were hurt some in the melee, but succeeded in driving the negroes from the boat …"

Lincoln spent his 20th birthday in the busy international port of New Orleans, where schooners from the East Coast, Europe, South America, and the Caribbean off-loaded their own cargoes and took aboard southern cotton and sugar. There was trade of another kind—human beings—but whether the boys saw slaves being sold is not reliably recorded. Lincoln had absorbed his parents' dislike of slavery, declaring himself "naturally anti-slavery." As an adult, he contended that he could not "remember when I did not so think, and feel." But in the New Orleans he visited and throughout the antebellum South, slavery was intricately woven into the fabric of life.

The "peculiar institution," as Southerners called it with some pride in its distinctive character, fueled the Deep South's cotton-based, labor-intensive economy at the same time that it encouraged a class-based society. Owning another human being gave a Southerner social status, and the more one owned the better. Wealthy planters sat at the top of the social pyramid, their plantations often home to hundreds of slaves, who over time had created their own uniquely African American culture.

As the 19th century progressed, the South's tenacious love of its agrarian, slave-based culture was leaving it isolated from the North and much of the Western world, where the focus lay on a progressive, industrialized future. Even as Lincoln made his first foray into the Deep South, the division between North and South was widening.

Home again with his family, Lincoln grew restless. His sister, Sarah, had died in childbirth the year before, and his ties to the area were breaking. But he was not yet 21, so he was legally beholden to Thomas

---

WORLD PERSPECTIVE

The Great Age of Whaling

This whale-fishing [is] a costly conclusion. We saw many and spent much time in chasing them, but could not kill any," John Smith wrote after an unsuccessful whaling trip in 1614. By the 18th century, though, America's whalers had perfected their craft, and the oil harvested from the deep-sea leviathans lit the city of London, changing its dark and dangerous nighttime streets into more hospitable places for its citizens. Britain, too, began to build a whaling industry, competing with Americans for the rich new whaling grounds in the Pacific. During the War of 1812, whaling captains from both nations sparred with one another, hoping to take enemy ships as prizes.

When peace returned, New England whaling merchants began to build the largest fleet ever. By 1826, Nantucket Harbor was packed with "whale ships on every side and hardly a man to be seen on the wharves who had not circumnavigated the globe, and chased a whale." Each voyage took about four years, bringing the New Englanders into contact with faraway cultures.

What the whalers brought back fueled life in early 19th-century America. Whale oil fired lamps and greased the wheels of industry; spermaceti created the cleanest, brightest-burning candles; baleen from whale jaws gave structure to corsets and shape to women; ambergris from whale excrement made perfumes last longer; and tales of whaling adventures kept the public entertained.

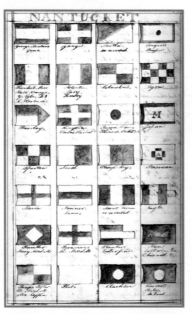

The colorful signals flown by whaling ships setting sail from Nantucket, Massachusetts, in the glory days of American whaling.

In New England, former whaler Herman Melville told stories of the long, harrowing days aboard the "blubber hunters," although his great whaling novel *Moby-Dick* was unsuccessful when published in 1851. One critic called it "a crazy sort of affair … stuffed with oddities."

By 1843, a magazine proclaimed that "the enterprise and success of this fishery … totally disables any other nation from competing." In the 1850s, whaling was America's fifth largest industry, providing a livelihood for some 70,000 people.

to work another year on the family farm. In 1830, milk sickness rumors pushed Thomas to move the family again, this time into central Illinois to a tract on the Sangamon River.

> "ABRAHAM LINCOLN
> IS MY NAME,
> AND WITH MY PEN
> I WROTE THE SAME,
> I WROTE IN BOTH
> HAST[E] AND SPEED,
> AND LEFT IT HERE
> FOR FOOLS TO READ."
> LINCOLN, BOYHOOD POEM

Illinois was then a free state, at least by law. The new state suited Abraham, nearly 21 years old, and he began following local politics. That summer, he went to hear two politicians speak at a store in Decatur. When he took the floor himself, the audience expected jokes and banter. Instead, he spoke convincingly of the need for improvements on the Sangamon River that would aid commerce. Even as a child he had had a knack for storytelling. Dennis Hanks recalled that when "he would commence his pranks, tricks, jokes, stories … all would stop, gather around Abe and listen, sometimes crying and sometimes bursting their sides with laughter." Now he captured the ear of the crowd, and the experience must have stuck in the mind of this ambitious young farm boy, who hoped to set his own course in the world. He could put his speaking talents to use.

In 1831, Lincoln left Thomas's home for good. A businessman named Denton Offutt hired him to take a load of bacon, wheat, and corn downriver to New Orleans. When he returned, he did not go back to the family farm, but landed like "a piece of floating driftwood" in the village of New Salem.

"The Railsplitter" portrays Lincoln in his hardworking, backwoods boyhood and early manhood. Pages 30-31: The grid-lined plan of 1815 New Orleans, with its Spanish and Creole influences, reveals the arc of the Crescent City along the Mississippi, which Lincoln first visited in 1828.

(A) HALLE DES BOUCHERIES construite en l'année 1813

(B) HOTEL DE VILLE construite en l'année 1795   (C) EGLISE PAROIS...

(F) THEATRE D'ORLEANS année 1813

(I) DOUANE année 1809

(M) GOUVERNEMENT année 1761

PLAN of the City and Suburbs of NEW ORLEANS from an actual Survey made in 1815 by J. Tanesse City Surveyor.

MISSISSIPI

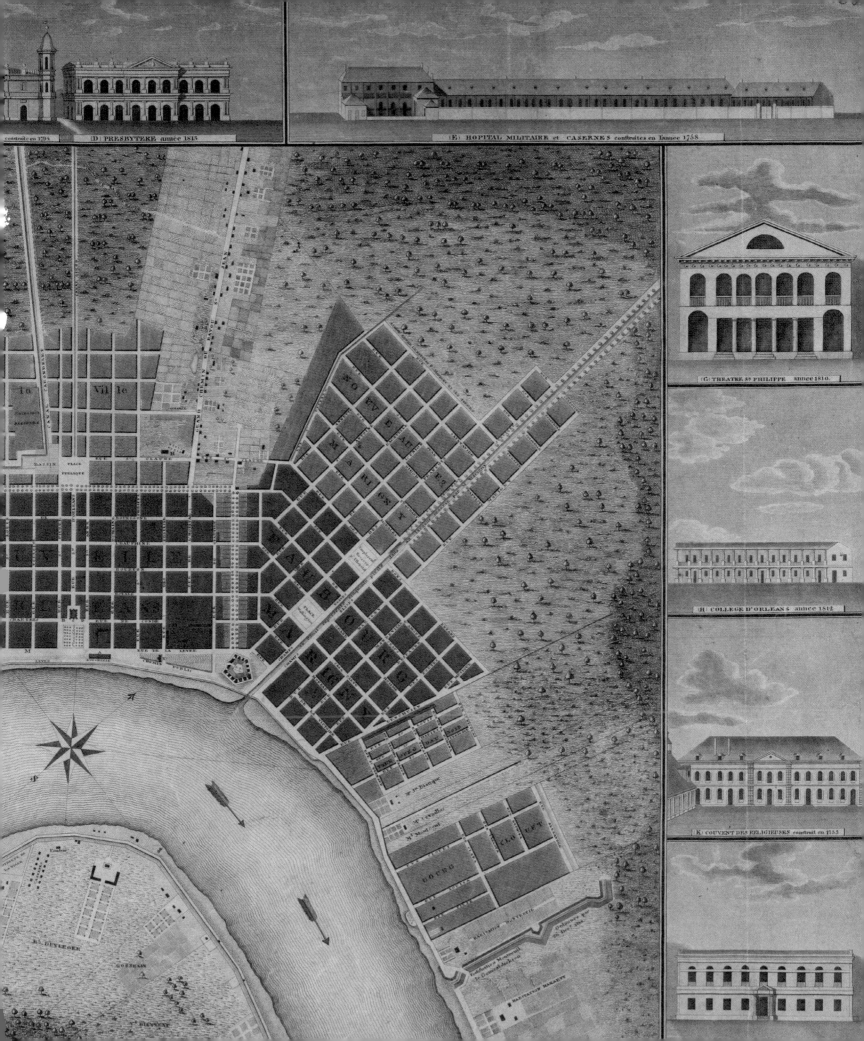

construite en 1794   (D) PRESBYTERE année 1813

(E) HOPITAL MILITAIRE et CASERNES construites en l'année 1758

(G) THEATRE St PHILIPPE année 1810.

(H) COLLEGE D'ORLEANS année 1812

(K) COUVENT DES RELIGIEUSES construit en 1753

"MR. LINCOLN WAS A SOCIAL MAN, THOUGH HE DID NOT SEEK COMPANY; IT SOUGHT HIM."

JOSHUA SPEED, LINCOLN'S LONGTIME FRIEND

[CHAPTER TWO]

I AM YOUNG AND UNKNOWN
1831-1846

ON THE POLITICAL FRONT, ABRAHAM LINCOLN AND THE NATION CAME of age together. The era of Jacksonian democracy was in full throttle as the 21-year-old embarked on an independent life, free from his father's harness. Andrew Jackson had run as a Populist in the 1828 presidential race, decisively beating the incumbent, President John Quincy Adams. Jackson, a Democratic Republican, promised to usher in the "era of the common man"—though in fact he was far from egalitarian. His victory was, in part, owed to the fact that all states, except South Carolina, had given every white male the right to vote. In the past, only men who owned property or paid taxes had the vote in most areas of the country. But by 1828 America had matured enough not to make those distinctions—at least not among white males. Women, blacks, and Native Americans were not part of the nation's expanding notion of democracy. But the party system was.

This politics of parties was just beginning to trickle down to the state level as Abraham Lincoln took up his new life in the village on the wooded bluff above the Sangamon River. New Salem had been established only two years before. Now it was an opportunistic little commercial hub, whose businesses served the needs of nearby farms. With a hundred residents and a dozen buildings—most important a gristmill and sawmill—it was the biggest burg Lincoln had ever lived in. And its residents were far from inward-looking frontier settlers. They imported fine Staffordshire china from England and kept up with the news from the greater world—even if it often came to them weeks late.

BORN TO COMMAND.

OF VETO MEMORY.

HAD I BEEN CONSULTED.

KING ANDREW THE FIRST.

Covered wagons pass through the heart of Springfield, Illinois, on their way west (opposite). Above, a cartoonist depicts President Andrew Jackson, who some accused of ruling over "Jacksonian" America as king.

At six foot four, Lincoln made an impression on the townsfolk as an awkward but affable giant. He had come to the village in July 1831 because of an offer from Denton Offutt to work in a new store Offutt was opening. But Offutt, described by an acquaintance as a "gasy—windy—brain-rattling man," didn't have the store ready for business until several months after Lincoln arrived. In the interim, the young man supported himself doing odd jobs around New Salem, and he quickly established himself as a genial hard worker and a good storyteller with a knack for sometimes bawdy frontier humor.

Lincoln may have been a young man of "kindness and honesty," but he could also be as tough as circumstances required. In a famous episode with a group of young rowdies called the Clary's Grove boys, Lincoln took on their leader in a wrestling match. The match became the stuff of legend, with Lincoln sometimes besting his opponent, and in other versions, taking on the whole gang. Whatever actually happened, the fight established Lincoln's reputation as someone not to be tampered with. And it won him the loyalty of the Clary's Grove boys for years to come.

Lincoln also impressed his fellow villagers as a young man with "a future" beyond clerking in Offutt's store and weaving tales around the cracker barrel. In 1832, locals approached the 23-year-old to run for the state legislature. Lincoln agreed, though with no money for a campaign, his chances were slim. Both money and chances grew slimmer as Offutt's fortunes collapsed and the store closed; Lincoln was left jobless and virtually penniless.

Like many young men in his position, he joined the military. For two years, Sioux and Fox Indians, under the warrior Black Hawk, had been sparring with settlers in northwestern Illinois over their traditional lands. In

Europe's colonialism led to worldwide conflict. In the Pacific, the Java War between the Dutch and Javanese, led by Prince Diponegoro, claimed many lives and ended when Dutch general de Kock (above, pointing) captured the prince (in turban).

1832, Governor John Reynolds called up the militia, and white settlers joined to rid Illinois of the "bandit collection." For Lincoln, this was a paying job, and as an aspiring politician, serving in the popular Black Hawk War couldn't hurt. He was elected captain of his company, "a success," he said, "which gave me more pleasure than any I have had since."

Throughout the short conflict, the white soldiers were brutal to the Indians, attacking even when Black Hawk tried to surrender. If Lincoln had not liked killing wild game as a child, he had no better taste for brutalizing his fellow humans. When an elderly Indian stumbled into his camp, the soldiers clamored for the old man's life. Lincoln would not have it, declaring he would fight anyone who tried to hurt the man. That was likely the young captain's most decisive moment in his two months at war. He mainly recalled being bloodied by "musquetoes" and being "often very hungry." For Black Hawk, the war was a tragic loss. Captured by U.S. troops, he was sent on a humiliating tour by President Jackson, who had the warrior and his son Whirling Thunder displayed as trophies of war.

After the war, with a little money in his pocket, Lincoln resumed his campaign for the seat in the state legislature. He described himself as "a staunch anti-Jackson, or Clay man"—a reference to Henry Clay, the Kentucky senator who was running against Jackson in the presidential campaign. In an open letter "To the People of Sangamon County," he wrote eloquently and wisely for a man of only 23 years: "Every man is said to have his peculiar ambition … I have no other so great as that of being truly esteemed of my fellow men." He also admitted that "I was born and have ever remained in the most humble walks of life." The sentiments and the cadence of this first public appeal would echo through Lincoln's later speeches. But the election was not to be Lincoln's moment. His anti-Jackson views were not shared by

his constituency; he came in eighth in a field of thirteen. Still, his appetite had been whetted for the sport.

Andrew Jackson had better luck than Lincoln, winning reelection in 1832 over his three opponents. The campaign had begun with the first-ever national presidential convention, staged by Jackson's Democratic Republican Party. In the next four years, his administration pursued its policies against a stronger central government—it opposed a national banking system and federal funding for such internal improvements as turnpikes, canals, and railroads, the newest form

In 1831, Sioux warrior Black Hawk took on the white man. Believing that a treaty expelling his people from their tribal lands in Illinois was fraudulent, he led an alliance of Sioux and Fox Indians back into the state, sparking the Black Hawk War, the only conflict in which Lincoln ever served as a soldier.

of transportation. Jackson's policies were beginning to affect Lincoln's life directly.

After the Black Hawk War and his political defeat, Lincoln and a friend, William Berry, opened a general store in New Salem, an enterprising thing for a young man with little money to attempt. Lincoln paid for his half by signing a note, which the former owner accepted because Lincoln was so "thoroughly honest." The store struggled along, and after a year Berry applied for a

Lincoln signed this promissory note in October 1833, so that he and William Berry could establish a general store. The store ultimately failed, leaving Lincoln saddled for years with what he called his "national debt."

license to sell liquor by the drink, as a way to bolster profits. Lincoln, a nondrinker, was opposed to it, and only Berry doled out the liquor. But even with the liquor license, the store did not prosper because the town itself was in decline. No major roads or railroads connected New Salem with the outside world, and the flow of the Sangamon River was too unreliable for ships to ferry merchandise regularly in and out. A canal, as Lincoln often argued, would have made the Sangamon navigable and reinvigorated the town. The Erie Canal, completed the decade before, was an engineering marvel and a commercial success, connecting Lake Erie in the west with the Hudson River. Lincoln

believed canals could improve the economies of small towns and the nation. But no canal on the Sangamon would be built, and New Salem continued its decline. In less than a year the Lincoln-Berry store, as Lincoln put it, "winked out."

> "I OFTEN ADMIRED THE INFINITE ART WITH WHICH THE INHABITANTS OF THE UNITED STATES MANAGED TO FIX A COMMON GOAL TO THE EFFORTS OF MANY MEN AND TO GET THEM TO ADVANCE TO IT FREELY."
>
> ALEXIS DE TOCQUEVILLE,
> *DEMOCRACY IN AMERICA*

Despite New Salem's limited prospects, the young Lincoln stayed on, probably because he felt at home in the town. Appointed postmaster, he also took on surveying work to supplement his meager income. Surveying gave him an intimate knowledge of the land, which he would use later as a legislator to debate internal improvement projects. As postmaster, he was more accommodating to his customers than he was efficient as a bureaucrat, but the job had an additional benefit—"access to all the News papers."

During this period, records show that Lincoln had part ownership in two lots that may have had a building on them—perhaps the Offut store where he had originally worked. Lincoln may have planned to use the site to warehouse goods from inland farms and establish himself as a middleman for cargo being shipped from New Salem down the Sangamon, then on to the Ohio. It was another enterprising move. Had the plan succeeded, Lincoln's destiny could have been very different, and with it the destiny of the country. But there is no evidence that

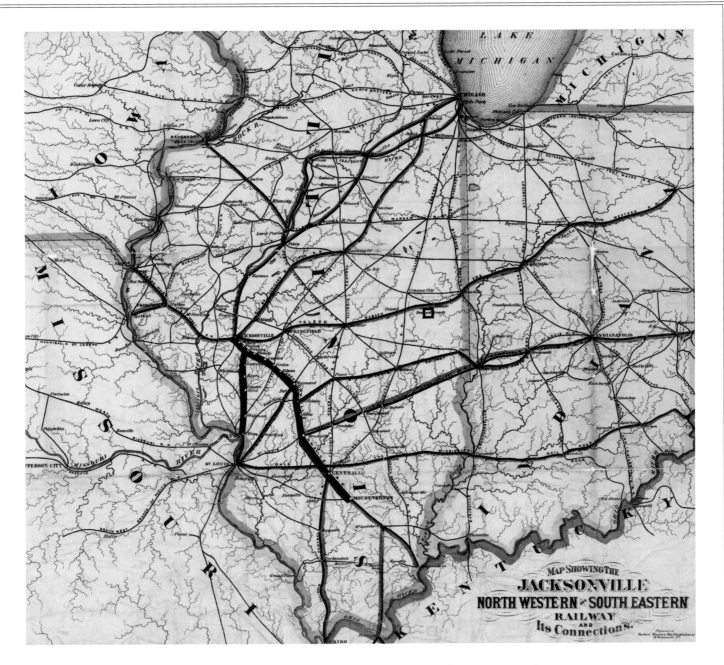

MAP SHOWING THE
JACKSONVILLE
NORTH WESTERN *and* **SOUTH EASTERN**
RAILWAY
and
Its Connections.

anything came of the business. Instead, his ambitions returned to politics and the state legislature, in part because of the salary a representative would receive. In 1834, he won a seat in the legislature, and he suddenly found himself a man of some standing. Anxious "to make a decent appearance in the legislature," he bought the first suit he had ever owned.

Lincoln understood that his background had not groomed him for the niceties of society. He had been teaching himself grammar

and the subtleties of language for some time. Now, he began to study the law as well. John Todd Stuart, a fellow legislator and powerful lawyer whom Lincoln had met in the Black Hawk War, loaned him both books and encouragement. Stuart's partner, on the other hand, considered Lincoln "the most uncouth looking young man I ever saw." But Lincoln seemed to have a talent for the law. In Vandalia, the Illinois capital and Lincoln's home while the legislature was in session, his

A great advocate of railroads and canals, Lincoln pressed for their construction in Illinois, and by mid-century the state was crisscrossed by rail lines. The success of the railroads, however, spelled an end to the age of canals.

Surveying was lucrative work for Lincoln, since surveyors were in demand to lay out the new towns springing up in the Midwest. Lincoln plotted the Illinois town of Huron (opposite) and even invested in property there. He lost his investment when Huron, like other towns in that overly optimistic period, never got off the ground.
Pages 40-41: Connecting the Hudson River and the Great Lakes with the East, the Erie Canal opened in 1825 and carried barges laden with goods.

fellow congressmen sought out their bright young colleague to draft bills for passage.

The logic of the law had always appealed to Lincoln's rational mind, and being a lawyer promised a way out of the tedious physical labor that had marked the lives of his father and so many other early 19th-century men. He bought a copy of Blackstone's *Commentaries* on the law, and "went at it in good earnest." He still had to support himself, so he continued to survey a bit and to act as post-

master, but he took time for his own studies as well. "He read so much … was so laborious in his studies," one acquaintance noted, "that he became emaciated and his best friends were afraid that he would craze himself."

If the law did not in fact craze Lincoln, a personal episode may have. In 1835, he reportedly fell in love with the local tavernkeeper's daughter, Ann Rutledge, a young woman a few years younger than he. He sometimes boarded at Rutledge Tavern, and Ann was a

---

WORLD PERSPECTIVE

Britain Abolishes Slavery

Britain lay at the heart of international slave trade during the 18th century, and Liverpool ranked as the world's busiest slave port. In just the ten-year period from 1783 to 1793, British ships transported over 300,000 Africans into slavery. But Britain was not alone in its slave interests. The 40 "slave factories" along the coast of West Africa represented British, French, Dutch, Danish, and Portuguese interests. The captive Africans were transported to the Americas, particularly the West Indies and Jamaica. Half of the bondsmen and women who made the Middle Passage aboard the cramped, godforsaken slavers either died en route or arrived too ill to work. Still, in the colonies of the British West Indies, slaves outnumbered whites by up to 15 to 1.

As the horrors of slavery gradually became more publicized in Britain, an abolitionist movement began to grow. In 1769 Granville Sharp sounded the moral alarm against slavery with a pamphlet whose lengthy title warned of the "Dangerous Tendency of Tolerating Slavery in England." Three years later Sharp won the now famous case for former slave James Somerset. In the court's decision, the Lord Chief Justice ruled that English law had no precedent of slaveholding. Other British abolitionists, with

Quakers leading the charge, soon rallied to the antislavery cause. American Quaker John Woolman came to England to exhort against the peculiar institution. He had traveled the American South and recorded his observations in his now legendary *Journal:* "The love of ease and gain are the motives in general of keeping slaves, and men are wont to take hold of weak arguments to support a cause which

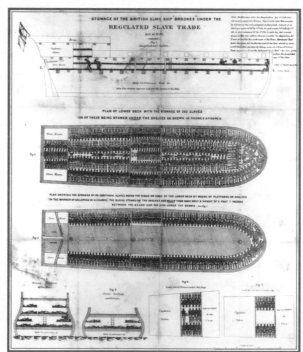

Before Britain abolished slavery, humans were crammed like cargo into ships' hulls. Many Africans died crossing the Atlantic.

is unreasonable … I believe liberty is their [the slaves'] right."

As public sentiment against slavery grew louder, the British Parliament considered a resolution put forth by William Wilberforce to abolish the slave trade. It was ultimately defeated. But the issue would not die, and after several more attempts, an 1807 bill decreed that "all manner of dealing and trading in slaves … [is] utterly abolished, prohibited and declared to be unlawful." The same year, the U.S. passed an act prohibiting the importation of African slaves. Neither law, however, abolished slavery itself, and the British law actually failed to end the lucrative trade. A final bill in 1811 made slave trading punishable by execution or exile. By this time, about 2.8 million bondsmen had been transported by the British.

Finally, in 1833 Britain moved decisively to end slavery in its lands. Planters were to be compensated for the loss of their slaves, and slaves were required to work seven years in apprenticeship to their former masters, as a transition to complete freedom. Eventually, the transition period was reduced to five years. France soon enacted its own antislavery laws, as did Portugal and the governments of Argentina and Colombia. In the Western world, only the U.S., Cuba, and Brazil continued to perpetuate the peculiar institution into the mid- and late 19th century.

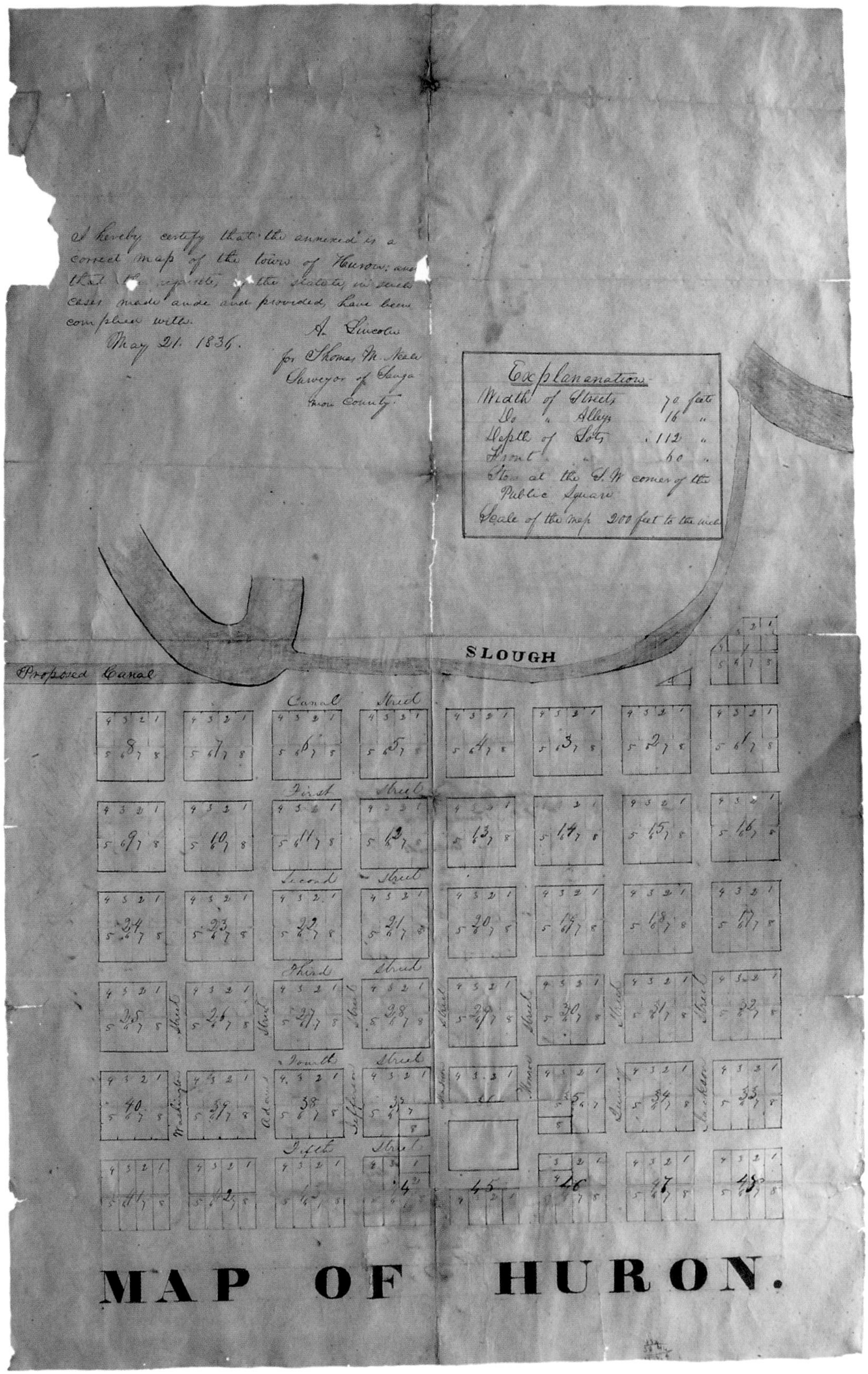

I hereby certify that the annexed is a
correct map of the town of Huron; and
that the requisite, by the statute, in such
cases made and provided, have been
complied with.

May 21. 1836.

A. Lincoln
for Thomas M. Neale
Surveyor of Sanga-
mon County.

Explanations
Width of Streets   70 feet
Do   "   Alleys   16 "
Depth of Lots   112 "
Front   "   60 "
Store at the S.W. corner of the
Public Square

Scale of the map 200 feet to the inch

SLOUGH

Proposed Canal

Canal   Street

First   Street

Second   Street

Third   Street

Fourth   Street

Fifth   Street

MAP OF HURON.

winsome, pleasant young woman, generally described as "social" and "goodhearted." She had been engaged to a man who went East and never returned. That left the field open for Lincoln, who may have felt more comfortable around Ann than he did with most women.

To her, he must have seemed a mixed blessing. Tall and awkward, with unruly hair that generally stuck up in a variety of directions, he was a young man without real means and with debts that would hobble him for years to come. But he was also well liked, admired despite his eccentricities, and ambitious. By some accounts, Ann and Abraham made plans to marry the following year, once he was admitted to the bar and had the means to support a wife.

That summer, as record heat and flooding hit the area, Ann fell fatally ill with a fever, probably typhoid, and by August she was gone. Distraught, Lincoln apparently sank into a deep depression. Depression struck him periodically throughout his life, but in his younger years, it seemed to take a greater toll. With time, though, the black moods always abated. A month after Ann's death, he had resumed his life and again focused his energies on politics.

In the winter, he attended a special session of the legislature, called to authorize a loan to build the Illinois and Michigan Canal. Canal-building had been an obsession not just with Lincoln but with the nation since the days of George Washington—a way to link the country north to south and east to west. The new canal on the Illinois and Chicago Rivers would do both, connecting Lake Michigan to the Mississippi and encouraging

PLAIN SEWING DONE HERE

SYMPTOMS OF A LOCKED JAW

"Might stop a hole, to keep the wind away."

In an 1834 cartoon, Kentucky senator Henry Clay holds down President Andrew Jackson and tries to sew his jaw shut. The two men, contenders in the 1832 presidential election, were on opposite sides in the bitter war over the rechartering of the national bank. Jackson's high-handed actions against the bank led to financial turmoil in the 1830s and the end of the Bank of the United States.

commerce and new growth. This was exactly the kind of internal improvement project Lincoln firmly believed in. It was also what the newly created Whig Party stood for—an industrialized, interconnected America that would become a manufacturing giant.

When Lincoln campaigned for his next term in the Illinois Legislature, he ran as a Whig. With his reelection, he returned to the capitol in Vandalia ready to push for more internal improvements for the state. An impressive young Democrat in the House had similar ideas. Stephen A. Douglas spoke out eloquently for a central railroad to connect with the Illinois and Michigan Canal. The potential of these new webs of transportation promised to expand across the nation and change its very nature, and Illinois did not want to be left behind.

Changing Fortune

In 1837, the nation's buoyant mood was drowned by a financial panic that could be traced to the "banking wars" waged by President Jackson and Nicholas Biddle, president of the Bank of the United States. The bank was the repository for all federal deposits; it issued notes that served as a dependable currency exchange from state to state; and it had branches in 29 cities. It stood for the kind of federally centered institution Jackson abhorred. Until the bank's charter expired in 1836, the most Jackson could do was to weaken it. He ordered his secretary of the treasury to withdraw all federal deposits. When the secretary refused, he appointed a new one. That secretary, also aware of the financial chaos that could ensue, refused to remove federal deposits as well. Finally, Jackson turned to his friend, Attorney General Roger B. Taney, and appointed him to Treasury. Taney did Jackson's bidding (and was soon rewarded with appointment as Chief Justice of the United States), while Biddle fought back to save the bank by calling in loans and raising interest rates. In 1836, the bank charter expired and Jackson did not renew it; another century would pass before the U.S. had a central banking system again.

By 1837, the financial chaos that had been predicted was under way. Within months, banks and businesses failed, and men were left jobless. Half-dug canals and partially built roads were sad reminders of a boom gone bust. It would take seven years for the country to pull out of the depression that followed.

In the midst of this economic crisis, Lincoln had the gumption to leave behind the life he had known in New Salem and begin a career

> "[THE FOUNDERS] *WERE*
> THE PILLARS OF THE TEMPLE
> OF LIBERTY ... WE, THEIR
> DESCENDANTS, [MUST] SUPPLY
> THEIR PLACES WITH OTHER
> PILLARS, HEWN FROM
> THE SOLID QUARRY
> OF SOBER REASON."
> ABRAHAM LINCOLN

as a lawyer. During the previous legislative session, he had led a group of Sangamon County colleagues known as the Long Nine, because they were all over six feet tall. The nine had successfully put a bill through that changed the capital to Springfield. Now Lincoln himself moved to the new state capital, a place that promised opportunity. John Todd Stuart, who had loaned him law books and seemed to understand his potential, took the self-taught Lincoln on as a junior partner, not an uncommon practice in those days. The well-bred Stuart was a respected member of Springfield society, while his younger partner was too poor to own his own horse. The 28-year-old Lincoln rode into Springfield on a borrowed one.

An aspiring prairie town, Springfield boasted 1,500 residents. Its broad streets were unpaved and roamed by livestock but its citizens energetic and proud. It was a far cry from the dying New Salem Lincoln had left behind, and he was far from the uncouth country boy who had first arrived in New Salem. He had put his years in the quiet village to good use, teaching himself proper

WORLD PERSPECTIVE

Railroading into the Future

It was the marriage of rail and steam that led to the great age of railroads. Early in the 19th century, several inventors tried to make that marriage work, with varying degrees of success. The obstacle was in finding ways to force the wheels to adhere to the rails and the rails to support a steam locomotive. By the 1820s the first public railway was commissioned, and in 1825 the Stockton-to-Darlington line opened to great fanfare. While still far from perfect, railroads were seen as the way of the future. In just a few decades, they eclipsed canals as the most efficient form of transportation.

America's first major rail line was the Baltimore and Ohio. At its dedication, nonagenarian Charles Carroll, prominent Marylander and signer of the Declaration of Independence, broke ground declaring, "I consider this among the most important acts of my life, second only to signing the Declaration of Independence." A decade later some 3,200 miles of track traversed America.

U.S. railroad companies got a bit of a free ride, with land grants given for rights-of-way and wood a cheap fuel. Railroading stimulated the economy with its needs for iron, steel, and wood, but it also made transport to market quick and inexpensive. Trips that had taken weeks now took days, knitting the country closer.

In the early 1850s, several trunk lines leaped the Appalachian barrier, connecting the North with what was then called the Northwest (Illinois, Indiana, and Ohio). But there were dreams of greater things to come. In 1853 money was appropriated "to ascertain the most practicable and economical route for a railroad from the Mississippi River to the Pacific Ocean." Soon the dream extended to a transcontinental line connecting coast to coast.

Few lines, though, were planned for the South; the great trade link between North, South, and West—the Mississippi—was no longer the vital corridor it had been. The disconnect between the South and the rest of the nation seemed to grow with every innovation.

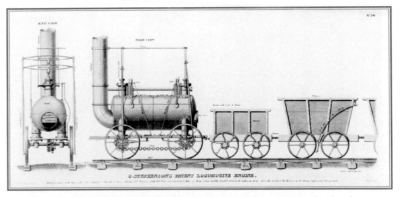

George Stephenson's drawings for the innovative steam locomotive and railroad cars that operated on the Stockton and Darlington Railway.

TEXAS REVOLUTION 1835-1836

The vast area known as Texas was always a borderland between the U.S. and Mexico. With the Louisiana Purchase in 1803, America claimed it but renounced the claim in 1819. That didn't stop American settlers from moving into Mexico's northern hinterland, encouraged by the Mexican government. These Texians, as they were called, were mostly Southerners, hoping to grow cotton in the rich Texas soil. By 1835, their numbers had reached 30,000, and Mexico's new president, Gen. Antonio López de Santa Anna, no longer welcomed them. They, in turn, were readying for open revolt against his autocratic rule. By December, they had captured San Antonio.

In 1836 Santa Anna led an army into Texas, aimed at retaking San Antonio. Internal bickering had weakened the insurgents, and Santa Anna pushed forward with ease. A poorly manned mission named the Alamo stood in his path; by early March his force of several thousand had reached it. Fewer than 200 men, including stalwarts Jim Bowie and David Crockett, defended the fort, and, although outnumbered, they refused to desert. After the Alamo massacre, Santa Anna tangled repeatedly with the Texan army and its famed commander, Sam Houston.

Though the fighting went on for years, Houston was elected president of the Texas Republic in 1836, and for ten years Texas remained independent. In 1845, it was annexed by the U.S. as a slave state, adding to the inevitable war brewing on the distant horizon. ■

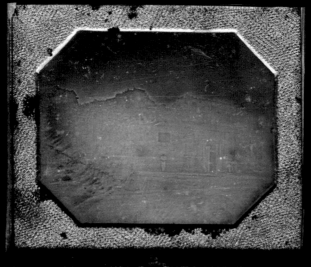

A Virginian by birth, Sam Houston (above) became the "founding father" of the Republic of Texas and twice its president. When Texas joined the U.S., he became a U.S. senator, then in 1861 Governor of Texas. After Lincoln's election, he strongly opposed Texas's secession from the Union, and that unpopular position forced him from office. At left, an 1849 daguerreotype depicts the old Spanish mission that has gone down in history as the Alamo.

CROCKETT AT THE ALAMO.

When I war at the battle of the Alamo, whar the creturs thought to catch us like a weazel asleep, I heated my gun red hot in firing so quick, and thar war no need in pulling a trigger, and drawin a lead, for the gun went off nat'ral and kilt a Mexican sojer every time Arter my ammunition war gone, I swept down twelve of 'em with one sweep of my musket. It war the best job that kill-devil ever did. I think it war a duty to clear the country of setch varmint's as much as foxes and wolves and crocodiles. Arter that battle, I counted about fifty that had killdevil's mark on 'em, f r I knowed every bullet-hole that cum from them balls of killdevils. Luke Wing took off scalps enough to make his wife a Sunday petticoat with the hair hangin' down, and she said it was the warmest Sunday petticoat she ever had on. I never fout so hard before but wonst, and that war when thar war a feller running agin me for Kongress, and I dared out all that voted for him. That time I put seventeen eyes into my pocket, but at the Alamo, I might have took a smart chance of eyes if I had wanted to do it: but thar eyes war so far in the head, it war not worth my trouble to dig 'em out ; so I let 'em lay and rot on the field ; but I took a bundle of scalps and sent 'em home to Mrs. Crockett, to sew 'em together and make a patchwork bed-quilt of 'em.

Among those who gave their lives at the Alamo, David Crockett (left), a former Whig congressman from Tennessee, went down in history as the courageous Davey Crockett. Hardly the coonskin-wearing frontiersman of legend, he dressed "like a gentleman and not a backwoosman," according to a contemporary. Having bested Santa Anna (top), Texas established itself as an independent republic and issued its own currency (above).

As young men starting out in Springfield, Lincoln and Joshua Speed became close companions and remained friends throughout their lives. In later life, Speed (above) refused Lincoln's offers to appoint him to a government position, although his brother James became Lincoln's attorney general in 1864.

grammar, surveying, political skills, and the law. As one friend from New Salem described him, "His mind was full of terrible enquiry—and was skeptical in a good sense." Now he was a respected Whig politician, and the new state capital fit his own ambitions nicely. The one thing he lacked was, as always, money.

When he arrived in town, Lincoln stopped at a general store, where he tried to buy a bed on credit. He warned the young shop clerk, Joshua Speed, that he was beginning "an experiment as a lawyer," and that if he failed, "I do not know that I can ever repay you." Speed made him a counteroffer. He had, he said, a room above the store with a double bed "which you are very welcome to share with me." The room with Speed would be

Lincoln's home for the next four years. Other young men, too, would wander in and out when they had no other place to call home.

Lincoln may have anticipated that the arrangement with Speed would last a far shorter time than it did. Before leaving New Salem, he had come to another "understanding" with a young woman visiting from Kentucky. Mary Owens was accomplished and vivacious, and Lincoln was no doubt drawn to her energetic charm. Whatever the motive, Lincoln had committed to her. But doubts

> "THE MAN WHO IS OF
> NEITHER PARTY IS NOT
> —CANNOT BE—
> OF ANY CONSEQUENCE."
> ABRAHAM LINCOLN

soon cropped up on both sides. Lincoln's lack of manners led Mary to comment that he "was deficient in those little links which make up the chain of woman's happiness." Lincoln did indeed display the very lack of gallantry that Mary had complained about. After seeing her again in New Salem, he described to a friend Mary's "want of teeth, weather-beaten appearance in general," and her size. "Nothing could have commenced at the size of infancy, and reached her present bulk in less than 35 or 40 years." His comments may well have masked his own lack of confidence and standing. Still, he continued the courtship halfheartedly from Springfield, warning her in a letter that if the relationship with him came to marriage, "You would have to be poor without the means of hiding your poverty. Do you believe you could bear that patiently? Whatever woman may cast her lot with mine, should any ever do so, it is my intention to do all in my power to make her happy and contented." Lincoln vowed he would "most positively abide by" their understanding, "provided you wish it.

My opinion is that you had better not do it." Mary apparently shared his opinion—she rejected his halfhearted proposal. "My vanity was deeply wounded by the rejection," Lincoln admitted, "that she whom I had taught myself to believe no body else would have, had actually rejected me, with all my fancied greatness; and to cap the whole, I then, for the first time, began to suspect that I was really a little in love with her."

The wounded vanity passed soon enough, as Lincoln immersed himself in his new life. At first, he had found Springfield "a busy wilderness," and admitted that he was "quite as lonely here as … anywhere in my life." But he began frequenting the nightly gathering of young professionals at Speed's store, where talk was about Lincoln's first love, politics.

The law also kept Lincoln busy and away from Springfield for up to six months a year, riding circuit. The Eighth Judicial Circuit that he served sprawled across 10,000 square miles in north-central Illinois, and "riding" it for months was one of the things most lawyers disliked about their profession. But Lincoln seemed not to mind the unpaved county roads that could dissolve into muddy morasses or having to share a bed with one or two other men each night. The small cases he took while riding circuit accounted for a substantial part of his income, and the courts provided entertainment for the isolated communities where they were held, spotlighting the lawyers and giving aspiring young politicians a chance to build up a reputation and a following. Lincoln also liked hearing firsthand the concerns of his fellow Illinoisans, and he enjoyed the camaraderie with other lawyers on the circuit. The rubbing elbows, he realized, only helped his political career.

Now in his third term in the legislature, Lincoln had become a loyal Whig partisan, organizing the party throughout the state and twice running as the Whig candidate for speaker of the house, each time without success. In the legislature he continued to press for the completion of the new statehouse in Springfield—the legislature still met in Vandalia—and for internal improvements throughout the state. Despite the financial depression that still hung over the country, Lincoln was convinced the state needed better roads and canals, and he introduced several plans for financing them. Though his plans were never implemented, they echoed the kind of optimism he had for the state, and for the future in general. He believed that "all again will be well," and his personal drive reflected his deep belief that endurance and hard work would bring individual citizens and the nation success— particularly if guided by a "sober reason" and a respect for what today is called the rule of law, also a Whig tenet. In a speech he made at the local lyceum in 1838, he spoke eloquently for a nation of laws. "Let reverence for the laws, be breathed by every American mother, to the lisping babe … let it be taught in schools, in seminaries, and in colleges … In short, let it become the *political religion* of the nation."

Lincoln's choice of words was no doubt intentional. He was never a man drawn to organized religion, but he was living in a time of Christian fervor known as the Second Great Awakening. Itinerant preachers, mostly Baptist and Methodist, traveled throughout the countryside, holding revivals that attracted hundreds of followers and new converts. Some prophets preached the end of the millennium and the Second Coming of Christ. One historian described it as a period of "stark emotionalism, disorder, extremism, and crudeness that accompanied expressions of the faith fed by the passions of ordinary people."

The belle of Springfield, Kentucky native Mary Todd had the social grace to put the awkward lawyer Lincoln at his ease. But her sharp mind for politics may have been her most attractive feature to the aspiring young politician.

This kind of passionate rousing of the masses, far from the sober reason Lincoln himself preached, sometimes led to conflict and persecution. In nearby Missouri, members of a new religion calling itself the Church of Jesus Christ of Latter-day Saints had suffered serious persecution. The prophet and founder of the Mormons, as they were more commonly called, was a New York–born visionary named Joseph Smith. He had steadily moved his flock west, to Ohio then Missouri, where their numbers swelled to 10,000. The new religion attracted converts who felt overwhelmed by a society that was changing before their eyes. New machinery, steam-powered factories and transportation, a wave of immigrants, and a world of quickly communicated ideas had energized the country, but it had also threatened the traditional life of farming families. Mormonism, with its family focus and rigid structure, promised security and reliability.

The very success of Joseph Smith's burgeoning religion was threatening to other people, particularly as Mormon numbers grew. Persecution dogged them as they moved west and settled into new areas, and in their early years they just moved on. But in Missouri, when their frontier neighbors repeatedly harassed them, burning their homes and denying them the right to vote, they fought back. Non-Mormon farms were burned and pillaged.

The governor called up the militia, with orders that the Mormons must "be treated as enemies, and must be exterminated or driven from the State." Forced out yet again, the Mormons moved across the Mississippi River and settled in Lincoln's own state, Illinois, industriously creating a new community they called Nauvoo.

Putting Down Roots

As the state capital, Springfield was a place of political and social aspirations, and the pivot

point for much of the town's socializing was the home of Ninian and Elizabeth Edwards. Abraham Lincoln, despite his graceless appearance and questionable manners, was included in the Edwardses' gatherings. The young lawyer, recalled Elizabeth Edwards, "could not hold a lengthy conversation with a lady—was not sufficiently educated and intelligent in the female line to do so." Yet he yearned for female companionship, and that yearning soon became concentrated on one woman, Elizabeth's engaging younger sister, Mary Todd, nine years Lincoln's junior.

Miss Todd was the toast of the Edwardses' social crowd and much sought after by Springfield's eligible young men. She had a knack for putting Lincoln at ease, as she did most of the talking—and much of that talk was about their shared mutual love, politics. Like him, she was a Whig and supporter of fellow Kentuckian Henry Clay, who was in fact a longtime friend of her family.

The Todds were a prominent clan in Lexington, Kentucky. Mary's father, Robert, was a merchant and lawyer with his hand firmly placed in Kentucky politics. In 1833 he had strongly endorsed Henry Clay's law prohibiting slaves being brought into the state for the purposes of selling them.

Despite his objection to the "peculiar institution," Robert Todd's household ran on slave labor, and Mary Ann Todd's earliest years were those of a pampered southern child, the fourth of six siblings. But when she was six, her mother died of complications of childbirth and life changed forever. A year and a half later, Robert Todd remarried, choosing a younger woman who was no doubt overwhelmed to find herself the mother of six relatively unruly stepchildren. To control them, Ma, as they called her, used shame and embarrassment, telling them they were the "limb of Satan." Ma grew even more overburdened as the years went on and she

In 1844, the Mormon prophet, Joseph Smith, ran for President, proclaiming the urgent need for a "theo-democracy" in the United States. Later the same year, he was assassinated by Illinois vigilantes. In 1845-46, the Latter-day Saints abandoned their Illinois settlement of Nauvoo and began the trek on the Mormon Trail (below), finally settling in Utah.

had eight children of her own. In later years, Mary characterized her childhood as "desolate" and said that her "early home … was truly at a *boarding* school."

In the years before the boarding school, Mary and her sister walked to Dr. John Ward's academy, where Mary did well in her classes, which included English, math, the sciences, and French. Most young women in her social world would have ended their schooling at 12 or 13 and spent several years of relative idleness before marrying. But Mary was independent-minded and ambitious. After finishing at Ward's academy, she enrolled at Madame Mentelle's, a boarding and day school a mile and a half from the Todd home. Local girls typically attended as day students, but during the week, Mary boarded, no doubt to escape tensions with Ma.

The Mentelles, French refugees, had a disdain for the "terrible manners" of their fellow citizens, and they probably instilled

---

WORLD PERSPECTIVE

Moving Against the Indians

Andrew Jackson ran for President in 1828 on a platform of "Indian removal." Sharp Knife, as the Indians called him, had been the hero of several wars against Native American tribes, and ridding the Southeast of them was a burning issue for him. Jackson's attitude reflected white supremacist beliefs common then—that Indians, like blacks, were "savages" who had no rights, if those rights got in the way of the desires of white men.

Jackson sought to force the Five Civilized Tribes of the South—the Cherokee, Creek, Choctaw, Chickasaw, and Seminole—off their lands. Indian land reclaimed by whites could be put into cotton production, or in the case of Cherokee lands, prospected for gold, he believed.

In his first message to Congress, Jackson urged the passage of an Indian removal bill that would be "voluntary." Indians could, he explained, either "emigrate beyond the Mississippi or submit to the laws" of the southern states in which they lived.

Reaction against the bill was strong in some quarters. Catharine Beecher, sister of Harriett Beecher Stowe, spoke out forcefully, saying that the "domestic altar" should not "be thrown down before the avaricious god of power." The bill passed the House by a thin margin and was signed into law. All Indians east of the Mississippi would move to the newly created Indian Territory (now Oklahoma).

Seminole warrior Osceola fought many successful battles against U.S. forces before his capture in 1837.

In Mississippi, a large party of Choctaw was the first to leave its homeland during the 1831-32 winter. Within 20 years, some 100,000 Indians were forced from their homes, and the 100 million acres they vacated were opened to white settlement. Some went quietly, others did not. The Seminole in Florida, who had fought Sharp Knife earlier, put up a struggle. After a protracted war that cost the government 20 million dollars, the U.S. gave up in 1842. There are Seminole in Florida to this day.

The Cherokee also took a stand. In 1823, a council of chiefs had declared that "It is the … unalterable determination of this nation never to cede *one foot* more of our land." In 1831 the tribe took its first case to the Supreme Court. In a ruling that became famous as the origin of the "trust relationship" between the U.S. and Native Americans, Chief Justice John Marshall ruled that the relation of the tribes "to the United States resembles that of a ward to his guardian." He reversed himself the following year, ruling in favor of the Indians, calling them "distinct political communities, having territorial boundaries within which their authority is exclusive." The President declared the court's ruling "absurd." "John Marshall made his decision," Jackson said, "Now let him enforce it."

By the spring of 1838, U.S. soldiers were on the doorsteps of Cherokee families, forcing them out. Herded into festering camps, most did not begin the 800-mile march west until the fall and winter of 1838-39. Cold and malnutrition claimed some 4,000 of the Cherokee who set out. As one soldier wrote years later, "I fought through the Civil War and have seen men … slaughtered by the thousands, but the Cherokee removal was the cruelest work I ever knew."

a certain air of superiority in their students. Madame certainly inspired the young women with her freedom of thought, her hauteur, and her theatricality—all characteristics that the young Miss Todd exhibited when Abraham met her.

She had come to Springfield for a prolonged stay with her sister, once her schooling had ended. The prairie town was not exactly the well-heeled world of Lexington, but as her sister Elizabeth later explained, "Mary left home to avoid living under the same roof with her stepmother." Aside from two sisters in Springfield, Elizabeth and Frances, Mary had several other relatives who were part of the migration of upland southerners from Kentucky and Tennessee into Illinois. Lincoln's partner, John Todd Stuart, was her cousin.

Even the independent Mary no doubt knew it was time for her to find a husband. Almost no other course but marriage was open to a young woman, and Mary wanted a man with as much drive as she had. In Kentucky, she had jokingly proclaimed that she planned to marry a man who would one day be President. In Springfield, the refined and attractive young woman must have seemed almost exotic. According to her brother-in-law Ninian, she "could make a bishop forget his prayers." Among her admirers was the redoubtable Stephen A. Douglas, who was clearly a rising star in the political world, but their relationship was more a flirtation than a serious affair. She was also pursued by an older widower, Edwin Webb, who had two children—Mary called them his "two *sweet little objections*." And then there was Abraham, the six-foot-four giant (Mary was five foot four), whom her sister Frances considered the "plainest man" in Springfield.

Miss Todd apparently could see beyond Lincoln's plainness to his potential, and by 1840, the two were exchanging, as she put it "lovers' eyes" and an understanding that they would marry. Elizabeth was not pleased.

"I warned Mary that she and Mr. Lincoln were not suitable … They were different in nature, and education and raising. They had no feelings alike. They were so different that they could not live happily as man and wife." During the holiday season that year, Elizabeth's objections seem to have been borne out, because the engagement ended. Some historians blame it on a quarrel the couple had when Lincoln showed up late to escort Mary to a party and she went on her own, flirting openly with another admirer. According to that account, a "grim and determined" Lincoln confronted her and the resulting argument ended the courtship. Others historians believe Lincoln simply lost his nerve and told Mary he did not love her. An oft-repeated but apocryphal tale claims that Lincoln stood her up at the altar.

Whatever caused the broken engagement, Lincoln was devastated by it and again fell into a depression, this one so severe that he spent days in bed. His friend and roommate Speed claimed that he removed "razors … all knives and other such dangerous things" from Lincoln's reach. That may have been an exaggeration, but to his partner and Mary's cousin, John Todd Stuart, Lincoln confessed, "I am now the most miserable man living. If what I feel were equally distributed to the whole human family, there would not be one cheerful face on the earth."

By late January, Lincoln was beginning to come out of his depression, though it would take more months before he was fully recovered. In the intervening time, he and Stuart dissolved their partnership. The older man had not been much of a legal mentor to Lincoln, because he was often away pursu-

Lincoln's first law partner, the courtly and connected John Todd Stuart, was a favorite cousin of Mary Todd. A prominent Whig and member of Congress from 1839 until 1843, he returned to Congress as an antislavery Democrat in the early 1860s.

"I SHALL BECOME
MRS. PRESIDENT,
OR I AM THE VICTIM
OF FALSE PROPHETS."

MARY TODD

ing his own political career. And the kinds of cases Lincoln was handling as Stuart's junior parent weren't moving him forward professionally. The partnership ended amicably. It may not have been all Lincoln had hoped it would be, but it had given him an entrée into Springfield society and cemented his standing as a lawyer. After Stuart, he went into partnership with Stephen Logan, one of the leading lawyers in the county. Again Lincoln was the junior partner, but Logan honed Lincoln's skills, teaching him to rely on precedents and procedures in making his cases. The time with Logan was well spent, giving Lincoln a richer understanding of the law.

The summer after his broken engagement, Lincoln took what was surely his first true vacation. He went to Kentucky to spend a month with his longtime roommate Joshua Speed at the Speed family home. Their gracious house outside Louisville was a far cry from the one-room Kentucky cabin where Lincoln spent his own early childhood, and he had time to relax there and experience a life of wealth he had never known. On a riverboat trip during this time, Lincoln saw

The small Springfield house purchased by the Lincolns in 1845 would be their only true home; they expanded it to a stately, Georgian two-story (left) during the 1850s. In the days before street numbers, a name plate (above) identified homes for visitors.

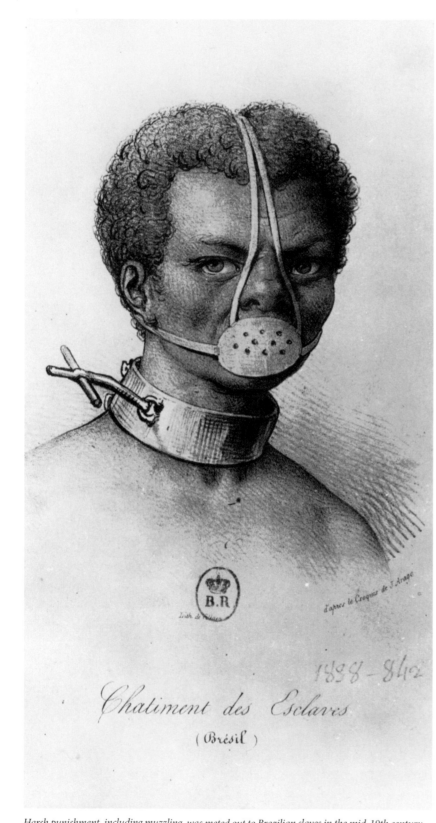

Harsh punishment, including muzzling, was meted out to Brazilian slaves in the mid-19th century. The last nation in the New World to prohibit slavery, Brazil permitted the institution to continue until 1888.

"twelve negroes … strung together precisely like so many fish upon a trotline … being separated forever from scenes of their childhood, their friends, their fathers and mothers." But, he went on in a letter to Speed's sister, "they were the most cheerful and apparently happy creatures on board." Lincoln spent much of his visit encouraging Speed to follow through on his own engagement and to marry his fiancé. Like Lincoln, Speed was having second thoughts. But Lincoln reassured him. "In two or three months, to say the most," Lincoln wrote, Speed would be "the happiest of men."

Lincoln returned to Springfield with his spirits restored, and by the following year, he and Mary were courting again, this time in secret. The two met at the home of Simeon Francis, the editor of the Whig-leaning *Sangamo Journal.* Their mutual interest in politics probably helped heal past wounds and bring the two back together. One of Lincoln's few gifts to the woman he was courting was a list of election returns in the last three legislative sessions. Mary accepted it enthusiastically and tied it with a pink ribbon.

Over the course of the next fall the couple indulged in a political scheme that backfired badly. Lincoln began it by writing satirical letters to the *Sangamo Journal,* presumably from a widow named Rebecca, who lamented the hard times brought on by the "rascally" Democrats. The letters took delight in ridiculing James Shields, the state auditor and a Democrat. Mary and a friend of hers joined in the fun and wrote several scathing Rebecca letters themselves. The humiliated Shields forced Simeon Francis to give up the name of the anonymous writer. Lincoln insisted that only his name be given, and after refusing to retract the letters, he found himself challenged to a duel.

On the appointed day, the two men and their respective entourages crossed the Mississippi to Blood Island, Missouri, as dueling was illegal in Illinois. Before any true damage could be done by the broadswords that Lincoln had chosen as weapons, cooler heads intervened and stopped the conflict.

> "TO REMAIN AS I AM
> IS IMPOSSIBLE;
> I MUST DIE OR BE BETTER,
> IT APPEARS TO ME."
>
> LINCOLN, AFTER HIS BROKEN ENGAGEMENT

Though he did have some fun with the incident in a letter to Speed, Lincoln found the whole experience humiliating, and he discouraged any mention of it as time went on. Less than a week after the duel, on a rainy November night, Abraham Lincoln and Mary Todd married without fanfare. The Edwards—who had never felt comfortable with Lincoln as Mary's suitor—nonetheless lent their home for the ceremony. The date apparently had been fixed only the week before, and not many guests attended. Weddings were much simpler in those days, but this one was simple even by 19th-century standards.

Whatever the ceremony may have lacked, the marriage seems to have made up for. Lincoln wrote Speed with typical humor, "Nothing new here, except my marrying, which to me, is a matter of profound wonder." He and his bride "Molly," as he affectionately called her in private, were "not keeping house," he told Speed, "but boarding at the Globe tavern, which is very well kept now by a widow lady of the name of Beck. Our room … and boarding only costs four dollars a week." Lincoln may have found the Globe acceptable, but Mary was used to fine homes and personal servants. Now she lived in an 8-by-14 foot room in a boarding house that catered mostly to males. She had little to occupy her time—no household duties and a reduced social life. Her sisters Frances and Elizabeth found her marriage unacceptable and

no longer included her in their social circle. With no room in which to receive guests and Lincoln preoccupied by work, Mary was left largely on her own. Despite that, the couple was deeply in love, and Mary put up with her new circumstances uncomplainingly.

In August 1843, Robert Todd Lincoln was born, and the family soon rented a four-room frame cottage, where they lived through the following winter and spring. In May, they bought the only home they would ever own—a five-room cottage with a sleeping loft and a few outbuildings for animals. Att the corner of Eighth and Jackson Streets, it was only a four-block walk from the courthouse and the law office that Lincoln would soon open with a new partner, a young man who had been studying law under him and Stephen Logan.

Why exactly Lincoln chose William Herndon over more established lawyers

Lincoln's second law partner, Stephen T. Logan, later became a judge and legislator. In 1861, Logan represented Illinois at the failed Washington Peace Convention, which sought a way to avoid war between the North and the South and preserve the Union.

The original Robert Mills design for the Washington Monument was reduced to just a marble shaft. Begun in 1848, monument construction came to a halt during the Civil War, and the shaft stood half-finished until work resumed in 1876. Pages 58-59: A map from an 1844 atlas reflects an evolving world, where empires and kingdoms dominate, but young republics, like the United States, are slowly taking form.

politics. Herndon would also become one of the earliest chroniclers of Lincoln's life.

Despite a genuine affection and admiration for his senior partner, Herndon was not always flattering in his comments, probably because he envied Lincoln. Herndon frequently mentioned Lincoln's ambition, calling it "the little engine that knew no rest," and he could be disdainful of Lincoln's sometimes eccentric behavior and appearance. "Mr. Lincoln," as Herndon always called him, had hair that was "almost black and lay floating where the fingers or the winds left it, piled up at random … His nose was large … and a little awry toward the right eye … His face was long—sallow—cadaverous—shrunk—shriveled—wrinkled and dry … His cheeks were leathery and flabby, falling in loose folds at places, looking sorrowful and sad."

If Billy—as Lincoln called Herndon—could be critical of Lincoln, he was merciless when it came to Mary. Herndon claimed the couple quarreled often and that Lincoln's sometimes distraught or depressed periods were due to the strain of his marriage. All Springfield seemed to know that Mary was difficult and given to bursts of temper—and the demands on her probably didn't help her mood swings. By 1846, the Lincolns had two sons, Robert and Edward, and Mary often had the full weight of the household on her, from carrying water (the house had no plumbing) and keeping the wood fires going, to cooking, sewing, and cleaning, as Lincoln was away riding the circuit for months each year. Mary had a hard time finding a "hired girl" that either suited her or that she suited. One of them claimed that Mary talked to her domestic help "as if we had no feelings and I was never so unhappy in my life as while living with her." Neighbors and others in Springfield were not spared her tongue or her haughty manner, and in general her difficult personality seems to have been almost the opposite of Lincoln's easy geniality. "Mrs. Lincoln was a very nervous, hysterical woman who was incessantly

who would have been happy to partner with him is unclear. One morning Lincoln simply appeared at Herndon's door and asked without fanfare but with obvious enthusiasm, "Billy, do you want to enter into partnership with me in the law business?" Herndon was taken completely by surprise, but he accepted without hesitation. "It is an undeserved honor; and yet I will kindly and generously accept." It was the beginning of a lifelong friendship and partnership, both in law and alarming the neighborhood with her outcries," a neighbor recalled.

Lincoln was more philosophical about his wife's temperament. After one of her outbursts in front of a guest to their home, Lincoln turned to the visitor and said, "If you knew how much good that little eruption did, what a relief it was to her, and if you knew her as well as I do, you would be glad she had had an opportunity to explode."

From all evidence the two loved each other and affectionately called one another "Mother" and "Father." They were lenient parents whose rambunctious, undisciplined younger children became legendary. Herndon called the boys "brats," and they disrupted the office on their visits. How they behaved at home Herndon would never know, as Mary refused to invite Lincoln's partner into her home. She felt Herndon was not of the same social standing as the Lincolns. And, as would become a pattern in their lives, Mary was jealous of close friendships that Lincoln developed.

National and Personal Ambitions

In 1844 the Whig candidate for President, the Lincolns' beloved Henry Clay, lost again, this time to Democrat James K. Polk. Lincoln had campaigned hard for his man, making speeches on Clay's behalf throughout the district. One Whig colleague called Lincoln "the best stump speaker in the state." But Polk was swept into office by America's growing belief in its Manifest Destiny. It was the nation's "manifest destiny," Democratic editor John O'Sullivan had explained, "to overspread and to possess the whole of the continent which Providence has given us for the development of the great experiment of liberty." Polk and the expansionist Democrats aimed to ensure that that happened, and their platform preached the annexation of Texas, then an independent country, and the addition of the Oregon Territory. After Polk's victory but before his inauguration, Texas was admitted to the Union as a slave state.

In 1845, Polk engineered a treaty with the British that gave America the Oregon lands south of the 49th parallel (where present-day Oregon lies) and east to the Rockies. But even as Polk negotiated for Oregon, he had his eye on new territory. The nation would not extend from sea to sea as long as California and the Southwest remained in Mexican hands. When Mexico refused to sell the lands outright, Polk maneuvered the situation until he got what he wanted—a declaration of war with Mexico.

The conflict became a proving ground for a generation of young American officers. As Robert E. Lee, Ulysses S. Grant, Thomas Jonathan (Stonewall) Jackson, George McClellan, George Pickett, James Longstreet, and other military men battled Santa Anna's troops through the deserts and mountains of Mexico, Lincoln was fighting his own political battle. Neither the military men nor Lincoln could have known that they were honing their individual skills for an epic battle over the fate of the nation.

In 1845, Lincoln ran as a Whig candidate for the U.S. Congress. His Democratic opponent, a Methodist minister named Peter Cartwright, used religion as his political weapon, painting Lincoln as an infidel because he was not a churchgoer. Lincoln didn't try to refute the charge; he had never been a churchgoer, but he had a strong faith in God. In answer to Cartwright's charge, Lincoln explained in a pamphlet he circulated: "I have never denied the truth of the Scriptures; and I have never spoken with intentional disrespect of religion," adding, "I do not think I could myself, be brought to support a man for office, whom I knew to be an open enemy of, and scoffer at, religion."

In the fall of 1846, the 37-year-old Lincoln won the congressional seat he was after. For years Whig politics in Illinois had been his life's blood. Now he would have to prove himself in a political arena larger and more complicated than any he had known before.

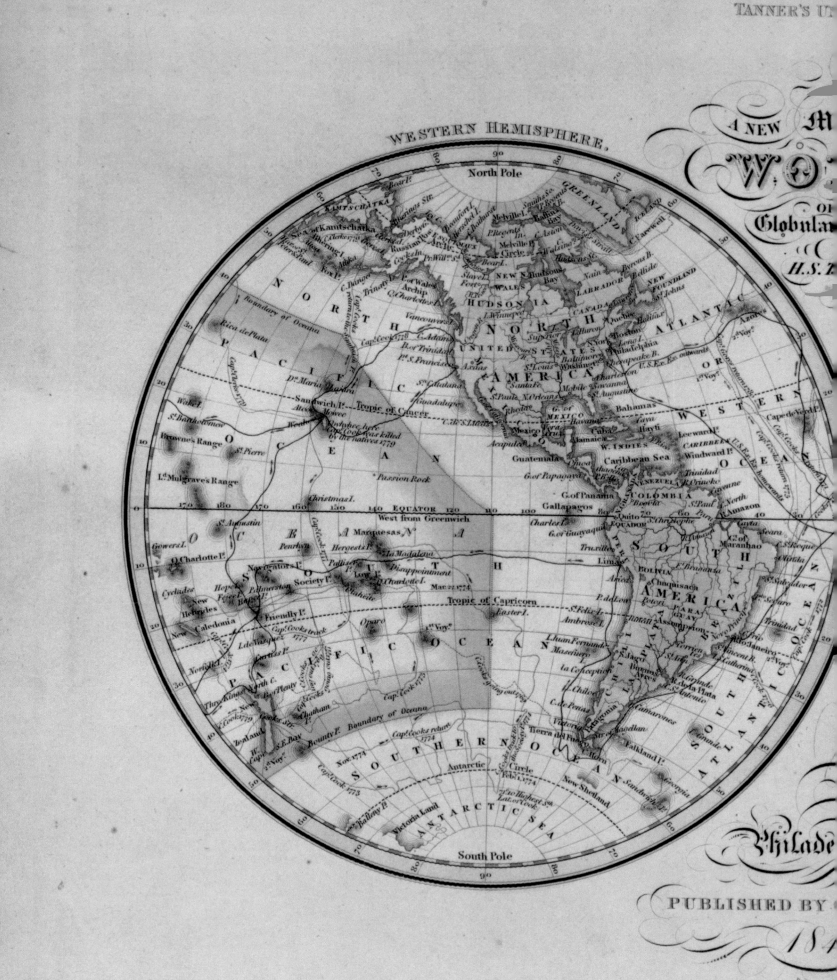

WESTERN HEMISPHERE,

A NEW M...
WO...
OF
Globular...
H.S.T...

North Pole

KAMTSCHATKA

GREENLAND

ICELAND

C. Farewell

NORTH

HUDSONIA

LABRADOR

NEWFOUNDLAND
St Johns

CANADA

NORTH

ATLANTIC

UNITED STATES

AMERICA

Washington
Philadelphia

PACIFIC

Tropic of Cancer

G. of
MEXICO

Bahamas

Havana

WESTERN

Mexico

Cuba

Hayti

CARIBBEE

Vera Cruz

Jamaica

Windward I.

OCEAN

Acapulco

W. INDIES

Guatemala

Caribbean Sea

Trinidad

OCEAN

G. of Papagaya

VENEZUELA

R. Orinoco

Cayenne

Christmas I.

G. of Panama

COLOMBIA

Bogota

St Paul

EQUATOR

West from Greenwich

Gallapagos

Quito

EQUADOR

Amazon

A Marquesas, N.

G. of Guayaquil

PERU

Truxillo

SOUTH

Society I.

Lima

BOLIVIA

AMERICA

Tropic of Capricorn

Easter I.

CHILI

PARAGUAY

BRAZIL

New Caledonia

Friendly I.

St Jago

Buenos Ayres

LA PLATA

Rio Janeiro

Zealand

Chatham

Concepcion

PATAGONIA

St of Magellan

Falkland I.

Boundary of Oceana

SOUTHERN OCEAN

Tierra del Fuego
C. Horn

ATLANTIC

Antarctic Circle

New Shetland

Georgia

Sandwich Land

Victoria Land

ANTARCTIC SEA

South Pole

PUBLISHED BY...

Philade...

18...

P OF THE

RLD

e

Projection

VER.

ohia.

AREY & HART.

EASTERN HEMISPHERE.

[CHAPTER THREE]

A HOUSE DIVIDED
1847-1861

IN HIS 37 YEARS, ABRAHAM LINCOLN HAD KNOWN WELL ONLY ONE CORNER OF America—the pocket of woodland and prairie where Kentucky, Indiana, and Illinois meet. But as Lincoln prepared to leave it behind in 1847, the prairie heartland was on the cusp of a revolution. The family farm that provided a livelihood for most Midwesterners was being transformed by the ingenuity of an Illinois blacksmith named John Deere, whose steel plow could churn through the tough prairie soil, opening it up to more planting. Another invention, the Virginia reaper, was about to make the nation's breadbasket more productive. The reaper's inventor, Cyrus McCormick, had just moved to Chicago from Virginia's Shenandoah Valley to mass produce his machine. And Chicago itself, with the burgeoning of the railroads, was poised to become a world-class city.

As Lincoln headed east, wagon trains of hopeful settlers were heading west on the 2,000-mile-long Oregon Trail, bound for the lands of the Oregon Territory and California. America was fulfilling the Manifest Destiny it believed to be its birthright. Good times seemed to lie ahead.

But the prosperity of America's heartland was a far cry from conditions in much of the world. In northern Europe, industrialization had brought misery to workers. For the past several decades, people had poured into factory towns in search of work. The new urbanization was changing the complexion of European society. Overcrowding, poverty, and disease—particularly cholera caused by bad water—plagued workers. Yet, their concentration in the cities also opened them to new ideas and greater possibilities.

One of those ideas was a growing belief in the rights of the masses. New social movements had rallied workers to demand more legal rights and better working

A Georgia family (opposite) poses in the cotton field amidst their labors. Cotton production in the Deep South increased 600 percent between 1820 and 1850. An 1831 slave tag (above) from Charleston, South Carolina, identified its owner as a bondsman, not to be confused with a free black man.

conditions. In England, the Chartist Movement had succeeded for a decade in forcing through the British Parliament factory legislation that helped improve working conditions and workers' rights. But across Europe, industrialists and monarchs fought against the populist groundswell. French social commentator Alexis de Tocqueville predicted that Europe was on the cusp of disaster: "Society was cut in two: those who had nothing united in common envy, and those who had anything united in common terror."

With unrest on the rise, two German intellectuals—Karl Marx and Frederick Engels—published a radical tract for workers. Their "Communist Manifesto," a 12,000-word pamphlet, declared that "two great hostile camps" were "directly facing each other: Bourgeoisie and Proleteriat…

> The discovery of America, the rounding of the Cape, opened up fresh ground for the rising bourgeoisie. The East-Indian and Chinese markets, the colonisation of America, trade with the colonies, the increase in the means of exchange and in commodities generally, gave to commerce, to navigation, to industry, an impulse never before known, and thereby, to the revolutionary element in the tottering feudal society, a rapid development.

Marx's and Engels's call, "Workers of the World, Unite," may not have been realized for another 70 years, but rebellion *was* in the air. The year their manifesto was published, 1848, became known as the Year of Revolution, as European monarchies faced insurrection. Both the king of France, Louis-Philippe, and of Bavaria, Frederick Wilhelm Ludwig, had been forced from their thrones, and the German Confederation, Austria, and Hungary erupted in rebellion.

As Europe battled and America prospered, Lincoln and his young family, surely and proudly part of the bourgeoisie by the standards of Marx and Engels, settled into their first year in the provincial capital of the U.S. To the Lincolns, Washington, D.C., was far from provincial. The largest city either had ever lived in, its population hovered at 40,000, compared with London's 2.5 million and Paris's 1 million. While Washingtonians attended concerts of the Marine Band on the President's grounds, Europeans thrilled to the operatic swells of Richard Wagner's *Lohengrin* staged in lavish opera houses.

> "A NEW REVOLUTION IS POSSIBLE ONLY IN CONSEQUENCE OF A NEW CRISIS. IT IS, HOWEVER, JUST AS CERTAIN AS THIS CRISIS."
>
> KARL MARX

Along with other Whig congressmen, the Lincolns took up residence at Mrs. Sprigg's boardinghouse, within sight of the unfinished Capitol. The couple and their two sons occupied one large room, taking their meals with other boarders. Always boisterous, the Lincoln children no doubt annoyed fellow lodgers, though Eddie was again sickly.

The talk at Mrs. Sprigg's was political, centered mostly on the growing schism in the country concerning slavery and the ongoing war with Mexico. Lincoln and his fellow Whigs held a narrow majority in the 30th Congress and were opposed to the war that Democratic President James Polk had been waging. Polk had insisted that Mexico had "commenced the war" by "invading the territory of the State of Texas, striking the first

A mid-19th century survey crew with the British North American Boundary Commission marks the boundary line between present-day Idaho and British Columbia. In 1867, eastern Canada became the independent Dominion of Canada, but it would take decades before other areas of northern North America joined the dominion.

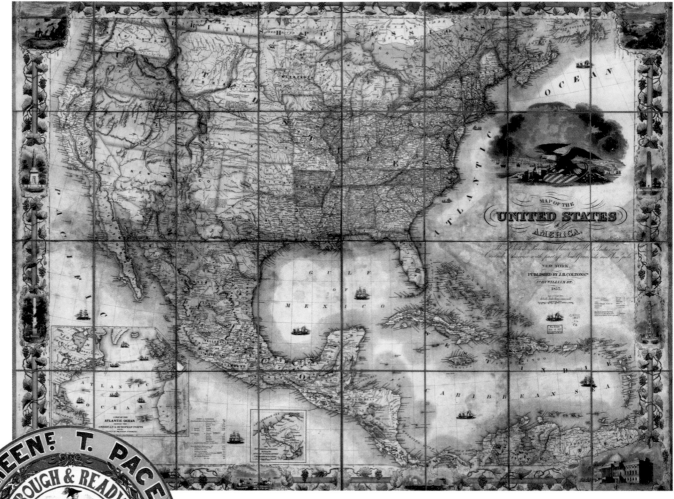

At the outbreak of the Mexican-American War, Mexico's territory included today's United States Southwest, as well as California (map, top). After the war, that vast expanse became part of the Union, and "Rough & Ready" war hero Zachary Taylor became President (campaign button, above).

blow, and shedding the blood of our citizens upon our own soil." With victory in sight Polk, in his annual message to Congress, had called for Mexico to relinquish the territories of New Mexico and California, where U.S. forces were already in control. The President also requested more funding to pursue the war.

In his first two months in the House of Representatives, Lincoln introduced resolutions against Polk's war. Relying on a distinctly lawyerly argument that he expected to gain him a firm footing as a Whig spokesman, Lincoln insisted Polk supply the House "all the facts which go to establish whether the particular spot of soil on which the blood of our citizens was so shed, was, or was not, our own soil." The freshman congressman

knew that the "spot" was actually a part of New Spain and its citizens held no allegiance to the U.S. On January 12, 1848, Lincoln told the House, "The President is, in no wise, satisfied with his own positions. He is a bewildered, confounded, and miserably perplexed man. God grant he may be able to show, there is not something about his conscience, more painful than all his mental perplexity!"

Lincoln's "spot resolutions," as they derisively came to be referred to, were never passed into law, and Polk never acknowledged them in any way. Even worse for Lincoln as an aspiring Whig politician was the reaction in Illinois, where fellow members of his party warned against an antiwar stance. Chicago Whig Justin Butterfield, who had opposed the War of 1812 and felt that his opposition "had ruined" him, heartily declared, "From now on I am for war, pestilence, and famine."

A Whig in the White House

By March, Congress had ratified the Treaty of Guadalupe Hidalgo. It ended the war and gave the U.S. California and what was then called New Mexico (it would eventually become the states of New Mexico, Utah, Arizona, and Nevada). Counting the accession of Oregon, Polk had brought more territory into the American fold than any other President. But he had also stirred an ever simmering pot of national dissension: Would the new lands be free or slave-holding?

When the Treaty of Guadalupe Hidalgo had been submitted to the Senate, Whigs had attempted to attach the Wilmot Proviso, to ban slavery in the new territories acquired from Mexico. Southern senators, along with Illinois senator Stephen A. Douglas and other Democrats, worked to keep that from happening and succeeded. But slavery was becoming a point of irreconcilable contention between the North and South.

Even in Africa, Americans were far slower than other countries to relinquish their control over Blacks. When the West African colony of Liberia, founded in the 1820s to take in freed Blacks from America, declared its independence from the U.S. in 1847, other nations recognized its sovereignty; America did not.

With the war with Mexico over and America victorious and land rich, the Whigs looked for a way to make up for their antiwar stance. As the presidential election of 1848 approached, some Whigs, including Lincoln, turned to a popular hero of the Mexican conflict as their man in the upcoming campaign. "Old Rough and Ready," as Zachary Taylor was known, had beaten back Santa Anna's forces, despite their overwhelming numbers, at the Battle of Buena Vista. When the Mexican general had advised the outnumbered

Americans to surrender, Taylor had replied, "Tell Santa Anna to go to Hell!"

Aside from Taylor's war popularity, he was a Southerner with cotton plantations in Louisiana. As the slavery question continued to fester throughout the country, Taylor looked like the one Whig who could carry the day against Polk. After time, even Lincoln embraced the Taylor candidacy, not because "he would make a better President

---

WORLD PERSPECTIVE

Irish Potato Famine

In one of history's many ironies, the agent that would force so many Irish refugees to America was itself American in origin. *Phytophthora infestans*, an airborne fungus, initially came to Europe in the holds of ships traveling from the Americas to England.

Most Europeans did not embrace the potato as a food for a couple of centuries after it was first introduced in the 1500s. Easy to grow in poor soil, it gradually became the centerpiece of the Irish diet. Reports claim that more than seven pounds per person were consumed daily by the 1800s.

In the summer of 1845, disaster struck. The moist conditions encouraged the blight to spread, and within a week the decimated crop gave off a nauseous stench. Believing that the potato crisis would end with the next year's harvest, the British government resorted to importing American corn. Though the Irish found the corn generally objectionable, it did stave off disaster for the first year. But the blight and resulting famine lasted 15 years.

A million Irish died from the famine, and 1.5 to 2 million more were forced to emigrate. In 1844, just before the blight struck, Ireland's population was 8.4 million; today it is less than half that. Many of the refugees came to the U.S. aboard horrific "coffin ships" that took thousands of lives. Unlike other European immigrants, the Irish often lacked resources to start anew. And the numbers were overwhelming.

A Harper's Weekly cover with the caption "We are starving in Ireland—the Herald of relief from America."

In 1847, some 37,000 arrived in Boston and roughly 52,000 landed in New York. Forced into slums, they were often maligned, and any employment they found was typically in service or hard labor.

By 1850, the Irish made up about 43 percent of the foreign-born population, most concentrated in eastern cities. The unprecedented flood of immigrants, German as well as Irish, led to the rise of nativist movements like the Know-Nothings. Even in Lincoln's heartland, nativism became a force that all aspiring politicians had to address.

"ANY PEOPLE ANYWHERE ... HAVE THE RIGHT TO RISE UP, AND SHAKE OFF THE EXISTING GOVERNMENT, AND FORM A NEW ONE OF THEIR OWN, OF SO MUCH OF THE TERRITORY AS THEY INHABIT."

LINCOLN, TO CONGRESS

than Clay"—Lincoln's political ideal—but "because Taylor seemed the only Whig likely to be elected."

With Lincoln as always absorbed in work, Mary, who had initially been charmed by Washington, soon found the days tedious. By spring, she and the children had gone to visit her family in Lexington, Kentucky. At first, Lincoln may have been relieved to work undisturbed, but by mid-April he confessed in a letter to Mary, "In this troublesome world, we are never quite satisfied. When you were here, I thought you hindered me some in attending to business; but now, having nothing but business—no variety—it has grown exceedingly tasteless to me." She wrote (in the only letter from the Kentucky stay that survives), "How very much I wish we were together this evening. I feel very sad away from you." That summer, the family reunited in New England where Lincoln was on a Whig campaign tour, then visited Niagara Falls before returning to Springfield.

During the previous spring, Lincoln had focused on uniting the Whig Party in a common platform. Anti-immigrant sentiment

As new states joined the Union in the early and mid-19th century and were given seats in Congress, the wooden-domed Capitol needed to expand. Mississippi senator Jefferson Davis introduced legislation to enlarge the building in 1850, and construction began soon after.

ran high as waves of refugees disembarked from Ireland, and Lincoln worried that those sentiments and the hotly debated antislavery issue would soon pull the party in different directions.

Lincoln took little part in the slavery debates going on in Congress. His driving political belief was "the principle of allowing the people to do as they please with their own business." But when the issue of abolishing slavery in Washington, D.C., began to pull his fellow Whig congressmen apart, he worked to find a compromise. After negotiating with opposing parties, he drafted a resolution calling for a referendum on slavery in the capital that would allow "every white male citizen" in the city to express their views on the issue. Should they vote to abolish slavery, slave owners would be compensated for loss of their "property." Support for the resolution evaporated, as the pro- and antislavery factions settled into their entrenched positions. Lincoln did not pursue it.

He did take the floor of the House to stump for his belief that the executive branch should concede most of its power to the legislative, who represented the people. "We, and our candidate, are in favor of making Presidential elections, and the legislation of the country, distinct matters; so that the people can elect whom they please, and afterwards, legislate just as they please, without any hindrance [from the President], save only so much as may guard against infractions of the constitution. ... We hold the true republican position. In leaving the people's business in their hands, we can not be wrong." His words would come back to haunt him.

Lincoln's Whig candidate, Zachary Taylor, carried the day in the presidential elections, and that had implications for Lincoln personally. Several Illinois Whigs lobbied the Taylor Administration to appoint Lincoln to

Lincoln's third and final law partner, William "Billy" Herndon, remained a lifelong friend, although the two were very different. After Lincoln's death, Herndon wrote one of the first Lincoln biographies, painting a realistic, and sometimes unflattering, portrait of his old friend.

a patronage position, as a reward for his hard work, since he could not run for another congressional term owing to Illinois restrictions. Lincoln had an interest in the Illinois commissioner of lands position, but he was offered instead the governorship of the Oregon Territory. He declined, blaming his decision on Mary's refusal to move. By March 1849, he was back in Springfield practicing law with Herndon, his political career apparently at an end.

The Quiet Years

An 1849 directory of Springfield businesses offers a picture of the commercial world:

"Corneau & Diller, and D. & I. P. Spear, dealt in drugs; P. C. Canedy and Birchall & Owen sold not only drugs but books and stationery as well. E. B. Pease & Co. confined themselves to hardware, cutlery and iron, but they were the only firm in Springfield which dealt exclusively in those commodities. There were three bakers and confectioners, three clothing dealers, two jewelers, two butchers and one milliner." Listed also were three livery stables and one bathhouse. (Concerning the latter, the directory commented: "The practice of bathing, has always been regarded as a great security and promoter of health, and it certainly is of comfort and cleanliness.")

That summer, the first railroad to Springfield began service. Expected to be a boon to the town, it ultimately proved a detriment. Now, legislatures and others coming to the isolated little capital on business could more easily return to their homes, even 200 miles away. And the city had a new and ever growing competitor, Chicago, less than 200 miles to the north. In just over a decade it had become a regional powerhouse, thanks in large part to the railroads and to its position on the Chicago River and Lake Michigan.

Lincoln apparently enjoyed the quiet world of Springfield, his law practice, and

his family. He showed no ill effects from the fever that had struck many American men at the end of the 1840s. In late January 1848, a glint in the water of Johann Sutter's millrace in Coloma, California, had turned out to be gold. The discovery stayed a secret until May, when a San Francisco merchant, hoping to outfit prospectors, ran through the streets, shouting, "Gold, gold, gold from the American River." Within six weeks, three-quarters of the men in the city headed for goldfields.

It would take several months for word to span the continent and reach the East. In fact,

men in the Far East and Mexico heard and flocked to California before Easterners did. It wasn't until Polk announced the discovery in December 1848 in his final address to Congress that the East knew. American men throughout the country left their homes for California. By 1850 the territory had become the 31st state and one free of slavery; by 1854 some 300,000 fortune seekers had been lured to its goldfields.

Lincoln and Mary were far removed from the thrill of gold. Tragedy struck them in the winter of 1850, when their youngest son,

Downtown Springfield's 19th century storefronts, including the spare, simple law office of Lincoln and Herndon, faced the central square, where the State Capitol stood.

Eddie, never a healthy child, took ill with what was at first thought to be diphtheria. The boy probably had the dread 19th-century "consumption," or pulmonary tuberculosis, for which there was no cure. After 52 days of fever, coughing, and progressive weakness, he died. Lincoln, though disconsolate, said only, "We miss him very much."

Eddie's funeral was held in the Lincoln home and presided over by the minister of the First Presbyterian Church, James Smith, because the minister of the Episcopal church that Mary normally attended was away. Mary was so moved and consoled by Smith that she began attending the Presbyterian church, where predestination was a tenet of the faith. "What is to be is to be and nothing we can say, or do, or be can divert an inexorable fate," she once said to her half-sister Emilie, adding with her characteristic determination, "but in spite of knowing this, one feels better even after losing, if one has had a brave, whole-hearted fight to get the better of destiny." Perhaps in a reflection of that spirit, Mary became pregnant again soon after Eddie's death, and in late December, another son, Willie, was born. The following year there was a fourth son, Thomas, named for Lincoln's father but affectionately called Tad.

As the family grew, so did Lincoln's law practice. He still rode the circuit in the spring, saying "I suppose now I am one of the old men," but he also had a growing case-load before Illinois's supreme court and the federal district court in Springfield. And he began to represent the railroads, whose networks throughout the state were complete. Now, when he was on the circuit, he could take a train home on weekends.

That no doubt comforted Mary. Her husband was at home more, and she was relieved of coping on her own for months at a time with the children and the demands of a 19th-century household. Cooking, cleaning (of which, for health reasons, she was rigorous),

and sewing still filled her days, and she liked to entertain, though the size of her dining room limited her to only a few guests for dinner. "Her table was famed for the excellence of its rare Kentucky dishes and in season was loaded with venison, wild turkeys, prairie chickens and quail and other game," recalled Isaac Arnold, a Chicago friend, who also praised Mary's "wit and kind manners."

The couple were indulgent and loving parents. Whatever reserve Lincoln had shown his older sons he lost with the younger boys. He took time to play with them or care for them himself, earning him a reputation in town as "hen pecked." Hand in hand, father and sons would occasionally walk the several blocks from their home to downtown Springfield, and on the return, Lincoln would hoist a tired boy high onto his shoulder and carry him home. Seeing this, his sister-in-law once admonished Lincoln to "put that great big boy down." But Lincoln worried, "Oh, don't you think his little feet get too tired?"

During the late 1840s and 1850s, as the Lincolns raised their sons, America—particularly the Northeast—was experiencing an intellectual renaissance. Reformist movements advocated new freedoms. One, the women's rights movement, challenged the prevailing "cult of domesticity" and demanded a visible place for women in society. At the 1848 convention in Seneca Falls, New York, feminists declared that "all men and women are created equal," and thus women should have the right to vote. Their

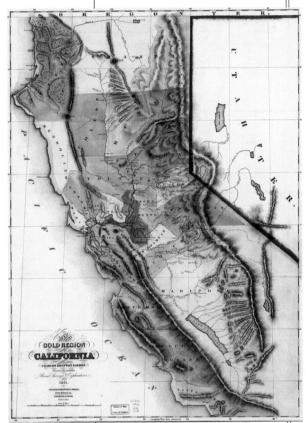

Thousands of men like this one (opposite) flocked to California during the mid-century gold rush, hoping to strike it rich in the Sierra foothills, where gold was first discovered in 1848. With new discoveries, "Gold Country" (above) spread throughout California.
Pages 72-73: Portraits of Abraham and Mary taken about four years after their marriage. Lincoln's expression reflects the melancholy that "dript from him as he walked," in the words of his partner Herndon. Marriage helped alleviate that state somewhat.

fight at the time was for women's rights; by "all men and women," they meant whites.

In New England, a group of writers and intellectuals centered in Concord, Massachusetts, sought to transcend the American drive for material success and seek a more profound reality. In the 1850s, the search for beauty, both in nature and the spirit, informed the writings of the Transcendentalists, whose leading voices were Ralph Waldo Emerson and Henry David Thoreau. In Emerson's *Nature* and "The Transcendentalist" and in Thoreau's *Walden,* the virtues of individualism and self-reliance were extolled. "Standing on the bare ground,—my head bathed by the blithe air, and uplifted into infinite space,—all mean egotism vanishes," Emerson wrote in "The Transcendentalist." Averse to creeds and any other conventions that confined the soul, the Transcendentalists were particularly offended

---

WORLD PERSPECTIVE

1848: Europe's Year of Revolution

On February 22, 1848, uprisings in Paris set off a year of revolution across the continent. Throughout the "Hungry '40s," the working class and emerging middle class of Europe had suffered, and their unrest came to a head first in France. Rallying behind the cause of universal male suffrage, angry Parisian mobs took to the streets.

Within two days, Louis-Philippe, the "Bourgeois Monarch" and last king of France had abdicated, permitting a provisional government to coalesce. Committed to universal male suffrage and to relieving unemployment, France's second republic ignited the passions and hopes of other disenfranchised Europeans.

During the Spring of Nations, as the spring of 1848 came to be called, Europe also witnessed a groundswell against the Habsburgs, whose Austrian Empire extended from the German states through present-day Italy to the Balkans. For decades, the repressive Habsburgs had quashed freedom of the press and assembly and exploited its subjects. But a growing nationalism began to fuel anti-Habsburg sentiment. On March 13, Viennese liberals rose up against the monarchy, forcing Emperor Ferdinand to dismiss the unpopular minister, Prince Metternich. Two days later, Buda and Pest revolted against Habsburg rule, and insurrection spread throughout Hungary. The Hungarians enjoyed the support of others oppressed by Austrian rule—German peoples, Poles, and Italians—but when the Russians, at the behest of the Austrians, invaded Hungary, they were forced back. The great leader of the Hungarian revolution, Lajos Kossuth, went into exile—and

Ferdinand I, Emperor of Austria, was plagued by epilepsy and forced to abdicate his throne during the 1848 revolution.

went on to serve the Union in the American Civil War.

In the German Confederation—a collection of Habsburg-dominated states—revolutionary demands followed those of the French: freedom of the press, freedom of assembly, and a national parliament representing the citizenry. In Bavaria, King Ludwig was forced to abdicate and in Prussia, Frederich Wilhelm ceded to revolutionary demands, if only briefly The Austrians also had to put down rebellion in northern Italy, where the Piedmont region ultimately won its independence; unrest also rocked other Italian states throughout the 1850s.

American reaction to European unrest was mixed. New Yorkers held a demonstration of solidarity and celebration, with immigrants singing native songs. Across the ocean, the Young Ireland movement fomented insurrection in Ireland as well.

The immediate reaction of American political parties to the revolutions of 1848 was predictable. The Whigs gave lip service to the cause of freedom but found mob rule and a disdain for law distasteful. Democrats applauded the Spring of Nations as a step toward popular sovereignty, their own battle cry.

But the greatest U.S. consequence of the European unrest hadn't yet emerged: In the 1840s and '50s some four million people immigrated to the U.S., twice as many as in the previous 250 years combined. By 1850, the foreign-born totaled 10 percent of the population. In Chicago and St. Louis, burgeoning cities of the heartland, foreign born outnumbered native-born. Their presence would change the American landscape, physically and politically, forever.

by human bondage, and they became increasingly ardent abolitionists.

Congressional Compromises

Lincoln's own philosophy remained hard-headed and firmly rooted in the pragmatic world. "It is best for all to leave each man free to acquire property as fast as he can," Lincoln said. "When one starts poor, as most do in the race of life, free society is such that he knows he can better his condition."

The overarching problem with America in the mid-19th century was simply that it was free for only a part of the population. Slavery, so long a thorn in the nation's side, was beginning to tear at the fabric of the nation. President Taylor tried to circumvent the slavery issue in newly acquired California and New Mexico by suggesting they forgo the territorial stage and apply directly for statehood. At the time, states could write their own constitutions, allowing or disallowing slavery as

> "SUCCESSFUL IN HIS PROFESSION, HAPPY IN HIS HOME, SECURE IN THE AFFECTION OF HIS NEIGHBORS, WITH BOOKS, COMPETENCE, AND LEISURE— AMBITION COULD NOT TEMPT HIM."
>
> LINCOLN, DESCRIBING HIMSELF

they chose. Taylor's suggestion had caused a backlash in both the North and South, and Southerners had threatened to secede from the Union. Old Rough and Ready would have none of it. He promised that he would personally lead the army against anyone who broke the laws of the land. But on July 4, 1850, Taylor suddenly died of typhoid fever, leaving his Vice President, Millard Fillmore, to grapple with the slavery impasse.

An advertisement for soap lampoons the Know-Nothing Party for its "nativist" sentiments by depicting only Native Americans.

In the U.S. Senate, Lincoln's "beau ideal of a statesman," Henry Clay, had been working to craft a compromise that would quell the rising sectional tensions surrounding slavery. Among other provisions, the Compromise of 1850, as it came to be called, gave California admission to the Union as a free state, but in the rest of the area acquired from Mexico, territorial governments could choose themselves whether to be free or slave. This would give the North 15 free states plus California, exactly the number of slave states in the South. This kind of delicate equilibrium between North and South had been maintained for decades. But the northern free territories were extensive, and with Clay's compromise the new territory acquired from Mexico could go either way.

UNCLE TOM'S CREATOR

The great classic of the mid-19th century was initially deemed unsalable. Who would read a book on a controversial subject, slavery, written by a woman? In fact, during the last century and a half, millions of people worldwide have read Harriet Beecher Stowe's *Uncle Tom's Cabin*.

From a liberal New England family, Harriet Beecher Stowe had social reform in her veins. Her father, husband, and brother were all reformist ministers, and brother Henry Ward Beecher was a leading abolitionist voice.

As a young mother, Stowe began to follow reports of the horrors inflicted on slaves after the passage of the 1850 Fugitive Slave Act. "I now feel," she wrote, "that the time has come when even a woman or a child who can speak a word for freedom and humanity is bound to speak." In June 1851, the first of 40 installments of *Uncle Tom's Cabin* began appearing in the abolitionist paper, the *National Era*. Stowe's portrayal humanized the plight of slaves in the South.

Boston publisher John Jewett printed and released *Uncle Tom's Cabin* in book form in March 1852. A resounding success, it sold 10,000 copies in the first week and 300,000 the first year. By 1857, it had sold two million copies worldwide .

Beyond its commercial success, *Uncle Tom's Cabin* "made Stowe's the single most powerful voice on behalf of slaves," according to one of her biographers. Later, when Stowe met Lincoln in the White House, the President is said to have greeted her with, "So this is the little lady who made this big war?" ■

Harriet Beecher Stowe (top) described herself as "a little bit of a woman—about as thin & dry as a pinch of snuff, never very much to look at." But her literary voice was large, and her Uncle Tom classic has been published in Italian (above), Danish (right), and a host of other languages since its release in 1852.

In Europe and America, dramatizations of Stowe's Uncle Tom's Cabin (top) brought to the stage the hardships and horrors of the lives of American slaves and continued to be featured on American stages into the 1920s (left). The book also inspired other artwork, including a lithograph, showing a dream inspired by Stowe's classic (above).

The advent of the telegraph and photography made coverage of the Crimean War an entirely new phenomenon. This shot, by British photographer Roger Fenton, shows a cavalry encampment on the Crimean Peninsula in 1855.

In order to placate the South, Clay promised a more stringent fugitive slave law.

For months the Senate's great elder statesmen—Clay, South Carolina's John C. Calhoun, and New Hampshire's Daniel Webster—debated the compromise in a war of words that ended in defeat for Clay's bill. But the bill's demise did not end the debate. A rising generation of legislators—William Seward of New York, Jefferson Davis of Mississippi, and Stephen A. Douglas, the Illinois senator and Mary's former suitor—entered the fray.

In 1854, Douglas stepped forward with what he considered a more workable compromise, the Kansas-Nebraska Act, which essentially repealed the long-standing Missouri Compromise. Since 1820 that bill had helped maintain the precarious balance between slave and nonslave states. It barred slavery from the northern regions of the Louisiana Purchase but allowed it in the South.

Henry Clay had shepherded the compromise through Congress, and it had helped mitigate the North-South divide for almost a quarter century. But as Thomas Jefferson and other founders had foreseen, the slavery conflict, then a "speck on the horizon," was about to "burst on us as a tornado."

Now Douglas was hoping to bend the tornado to his own will. His Kansas-Nebraska Act stipulated that territories "when admitted as a State or States … shall be received into the Union with or without slavery, as their constitution may prescribe at the time of the admission." Douglas, a Democrat, expected that the act would result in "a hell of a storm," and he was right.

Slavery had never been a burning political issue for Lincoln, but he was incensed by Douglas's proposed act, saying it drew him back into politics "like nothing before." Still, he remained publicly quiet for months.

Then, while stumping for a Whig candidate, he spoke out passionately against the act and slavery: "I hate it because of the monstrous injustice of slavery itself. I hate it because it deprives our republican example of its just influence in the world—enables the enemies of free institutions, with plausibility, to taunt us as hypocrites." Lincoln added that "the fathers of the republic eschewed and rejected" slavery, tolerating it only as a necessity, but

that with the Kansas-Nebraska Act, "it is to be transformed into a 'sacred right.' "

Herndon, who was there when Lincoln first delivered the speech in the House of Representatives in Springfield, reported that Lincoln's voice was, at first, "shrill piping and squeaky" but gradually, over the course of the three-hour presentation, it "became harmonious—melodious—musical." Lincoln repeated the speech soon again in Peoria, in

WORLD PERSPECTIVE

Commodore Perry and America's Imperial Ambitions

When we look at the possessions in the east of our great maritime rival England ... we should be admonished of the necessity of prompt measures on our part ... Fortunately the Japanese and many other islands in the Pacific are still left untouched by this unconscionable government," Commodore Matthew Perry wrote in the mid-19th century. By late 1852, he was on his way to Japan, dispatched by President Fillmore on a quasi-diplomatic mission. At the time, isolationist Japan permitted only limited trade with the West, and that exclusively through the Dutch. But Perry and others realized that the island kingdom could mean new trade opportunities, as well as a strategic site and safe harbor for reprovisioning and repairing American whalers, and now, in the age of steam, critical coaling stations for refueling.

After half a year, Perry's four steam-powered warships dropped anchor in Edo (now Tokyo) Bay. The bay was forbidden to foreigners, but Perry would not consent to budge, insisting that he present Fillmore's letter of friendship to a high official. On the day of the presentation, Perry's journal recorded the setting:

A straggling group of peaked roofed houses [was] built between the beach and the base of the high ground which ran in green acclivities behind, and ascended from height to height to the distant mountains. A luxuriant valley or gorge, walled in with richly wooded hills, opened at the

head of the bay, and breaking the uniformity of the curve of the shore gave a beautiful variety to the landscape. On the right some hundred Japanese boats, or more, were arranged in parallel lines along the

In an 1850s woodcut by a Japanese artist, Commodore Perry takes on a distinctly Japanese demeanor.

margin of the shore, with a red flag flying at the stern of each.

Perry met the Japanese fanfare with his own and succeeded in presenting the presidential letter to two princes represent-

ing the emperor. Contained in an elaborate rosewood box inlaid with gold, Fillmore's letter began, "GREAT AND GOOD FRIEND," and went on to assure the emperor that, "I entertain the kindest feelings toward your majesty's person and government, and that I have no other object ... but to propose to your imperial majesty that the United States and Japan should live in friendship and have commercial intercourse with each other."

Perry gave the Japanese a year to contemplate their answer, ominously promising to return with a larger squadron of the formidable "black ships." The veiled threat was not lost on the emperor or the Tokugawa shogunate, who were the real powers in Japan at the time. Realizing they possessed none of the might needed to resist American force, the Japanese capitulated and on Perry's return in 1854 signed the Treaty of Kanagawa, opening Japan to American ships. Later, the shogun also consented to an even broader treaty that opened some ports to trade but limited Japanese tariffs. Similar treaties, all favoring the foreign powers, soon followed with Russia, the Netherlands, Great Britain, and France.

The capitulation to the West rocked the foundation of the shogunate, but the opening of Japan's ports to commerce ultimately led to a transformation of the old feudal society during the era of the Meiji, or "enlightened rule," that began in November 1867, when the last shogun, Yoshinobu, resigned.

a debate with Douglas that the senator had hoped to avoid. He now saw in Lincoln "the most difficult and dangerous opponent that I have ever met." The Peoria speech earned Lincoln a place both in the political spotlight and in history.

Lincoln had never given up the political game and had been quietly pursuing it as a Whig operative in the five years since he returned from Washington. Now, he made

The first of the history-making Lincoln-Douglas debates was held in Ottawa, Illinois's Washington Square. Despite the heat of late August, it attracted a crowd of approximately 12,000 spectators—"an immense concourse of people from all parts of the state," reported New York journalist Henry Villard.

his move. At the time, the Illinois legislature not the voters elected U.S. senators. With a new, anti-Nebraska legislature opposed to slavery in place, he began to petition them. "It has come round that a whig may, by possibility, be elected to the U.S. Senate," he wrote a new member of the legislature, "and I want the chance of being that man." When he narrowly lost the contest, he commented simply that "I regret my defeat moderately, but … am not nervous about it." He had allowed the votes of his supporters to go to another candidate, and he knew he had built strategic bridges in the process. This time Lincoln was in the political game for good.

The Democrats suffered serious losses themselves, as a result of the strong anti-Nebraska backlash. But the Whig Party was far from healthy. It had never managed to achieve and hold the Presidency, since William Henry Harrison, the only Whig President, had died after a month in office. Now, two new parties appeared and gained ground. The Republican Party included former Whigs and echoed many old Whig beliefs. The other party, the American Party, was labeled by its detractors as the Know-Nothing Party.

Changing Loyalties

In 1854, a wave of Irish immigrants and German political refugees was just finishing the five-year naturalization period and would soon have the vote; anti-immigrant sentiment, particularly against Irish Catholics, ran high. Begun as a grassroots alternative to the two dominant parties, Know-Nothings rallied under the nativist, anti-immigrant banner; at the same time, they opposed the extension of slavery. Lincoln deeply disliked the party's stance against foreigners but welcomed their antislavery stance.

At times he was accused of being a Know-Nothing himself. In 1855, he strongly denied it in a letter to his friend Joshua Speed: "I think I am a Whig; but others say there are no whigs…. I am not a Know-Nothing. That is certain. How could I be? How can anyone who abhors the oppression of negroes, be in favor of degrading classes of white people?"

Lincoln "hoped that their organization would die out without the painful necessity of my taking an open stance against them." When that didn't happen, he increasingly understood that he had to appeal to their antislavery beliefs if he wanted to bring them into his party as allies against the Democrats.

In the next year, Lincoln admitted that his long-cherished Whig Party could not survive. But a new, as yet unnamed faction was beginning to take shape, comprised of free soilers—those who believed America stood for every citizen's right to own property, control their own labor, and prosper—more liberal democrats, and even antislavery Know-Nothings. Lincoln threw himself into organizing these strange bedfellows into a true party. By May they had come together to join the new Republican Party that was gaining ground across the northern U.S.

At the Republicans' first Illinois state convention, Lincoln, a delegate and recognized founder of the party, spoke eloquently against slavery. "The human heart *is* with us—God *is* with us. We shall again be able not to declare, that 'all States as States are equal' ... but ... that 'all *men* are created equal.' "

When the national convention was held, Lincoln was seriously considered for the vice presidential slot, to run with John C. Frémont, whose campaign slogan proclaimed, "Free soil, free labor, free speech, free men, and Frémont." The 1856 presidential race became a three-way contest among Know-Nothing candidate Millard Fillmore, Republican Frémont, and Democrat James Buchanan. Buchanan, who had run with a "Save the Union" message, narrowly won.

Almost immediately the new President was faced with crises. One was brought on by events in Europe. In 1854, imperial Russia, under Tsar Nicholas I, had squared off against the Ottoman Empire and its European allies in the Crimean War. It had begun over disputed religious sites in the Holy Lands. During the two years it lasted, the Crimean War drew European men off their farms and into battle, and the demand for American agricultural goods swelled as a result. But when the war ended with Russia forced to cede territory to the Ottomans, the farmers returned to their homes and American trade with Europe dropped. Panicked investors withdrew their

Mathew Brady's famous "Cooper Union portrait" of Lincoln was taken in the photographer's New York studio before Lincoln gave his 1860 Cooper Union speech. The speech and photograph helped solidify Lincoln's national appeal.

assets from businesses, setting off failures and a depression. Northerners blamed the depression on Buchanan's Democratic administration, which was under southern control.

Buchanan's problems with the North had been exacerbated by the Supreme Court. Two days after he took office in March 1857, the court handed down its long-awaited decision in the Dred Scott case. Scott had been a former slave with a complicated history, and, taking advantage of that history, abolitionists had convinced

> "THE AUTOCRAT OF
> ALL THE RUSSIAS WILL
> RESIGN HIS CROWN,
> AND PROCLAIM HIS SUBJECTS
> FREE REPUBLICANS SOONER
> THAN WILL OUR AMERICAN
> MASTERS VOLUNTARILY
> GIVE UP THEIR SLAVES."
>
> ABRAHAM LINCOLN

Scott to sue for his freedom, as a test case for the legality of slavery. The case became a legal tangle, with implications on many levels. The Supreme Court was divided in its opinions and released several decisions in the case. But Chief Justice Roger Taney's controversial ruling was the one that would change history. Taney, a Marylander and proslavery man, held that "Negroes [were] beings of an inferior order ... altogether unfit to associate with the white race" and with "no rights which the white man was bound to respect," including rights as citizens under the law. The Court also declared that Congress had no right to prohibit slavery in a state or territory. The decision had the effect of throwing gasoline on the smoldering slavery issue.

The previous year in "Bleeding Kansas," the slavery question had erupted in violence when an abolitionist named John Brown waged his own war against the proslavery settlers who had begun moving into the state since the passage of the Kansas-Nebraska Act. Believing himself to be an instrument of God, Brown killed five settlers and left their mutilated bodies as a warning to other proslavery supporters. The massacre gave rise to guerilla raids throughout the state. It was an ominous portent of things to come.

In June 1856, Lincoln spoke out against the Dred Scott decision. It flouted the founders' intention, he said. "In those days, the Declaration of Independence was held sacred by all, and thought to include all; but now, to aid in making the bondage of the negro universal and eternal, it is assailed, and sneered at, and construed, and hawked at, and torn, till, if its framers could rise from their graves, they could not at all recognize it."

The Great Debates

By the mid-1850s, Lincoln had become both a respected and seasoned Illinois politician and a successful lawyer. In 1855, he had been one of the attorneys representing Cyrus McCormick, the inventor of the reaper, in a patent infringement suit. He argued a number of other cases in the federal courts as well, though he still kept up his circuit court appearances. By 1856, the Lincolns could afford to expand the small cottage they had lived in for 13 years, and, as Springfield watched, the home was transformed into a respectable two-story Greek Revival. Returning home after riding the circuit, Lincoln joked to a neighbor, "Stranger do you know where Lincoln lives?" In the larger house as in the small cottage, politics was often the topic and entertaining often done with a political aim.

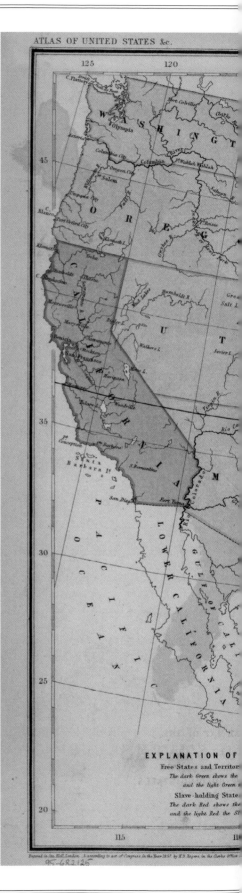

By 1857, the "united" states had divided themselves into factions based on their slavery stance. This map clearly shows the schisms: Dark red indicates slave-importing states, light red the slave-exporting ones; dark green represents the free states and light green colors the territories.

2

GENERAL MAP OF THE
UNITED STATES
Showing the area and extent of the
FREE & SLAVE-HOLDING STATES,
and the Territories of the
UNION.

Scale of English Miles.

Longitude West of Greenwich.

COLOURS.

Engraved by W. & A. K. Johnston, Edinburgh.

Mary's taste for the political game was stronger than ever, and she was devoted, sometimes vehemently so, to furthering Lincoln's career. Herndon claimed that she was "like a toothache, keeping her husband awake to politics day and night." When Lincoln, in a despondent moment, lamented, "No one knows me," she responded, "They will."

By 1858, all of Illinois—and most of the nation—did. At the state Republican conven-

> "ALL THE POWERS OF THE EARTH SEEM RAPIDLY COMBINING AGAINST [THE NEGRO] ... THEY HAVE HIM IN HIS PRISON HOUSE ... BOLTED IN WITH A HUNDRED KEYS."
>
> LINCOLN, ON THE
> DRED SCOTT DECISION

tion in June, delegates unanimously voted for a resolution declaring Lincoln "the first and only choice ... for the United States Senate, as the successor of Stephen A. Douglas." It was an unprecedented move, since at the time state legislators, not the electorate, voted for senators and parties did not choose a candidate in advance. In his speech to the delegation, Lincoln spoke directly to the slavery issue. "In my opinion, it [slavery agitation] will not cease until a crisis shall have been reached and passed. 'A house divided against itself cannot stand.' I believe that this government cannot endure permanently half slave and half free. I do not expect the Union to be dissolved—I do not expect the house to fall— but I do expect it will cease to be divided. It will become all one thing, or all the other."

It was the first of a series of great oratorical moments that year, as Lincoln and Democratic candidate Stephen A. Douglas sparred, each attempting to define exactly what America was and what it should become. A star of the Democratic firmament, Douglas was a

powerhouse in the U.S. Senate. He had tried for his party's presidential nomination in 1852 and had made a strong showing. Still, he didn't underestimate his opponent, whom he described as "full of wit, facts, dates and the best stump speaker, with his droll ways and dry wit, in the West. He is as honest as he is shrewd; and if I beat him my victory will be hard won." Lincoln understood how formidable the "Little Giant" was, commenting poignantly, "With *me,* the race of ambition

has been a failure—a flat failure; with *him* it has been one of splendid success."

Lincoln determined to follow Douglas around the state, offering a rebuttal to each of Douglas's speeches within hours—or at least by the following day. The pro-Democratic *Illinois State Register* called Lincoln a "poor, desperate creature" who "the people won't turn out to hear." Lincoln soon devised a new approach. He challenged Douglas to a series of debates, knowing that the senator would be reluctant to acquiesce but that he couldn't refuse without seeming to be intimidated. Ultimately, Douglas agreed to seven debates in the late summer and early fall of 1858.

Surely no one at the time could have anticipated the weight that history would

Lincoln's great oratorical opponent, Stephen A. Douglas (opposite) stood only five feet four inches tall, but his massive head and commanding presence earned him the title "Little Giant." A Vermont native by birth, he moved to Illinois when he was 20. Like Lincoln, he studied law and became a powerful force in American politics. Using the backdrop of the 32-star American flag, above, Lincoln and Hannibal Hamlin, his running mate, proclaim their candidacy in this campaign banner.

give the Lincoln-Douglas debates. Their oratory varied, but the themes they struck were consistent. Douglas propounded his belief in popular sovereignty—allowing the people of a territory to "vote up or down" on slavery without interference from the federal government. "I care more for the great principle of self-government, the right of the people to rule than I do for all the negroes in Christendom," Douglas thundered. He painted Lincoln as an abolitionist, and, appealing to an inherent "Negrophobia" among many Illinoisans, put Lincoln on the defensive regarding his own attitude toward the black man.

With his hand forced by Douglas, Lincoln stated flatly in one debate, "There is a physical difference between the white and black races which I believe will forever forbid the two races living together on terms of social and political equality." But he went on to insist that "there is no reason in the world why the negro is not entitled to all the natural rights enumerated in the Declaration of Independence, the right to life, liberty and the pursuit of happiness." As the debates reached culmination, Lincoln pressed the theme that slavery was "a moral, social, and political wrong." But, he made it clear he was no abolitionist. He did not believe in interference with slavery in the states where it existed.

The contrast between the style and delivery of Lincoln and Douglas on almost every level could not have been more pronounced. The rotund Douglas reached only to the top of Lincoln's shoulder, but what he lacked in height he made up for in bombast and bearing. He took the stage in crisp linens and a blue suit with silver buttons, generally accompanied by his beautiful, young second wife. His voice boomed across the audience and he made courtly bows to their applause. As he stumped across the state, he traveled in style in a private railroad car, followed by a retinue of supporters and reporters.

Lincoln on the other hand traveled alone as yet another train passenger, one bag containing all his needs. On stage, his worn black frockcoat and pants seemed too short for his long arms and legs, and his voice, particularly before he was warmed up, was high and penetrating. He "used singularly awkward, almost absurd, up-and-down and sidewise

WORLD PERSPECTIVE

A Changing China

Britain's imperial appetite had only been whetted by the loss of the American colonies in the 18th century. In the 19th century, it increasingly looked to the East, particularly to India and China, though China's isolationism made trade difficult. Until the 1830s, Chinese rulers limited foreign trade to Canton (now Guangzhou), and accepted payment only in silver for their gold, tea, silk, and porcelain. But the British began trading in an illicit commodity many Chinese wanted.

With ample supplies of opium from colonial India, Britain began shipping opium to Canton, and its use soon tore the fabric of Confucian society. A British doctor in China estimated that 12 million Chinese were addicted. In 1839, the Chinese commissioner appointed to stop opium commerce confiscated and burned some 20,000 opium chests, setting in motion the First Opium War. A second followed in the late 1850s, but in both wars China was forced to make concessions to the West. America benefited by an "open door policy" that guaranteed easy trade with China.

The West also made inroads into Chinese moral thinking by introducing Christianity. One convert believed that he was sent to restore the Taiping tienquo, the Heavenly Kingdom of Great Peace. With the country fighting a famine and the Q'ing Dynasty powerless to meet western demands, the Taiping Rebellion erupted in 1850 and continued for 14 years. Some 20 million died; countless villages were destroyed.

Despite the carnage, many of the Taiping leaders' reforms echoed modern values. They forbade opium smoking, polygamy, slave trade, and prostitution, and they valued women's rights and fair land distribution. The years of hardship and unrest led many to emigrate. And when news of the California gold discovery reached China in 1848, thousands of men, most from south China, found passage to *Gum Saan*–Gold Mountain.

Chinese militia waged the Opium Wars with the simplest of weapons and protective armor.

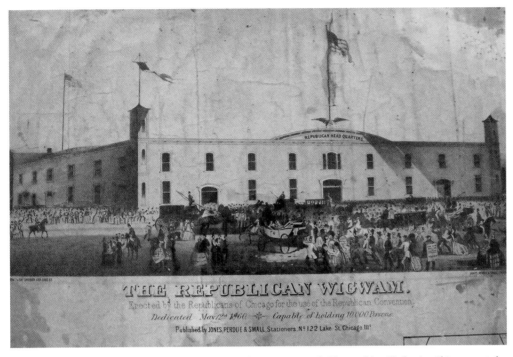

THE REPUBLICAN WIGWAM.
Erected by the Republicans of Chicago for the use of the Republican Convention.
Dedicated May 12th 1860 — Capable of holding 10,000 Persons.
Published by JONES, PERDUE & SMALL, Stationers. No 122 Lake St. Chicago, Ill.

Excited at the prospect of hosting the first national political convention ever held west of the Alleghenies, Chicago erected this "wigwam," to accommodate the Republican convention. Here, on May 18, 1860, Lincoln was nominated for President.

movements of his body to give emphasis to his arguments," reported a New York journalist. He concluded, "There was nothing in all Douglas's powerful effort that appealed to the higher instincts of human nature … Lincoln always touched sympathetic chords."

The Republican Ticket

Lincoln was well aware of the contrast he made with the elegant Douglas, describing his opponent's face to the audience as "round, jolly, fruitful," and full of patronage opportunities for his cronies. While his own face, he said, was "poor, lean, lank"—that of a man of the people. Throughout his campaign, Lincoln cultivated the image of a homespun, common man, of "Honest Old Abe."

Lincoln and Douglas crisscrossed the state in their campaigning, drawing huge crowds to hear their oratory—one of the great forms of entertainment at the time. As one reporter put it, "The prairie is on fire." Lincoln traveled more than 4,000 miles to make some 60 major speeches, fulminating over and over

against the moral outrage of slavery, while Douglas continued to hammer at the political premise that the people should decide for themselves how to handle slavery.

On January 5, 1858, the newly convened Illinois legislature elected Douglas by a vote of 54 to Lincoln's 46. Had it been a popular vote, the outcome might have been different.

The defeat left Lincoln dejected, but he hid his disappointment from the supporters. The race, he told one, "gave me a hearing on the great and durable question of the age, which I could have had in no other way; and though I now sink out of view, and shall be forgotten, I believe I have made some marks which will tell for the cause of civil liberty long after I am gone."

Politics was an expensive business for Lincoln, who was comfortably well off but far from wealthy. The money he made from his law practice supported him and his family, but when he took time off for campaigning, his finances suffered. After he lost the election, he told a friend, "I shall go to the wall for bread

THE 1860 PRESIDENTIAL CAMPAIGN

Campaign button from Lincoln's 1860 presidential race.

Campaign ribbon for Douglas and his running mate, Georgia senator Herschel Johnson.

Campaign banner for Lincoln and running mate, Maine senator Hannibal Hamlin.

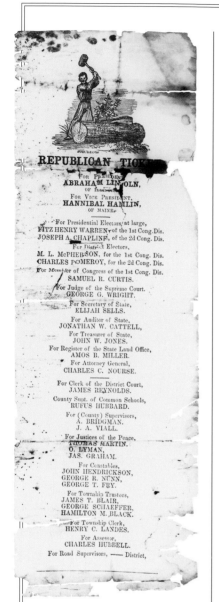

and meat if I neglect my business this year as well as last." Mary was no help in husbanding finances and sometimes shopped extravagantly by Springfield standards. As the years went on, Mary's spending would wreak havoc on her life and occasionally her husband's.

Lincoln was now well established as a prominent Republican, and in early 1860, he was openly mentioned as a strong presidential contender. To this, Lincoln replied, "I must, in candor, say I do not think myself fit for the Presidency." Yet, at the request of the prominent theologian and abolitionist Henry Ward Beecher, Lincoln traveled to New York to speak, knowing that an appearance in the East would help solidify his standing as a national politician. At Cooper Union in New York City, he told a large audience, "Let us have faith that right makes might." The speech gained him accolades and the wider recognition he had hoped for. From New York, he went on to New England, to visit his oldest son.

Probably at Mary's insistence, Robert had been sent east the previous fall to finish his education at a prestigious eastern school. Now, he was spending a year at Phillips Exeter Academy, preparing to enter Harvard.

Lincoln's relationship with Robert was always more formal than the one he enjoyed with his two younger sons. When Robert was young, Lincoln was often away riding the circuit or preoccupied with his own career or political aspirations. In fact, some scholars also speculate that the sickly Eddie made Lincoln more sensitive and responsive to the sons who came later.

In any case, Lincoln used the trip to New England both to visit with Robert and to speak at surrounding towns. By the time he returned to Springfield, he was willing to admit that he had presidential aspirations. "I will be entirely frank," he wrote to one colleague. "The taste *is* in my mouth a little."

The 1860 Republican National Convention was to be held in Chicago, in Lincoln's home state, giving him some natural political advantage. By the traditions of the day, Lincoln stayed in Springfield while his champions attended the May convention, because, as one of them put it, "You need a few trusty friends here to say words for you that may be necessary to be said."

> "GREAT EVENTS MAKE ME QUIET AND CALM; IT IS ONLY TRIFLES THAT IRRITATE MY NERVES."
> QUEEN VICTORIA, RULER OF THE BRITISH EMPIRE, 1837-1901

As the balloting began, Lincoln waited for the outcome in the offices of the *Illinois State Journal* in Springfield. On the first ballot, the names of five potential candidates appeared. William Seward, the senator from New York, took the lead in the vote count and Lincoln came in second. On the second ballot, the contest narrowed to just Seward and Lincoln, with Seward barely ahead. On the third ballot, Lincoln had the nomination. When word arrived, he joked with townsmen gathered there, "Gentlemen, there is a little woman at our house who is probably more interested in this than I am." Nearing home, he called out "Mary, Mary, *we* are elected."

To broaden the appeal of the Republican ticket, the convention also nominated a former Democrat and senator from Maine for Vice President, Hannibal Hamlin, a respected eastern politician, who had often opposed Lincoln's beloved Henry Clay. But Hamlin and Lincoln shared a concern about slavery expanding into the western U.S. They would not meet until after the election.

In June, Lincoln got more good news. The factionalized Democratic Party had split, with Southerners nominating John Breckenridge and Northerners Lincoln's old nemesis, Stephen Douglas.

Above, a sample Republican election ticket from the 1860 race is topped by an image of Lincoln, the "Railsplitter." Opposite, issued as a broadside, a national Republican chart shows former candidates and their platforms, as well as the disposition of free and slave states.

While the Republican Party promoted "Old Abe—the Railsplitter," Lincoln didn't campaign himself, as this was considered to be unseemly by the prevailing mid-19th century standards. Instead, he waited in Springfield, receiving the press and the curious. He admitted to his law partner Herndon that he was "bored—bored badly." Apparently, Mary was far from bored. A local minister commented that Mary "ought to be sent to the cooper's and well-secured against bursting by iron hoops."

Banners in the North celebrated Lincoln's victory as a great day for America, but in the Deep South newspapers proclaimed that "evil days . . . are upon us."

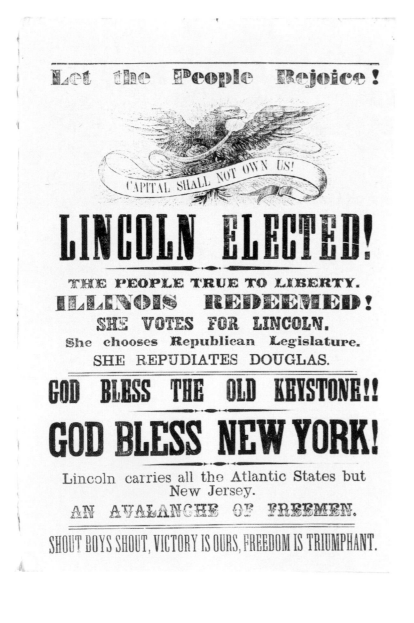

On November 6, 1860, the self-educated, self-improved frontier boy and prairie lawyer was elected 16th President of the United States. He had taken a handy majority in the electoral college, but he had received only 40 percent of the popular vote. He knew that he was facing a divided Washington—and nation. The day after his election, he joked to reporters in Springfield, "Well boys your troubles are over but mine are just beginning."

Almost immediately, Republicans flocked to Lincoln's door, hoping for patronage jobs. The press camped out in Springfield. Reams of correspondence descended upon the President-elect; among the letters, both he and Mary received death threats.

Lincoln had help managing the incessant demands on his time from a young newspaperman who had worked as his private secretary during the campaign. In his late 20s, John George Nicolay was a Bavarian by birth. His parents had immigrated to Illinois and died when he was young. Despite a childhood of poverty, Nicolay had learned the printing business and was owner of the *Pittsfield Free Press* when he came to Lincoln's attention. Lincoln's first official act as President was to appoint Nicolay his private secretary.

Brusque and efficient, the thin young man was generally considered "grim" and "acerbic." But he was protective of Lincoln and his time and was deeply loyal. Despite his efficiency, even Nicolay could not cope with the flood of correspondence, and he soon called on a friend, John Hay, to lend a hand. From a wealthy Illinois family, Hay had been educated in the East, at Brown University in Rhode Island. He was halfheartedly reading law in his uncle's Pittsfield office when he volunteered to help Nicolay. At the time, he was not the great Lincoln admirer that his friend was, sometimes referring to the President-elect as the "Cincinnatus of the prairie." Still, he would go with Nicolay to Washington as Lincoln's other private secretary.

In the four months before he took office, Lincoln watched from Springfield as the states of the Deep South seceded. John Calhoun's South Carolina, ever the hotbed of proslavery sentiment, led the charge, followed by Georgia, Mississippi, Florida, Alabama, Louisiana, and Texas. By February, they had declared themselves the Confederate States of America and elected Jefferson Davis their president. Not yet President himself, and believing that the secessionists represented only a minority of white Southerners, Lincoln spent his time contemplating his Cabinet and interviewing candidates.

In late January 1861, Lincoln took time to visit his 73-year-old stepmother, the woman who had encouraged and nurtured young Abraham. Sarah Bush Lincoln was living with her daughter in Goosenest Prairie, in east-central Illinois, and the President-elect made the hard winter trip alone, first by passenger train, then in the caboose of a freight train, and finally in a buggy. Thomas, Lincoln's father, had died years earlier, without ever having met Mary or his grandchildren.

In 1849, Lincoln's stepbrother had written that Thomas was critically ill, saying, "He Craves to See you all the time ... for you are his only Child that is of his own flesh and blood." Lincoln had rushed to his father's side, only to find that Thomas in fact was not at death's door. Later the same year, Lincoln again received an alarming letter about his father's health, but this time he wrote back telling his father "to call upon, and confide in, our great, and good, and merciful Maker." Thomas died in 1851, without seeing Abraham again. On the trip to Goosenest Prairie, Lincoln visited his father's gravesite and said that he would have a tombstone erected.

When he said his final good-bye to Sarah, she cried openly, worrying that they would never see each other again. Lincoln comforted her, "No No Mama. Trust in the Lord and all will be well. We will See each other

again." Later, Sarah admitted that she "did not want Abe to run for Presdt ... was afraid somehow or other."

Lincoln returned to Springfield for his final few days. He assured his partner Herndon, "If I live I'm coming back some time and then we'll go right on practicing law as if nothing had ever happened." On February 11, he boarded the train to Washington. Addressing the crowd who had come to see him off, he made an emotional farewell. "To this place, and the kindness of these people, I owe everything," he said, admitting that "I now leave not knowing when, or whether ever, I may return, with a task before me greater than that which rested upon Washington...."

On that he was surely correct.

On February 9, 1861, the Confederate States of America chose former United States Senator Jefferson Davis as their president, though the West Point graduate would have preferred to serve as army commander. Pages 92-93: The previous November, crowds gathered in Savannah, Georgia, to cheer for southern independence.

"I EXPECT TO MAINTAIN THIS CONTEST UNTIL
SUCCESSFUL, OR TILL I DIE OR AM CONQUERED ...
OR CONGRESS OR THE COUNTRY FORSAKES ME."

ABRAHAM LINCOLN

[CHAPTER FOUR]

I WOULD SAVE THE UNION
1861-1863

THE FOUR-CAR TRAIN CARRYING LINCOLN TOWARD HIS DESTINY PLOWED
through the barren winter heartland of America for 12 days. The
long, circuitous route was planned to give citizens a firsthand look
at their next President and his family. At whistle stops along the way,
admiring crowds gathered to hear Lincoln speak
and see Mrs. President Lincoln and the couple's young sons. Mary,
in high spirits, had been on a buying expedition to New York earlier
in the winter to equip herself properly for her role with the newest
fashions, and her efforts hadn't gone unnoticed. The *Home Journal,*
a national magazine, had crowned her the Illinois Queen. At most
stops along the way she appeared, dressed in her stylish new out-
fits, at Lincoln's side—but not always. In Ashtabula, Ohio, making
an appearance apparently didn't suit her, and Lincoln explained to
ladies there that he had "always found it very difficult to make her
do what she did not want to."

Even as the entourage made its way toward the capital, the newly
formed Confederates States of America inaugurated Jefferson Davis
as their president. What may have rankled Lincoln more was the
Confederacy's choice of vice president—Alexander Stephens, Lincoln's old friend from his days in Congress and a fellow Whig.

Lincoln's election may have been the precipitating event that led to the states of the
Deep South seceding, but the cleave in the country had been growing over decades,
and so had talk of "disunion." Even the New England Transcendentalist Ralph Waldo
Emerson had called the South a "barbarous community" and asked how it and the

*Crowds at the Alabama state
capitol in February 1861
(opposite) witness Jefferson
Davis's inauguration as president of the Confederacy. Above,
the second national flag of the
Confederacy—and its battle
flag—replaced the original Stars
and Bars in 1863.*

"civilized" North "could constitute one state." The very idea of a united country comprised of disparate states and regions was less than a hundred years old, and it had been a voluntary arrangement from the beginning. Since the Union's formation little had happened to cement the parts into a whole. Instead, the regions had grown apart culturally and economically. The North had industrialized, urbanized, experienced a great tide of immigrants, embraced a vision of a technological future. Meanwhile, the South still clung to the Jeffersonian ideals of a rural society modeled on noblesse oblige. Rich planters dominated culture and economy; poor whites and slaves held little hope for a different future.

Still, the North and South needed each other. Southern cotton fed northern mills and northern dollars helped sustain southern planters. But the slavery issue had become an increasingly heavy millstone around the nation's neck. Congress, through its many compromises, had attempted to deal with it, but to no avail. Now Lincoln was heading East to a destiny he could never have dreamed of—or wished for. He called himself "a mere instrument, an accidental instrument" of the Union. But he understood that he was the defender of the human dream of democracy for all, embodied in that Union.

On his trip to Washington, Lincoln assured the gathered crowds that all would be well. In Cleveland, he insisted that the secessionist crisis had been brought on by "designing politicians" and that it was "all artificial." But he never wavered from his message that the Union, at whatever cost, must be preserved.

In Philadelphia, Lincoln raised the flag at Independence Hall, telling the audience that the nation stood for liberty for all and the Declaration of Independence held the "promise that in due time the weights should be lifted from the shoulders of all men, and that *all* should have an equal chance." Then he continued, "if this country cannot be

saved without giving up that principle—I was about to say I would rather be assassinated on this spot than to surrender it."

> "I OFFER NEITHER PAY, NOR QUARTERS, NOR FOOD; I OFFER ONLY HUNGER, THIRST, FORCED MARCHES, BATTLES AND DEATH. LET HIM WHO LOVES HIS COUNTRY WITH HIS HEART, AND NOT MERELY WITH HIS LIPS, FOLLOW ME."
>
> GIUSEPPE GARIBALDI, ON THE 1860S STRUGGLE TO UNIFY ITALY

Assassination would have been uppermost on his mind that day particularly, because Allan Pinkerton, head of the Pinkerton National Detective Agency, had just uncovered a plot to assassinate Lincoln as he changed trains in pro-South Baltimore. Death threats were not new. In Springfield, Lincoln and Mary had been plagued with threatening letters, and this threat was being taken seriously by Lincoln's advisers, who persuaded him to alter his plans.

The next day in Harrisburg, Pennsylvania, Lincoln, accompanied by his Illinois friend and now bodyguard, Ward Hill Lamon, and Pinkerton, got off the presidential train, while Mary and the children continued on the official route. Secretly boarding a train that hurtled through the night to Washington, Lincoln traveled incognito, wearing a slouch hat pulled down around his unmistakable face. The sleeping berth he occupied that night didn't quite accommodate his long frame.

Arriving in Washington around five in the morning, the men stepped onto the train platform only to hear a voice saying, "Abe, you can't play that on me." Pinkerton turned, ready to attack, but Lincoln greeted the

speaker—his old Illinois compatriot, Elihu Washburne. The congressman accompanied the President-elect to Willard's Hotel. In the ten days before the Inauguration, it became the Lincoln home.

The President-elect had found the train-switching subterfuge an ignominious way to enter the capital, and the press lampooned him for "sneaking" into the capital city—and in disguise at that. But he had far greater concerns to occupy him as he re-immersed himself in the city he had first entered more than a dozen years before as a one-term freshman congressman. This time, official Washington courted him, and his time was filled with nonstop receptions and meetings.

Amid the socializing, Lincoln was preoccupied with Cabinet appointments. During the previous months in Springfield, he had contemplated Cabinet choices and interviewed candidates. Politics naturally was a major consideration—some of the men he entertained had helped him in his campaign and were major forces in the Republican Party. Four had contested him, and each other, for the 1860 Republican nomination. Regional considerations also affected his choices. In the precarious office Lincoln was about to inhabit, he needed a balance of ideas and approaches. As Inauguration Day neared, Lincoln completed his formal offers. The final choices left him with a "team of rivals."

Chief among the rivals was his secretary of state, William Seward, the strongest opponent Lincoln had faced for the Republican presidential nomination. A former governor

On March 4, 1861, Abraham Lincoln was sworn in as the 16th President of the United States in front of the East Portico of the Capitol, whose dome was then being replaced. As conflict gripped his Presidency, Lincoln insisted construction on the dome continue, "as a sign we intend the Union shall go on."

The "Tycoon," as his secretaries, John Nicolay (left) and John Hay, (right) affectionately called him, poses with the two young men in this well-known, though undated photograph. The businesslike Nicolay was fiercely protective of the President, while the affable Hay provided needed companionship to both Lincoln and his son Robert.

clear to others that Chase would stay—and so, in the end, did Seward. To his secretary Nicolay, Lincoln confided that he couldn't "afford to let Seward take the first trick."

Salmon Chase was no easier to handle than Seward. An elegant, self-important man and a respected U.S. senator, Chase had also been considered for the Republican nomination, and he fully expected to be President one day. As he did with most other mortals, Chase merely tolerated Lincoln. The President, for his part, found Chase's general bearing "about one and a half times bigger than any other man that I ever knew." An ardent abolitionist, Chase found his greatest rival would always be the southern-sympathizing Seward.

Another Seward rival was the bearded secretary of the Navy, Gideon Welles. A former Democrat who had become disgusted by his party's support of the "southern slaveocracy," he was now a Republican. But he held on to his old Jacksonian belief in small government. As the Presidency progressed, he would prove businesslike and stalwart, both in his duties and his loyalty to Lincoln. Another former Democrat, Postmaster General Montgomery Blair, was according to Nicolay, a "good and true man," but one deeply flawed by "violent personal antagonisms and indiscretions." Like Seward, he had strong southern sympathies. Attorney General Edward Bates, a respected senator from Missouri and another who had sought the presidential nomination, was not as obstreperous as Blair, but he wanted a conservative approach to the Union's dealings with the South, and he was as prickly and opinionated as most of the Cabinet. Secretary of the Interior Caleb Smith, easily swayed and little admired, was described by one acquaintance as a man with "neither heart nor sincerity … He cannot be a man of any convictions."

Most controversial of all in Lincoln's Cabinet was his secretary of war, Simon Cameron, the "czar of Pennsylvania," yet another Republican presidential contender. Tainted

of New York and a U.S. senator, Seward was seasoned, opinionated, and cunning. He was also sympathetic to the South and wanted to find a compromise with the slave states.

Betting on Lincoln's inexperience, Seward expected to be the real fountainhead of government, the "premier" working around a weak President. He quickly found that he was mistaken in that assumption when he opposed the appointment of Salmon Chase, a bitter rival of his, as secretary of the treasury. Sure he could force Lincoln to renege on the offer to Chase, Seward wrote a letter saying he would withdraw from the Cabinet if Chase were added. Lincoln did not try to dissuade Seward directly—except for a brief note asking him to reconsider. But the President-elect made it by rumors of corrupt political and business dealings, Cameron was strongly opposed by a number of Lincoln advisers; he also shared Seward's leanings toward the South. Cameron's presence on the Cabinet would reassure northern businessmen who worried that the administration was pro-free trade. As to accusations of business turpitude, Cameron, a self-made magnate, dismissed them saying, "If I have any ability whatever, it is an ability to make money. I do not have to steal it. I can go into the street any day, and as the world goes, make all the money I want."

These were the cohorts Lincoln would have to rely on in the hard days ahead. "No President ever had a Cabinet of which the members were so independent, had so large individual followings, and were so inharmonious," lamented New York politician Chancey Depew. Lincoln saw it this way:

WORLD PERSPECTIVE

Charles Darwin and the Voyage of the *Beagle*

On February 12, 1809—the same day in fact that Abraham Lincoln was born in a log cabin on the Kentucky frontier—Dr. and Mrs. Robert Darwin were delivered of a son in Shrewsbury, England. The boy, Charles, spent his days bird hunting and bug collecting before going off to Cambridge Divinity School. It did not inspire him, and when he gave up the notion of being a clergyman, he seemed to fulfill his father's prophecy that he would "be a disgrace to yourself and your family."

At the age of 22, Darwin was invited by Capt. Robert FitzRoy to join the H.M.S. *Beagle* as unofficial naturalist—there was already an official one. The ship was about to undertake a two-year survey of exotic locales around the world. Darwin accepted, pleased with the idea of adventure.

In December 1831, the *Beagle* set sail. By February it was off the coast of South America, surveying and collecting. Despite the original timetable, the *Beagle* stayed in the waters off South America until October 1835, and during that time, Darwin collected plant and animal specimens up and down the coasts, into the Andes, and on islands, including an isolated chain 600 miles offshore called the Galápagos Islands.

The ship then headed east into the Pacific, stopping at Tahiti, Australia, and South Africa, before again returning to South America, and, after five years away, home to England. "As far as I can judge of myself I worked to the utmost during the voyage

An 1850s photograph of the great naturalist, whose groundbreaking work on evolution haunted him throughout his life.

from the mere pleasure of investigation, and from my strong desire to add a few facts to the great mass of facts in natural science," Darwin later wrote.

He became pursued as a young naturalist/adventurer; his reputation grew when he published his *Journals*. He had also begun sorting the countless specimens he had collected. Among them were the beaks of birds from the Galápagos. When fellow naturalist John Gould examined them, he determined they were all beaks of finches—13 different species from different islands in the chain. Why so many beaks and so many species, each in a different habitat? The question came to haunt Darwin, and by 1844 he had written an essay he called *The Origin of Species*, but he did nothing with it.

Scholars debate the reason for "Darwin's delay" in publishing the essay, most attributing it to his conflict between his scientific beliefs and the prevailing religious views. "I am almost convinced . . . ," he wrote, "that species are not (it is like confessing a murder) immutable." If this was so, then the concept of God the Creator was at risk. When he later published his ideas, it shook the bedrock of Victorian society. During the 1860s, as Darwin's book was widely translated, scientists took up its cause, developing further the theory of natural selection. All the while, the Church of England opposed evolution. Even now, 150 years later, the controversy Darwin stirred has yet to settle.

"I had looked the party over and concluded that these were the strongest men ... I had no right to deprive the country of their services."

The Job of President

A cold, late winter wind blew through the streets of Washington on March 4, 1861, with the sun coming and going as the clouds separated. The Inaugural scene was far from celebratory—Gen. Winfield Scott had positioned soldiers at strategic locations and assigned sharpshooters to stand guard on rooftops, watching for anyone who might do harm to the tall ungainly man who was about to become President of the troubled nation. Some 30,000 people had gathered to witness the swearing in, but a wooden barricade stood between them and the Inaugural platform in front of the Capitol. Senator Edward Baker introduced Lincoln, who stood to take the oath of office, then seemed flummoxed when he had nowhere to place his stovepipe hat. Stephen Douglas, who had been gracious and helpful since Lincoln arrived in Washington, took the hat, saying "Permit me, sir." Chief Justice Roger Taney, whose Dred Scott decision had furthered the unraveling of the country Lincoln was now to lead, administered the oath of office. Then Lincoln began his Inaugural Address. His high voice was not resonant, yet it carried far across the crowds. "We are not enemies, but friends," he insisted. "The mystic chords of memory, stretching from every battlefield, and patriot grave, to every living heart and hearthstone, all over this broad land, will yet swell the chorus of the Union, when again touched, as surely they will be, by the better angels of our nature." The crowd reacted politely, and the northern press was less than effusive in its praise. But the southern press promised that Lincoln's stance would bring bloodshed.

At the Inaugural Ball, held in City Hall, Mary Lincoln appeared "dressed all in blue, with a necklace and bracelets of gold and pearls" and her signature flowers entwined in her hair. The ball was her crowning moment, and she charmed official Washington with her easy conversation and southern grace. The press gave her glowing reviews. "She is more self-possessed than Lincoln," the *New York Herald* reported.

From the first morning of his Presidency, Lincoln faced the turmoil of a nation facing war. Since South Carolina's secession the previous December, the Union had maintained a small garrison of 68 men under the command of Maj. Robert Anderson at Fort Sumter, near the mouth of Charleston Harbor. The Confederacy insisted that Anderson was occupying their sovereign soil. Now Anderson sent word that his garrison would be out of provisions within six weeks. If not resupplied, he would have to abandon the fort. To hold the fort, he said, would require 25,000 soldiers.

Lincoln approached General Scott for military advice, but he did not alert his Cabinet to Anderson's precarious situation until four days later. Their opinions were voluble and varied, but the choices were simple: Evacuate the fort or find a way to reprovision it—and that way could not entail a force of up to 25,000 because in early 1861, the Union had no such force. The U.S. Army totaled 16,000 men, most on the western frontier.

Whatever decision Lincoln made would have the direst of consequences. Capitulation, he believed, "would be our national destruction consummated." But he also did not want to risk alienating the states of the upper South, still in the Union. Through the weeks that followed, Lincoln heard advice

Self-assured Secretary of the Treasury Salmon Chase anticipated the day he himself would be President. His ambitions and political conniving created divisiveness in Lincoln's Cabinet and anguish for the President. Opposite, a map of Charleston Harbor details the South's bombardment of Fort Sumter.

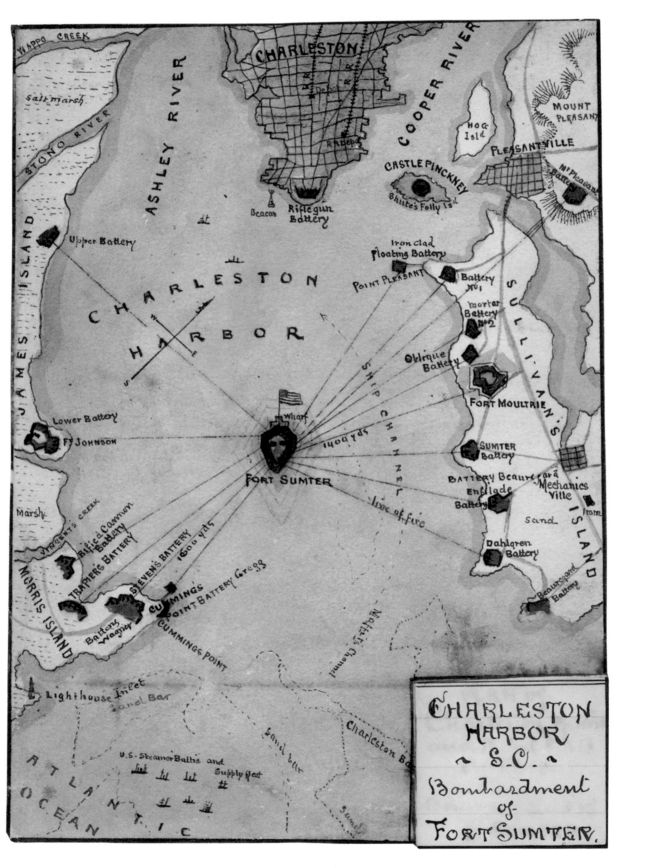

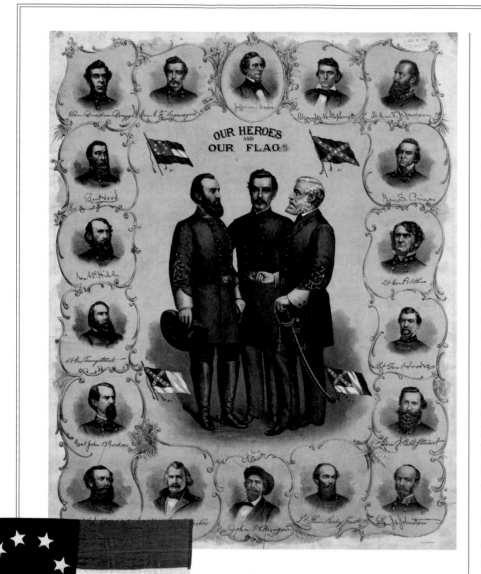

OUR HEROES
AND
OUR FLAGS

The coming war would make heroes of three Confederate generals (top): Thomas "Stonewall" Jackson (left), P. G. T. Beauregard (middle), and Robert E. Lee (right). Graduates of the U.S. Military Academy at West Point, all three had served in the Mexican-American War. Above, the original Stars and Bars flag of the Confederacy.

ciliation with the South by allowing slavery to continue there. Southerners had assured him that he was the man who could bring about "a peaceful adjustment of the difficulties." On April 1, he had sent Lincoln a remarkable memorandum suggesting that the North abandon Fort Sumter and instead reinforce the less controversial Fort Pickens, in northern Florida. Then, under the heading "For Foreign Nations," he asserted that public attention could be deflected away from the domestic stalemate by accusing France, and particularly Spain, of interfering in North American affairs, which to some extent they had. Spain had sent troops to reenforce rebels on Santo Domingo, and France had its eye on the unsettled situation in Mexico, where the populist president Benito Juárez was enacting land and social reforms that promised to stir up more trouble. Monarchist France disliked Juárez and saw intervention against him as an opportunity for their own empire-building. A "war with England, France, or Spain, … would be the best means of reestablishing internal peace," Seward believed.

He also believed the administration was "without a policy either domestic or foreign," but once a policy was adopted, "there must be an energetic prosecution of it. For this purpose it must be somebody's business to pursue and direct it incessantly. Either the President must do it himself, and be all the while active in it, or devolve it on some member of his cabinet"— of course Seward himself. Lincoln would have none of it. In a memorandum he assured his secretary of state that he, not Seward, would prosecute policy *and* that he had always had one.

In fact, Lincoln had little experience in foreign affairs and no real foreign policy. Though Seward had wildly overstepped his role, he did understand that the great European powers— Great Britain, France, and Russia—were considering intervening in the American conflict, on the side of the cotton-rich Confederacy.

from his military leaders, his Cabinet, and congressmen. Even as he worried over the crisis, he allowed office seekers to call on him throughout the day and into the night. Under such constant pressure, he finally collapsed with one of the migraine headaches that periodically attacked him.

While the Sumter crisis cost Lincoln both physically and politically, it taught him what it meant to be President—that all decisions ultimately resided with him. Realizing that, he reached his own decision—the Union would resupply Sumter by sea, forcing the South's hand, one way or the other. Seward objected.

Throughout the secession crisis, Seward had been meddling, working to bring recon-

He and Lincoln would walk a fine line to prevent that from happening.

Focused on the situation in the South, Lincoln began to plan for a force to reprovision Sumter, but he did make one concession to Seward's belief that the South could be mollified. He would send an emissary to inform South Carolina that a relief expedition was on its way. Lincoln's message was clear: "An attempt will be made to supply Fort Sumpter with provisions only."

> "THE STUFF OF WHICH
> HE IS MADE MUST BE
> AS STERN AS THE ASPECT
> OF OUR DAYS…. I DARE SAY
> THERE ARE DORMANT
> QUALITIES IN 'OLD ABE'
> WHICH OCCASION
> WILL DRAW FORTH."
>
> HENRY VILLARD,
> *NEW YORK HERALD*

For his part Confederate president Jefferson Davis faced the same charges of non-action that Lincoln had been facing. "The spirit and even the patriotism of the people is oozing out under this do-nothing policy," a Mobile newspaper lamented. On April 12, Davis acted. With the Union expeditionary fleet off Charleston Harbor, the South began bombarding Fort Sumter and kept at it for 33 hours. Anderson surrendered the fort on April 14. Lincoln had made his choice, and the Confederates had made theirs.

A day after Anderson's surrender, Lincoln called for 75,000 militiamen to serve for 90 days. Patriotic fervor swept the nation. A New York woman summed up the mood— "It seems as if we never were alive till now; never had a country till now."

But the proclamation also ensured more disunion, forcing the hand of the states of the upper South. The governors of those states weren't about to call up troops to march on their fellow Southerners. North Carolina, Virginia, Arkansas, and Tennessee seceded, and within weeks the Confederacy had declared its new capital to be Richmond, Virginia, only a hundred miles from Washington, D.C. The choice made sense. Virginia was the most populous and industrialized southern state. Richmond's Tredagar Iron Works could be converted to manufacture heavy ordnance, and the state's railroad system could transport men and matériel.

Virginia had a further military advantage—the man Winfield Scott had considered the best officer in the U.S. Army, Robert E. Lee. Lee had proved his leadership and tactical brilliance in the Mexican-American War and had risen steadily in the ranks. Scott had approached him to command the Union Army just as Lee heard of Virginia's secession. Lee could not accept. "I cannot raise my hand against my birthplace, my home, my children." Scott told Lee, as a friend, that he had "made the greatest mistake" of his life. Weeks later, Lee admitted that he saw disaster ahead: "I foresee that the country will have to pass through a terrible ordeal." Even knowing that, he accepted that he must play his own role in the ordeal, and he became a military adviser to Jefferson Davis.

Lincoln's call for troops had not been kindly received by the border slave states either. The governors of Missouri, Kentucky, Delaware, and Maryland spoke out vehemently against recruitment, but they did not leave the Union, much to Lincoln's relief. Maryland had the strongest reaction, insisting first that no Union

Virginia native Robert E. Lee had distinguished himself in the Mexican-American War but saw no battlefield action the entire first year of the Civil War. When he did take command in the field during the summer of 1862, he swiftly became the South's most formidable weapon.

militia cross through Baltimore on their way south, and later that none enter the state at all. Railroad bridges feeding into Baltimore from the north were destroyed and telegraph lines cut.

Washington became increasingly isolated and deserted, expecting daily that either reinforcements would arrive by sea or Confederate troops would attack the city. General Scott

> "THE CARDS ARE IN OUR HANDS, AND WE INTEND TO PLAY THEM OUT TO THE BANKRUPTCY OF EVERY COTTON FACTORY IN GREAT BRITAIN AND FRANCE OR THE ACKNOWLEDGMENT OF OUR INDEPENDENCE."
> JEFFERSON DAVIS

urged Mary Lincoln to take the two Lincoln boys and return to Springfield for safety. She refused. Troops encamped in the East Room of the President's House, as it was then called, and Lincoln became increasingly anxious at the delay of the northern troops. "Why don't they come? Why don't they come?" he asked repeatedly. Then, on April 25, the Seventh New York arrived by train from Annapolis, Maryland, and marched confidently through the streets of Washington. The next day Massachusetts and Rhode Island regiments arrived. The federal capital was secure, for the moment at least.

It was during the early tumultuous days of war that Lincoln made two controversial decisions. He later defended both by explaining that Congress had been adjourned at the time and he had had to act on his own accord. One of his orders suspended the right to the writ of habeas corpus along the corridor from Washington to Philadelphia. Those suspected of plotting against the Union or

aiding the Confederacy could be held without a court hearing. Chief Justice Taney, ever at odds with Lincoln, strongly objected, saying that the President's actions countermanded "a government of laws." But Lincoln would not back down: "Are all the laws, *but one,* to go unexecuted, and the government itself go to pieces, lest that one be violated."

Lincoln also ordered a blockade of all Confederate ports from Virginia to Texas. This order held a legal incongruity that would get him in trouble internationally. The President had also declared that the Confederacy was still a part of the U.S.—not a separate country but states in rebellion. By international law, a country could not blockade itself, but only "belligerent" nations. Secretaries Welles and Sumner had advised him to close the ports rather than blockade them, but Lincoln, despite his lawyer's training, insisted on the blockade. Predictably, European governments responded with harsh words. British diplomats worked hard to have the blockade lifted, but Lincoln would not budge. Britain then announced that she would consider it illegal for the U.S. to seize any of her vessels on the pretext that they had violated the blockade.

When Congress reconvened, Lincoln explained that the greater issue behind the war was "more than the fate of these United States. It represents to the whole family of man, the question, whether a constitutional republic, or a democracy … can or cannot, maintain its territorial integrity, against its own domestic foes."

With the first month of his Presidency behind him, Lincoln was no longer indecisive. By spring, he had called for additional volunteers and was expanding the armed

Federal uniforms were not standardized. These men of the 114th Pennsylvania Infantry chose the short, baggy pants of the French Army Zouaves, whose garb was inspired by North Africa. An early hero of the war, Elmer Ellsworth, wore such a uniform, and his death in 1861 helped popularize the look.

forces. Understanding how woefully equipped the country was for war, the President had taken charge. Even Seward approved, "Executive skill and vigor are rare qualities," he wrote. "The President is the best of us; but he needs constant and assiduous cooperation." With his new appreciation of the man who was his superior, Seward began to give that cooperation.

In Congress, Lincoln also had support from an unlikely source, Senator Stephen A. Douglas, who urged the Democrats to get behind the war effort. The senator toured the border slave states, encouraging them to back the Union cause. In June, Douglas was rallying support in his home state of Illinois when he was fatally stricken with typhoid fever. The Little Giant's last words were for his sons. "Tell them," he is said to have uttered, "to obey the laws and support the Constitution of the United States."

Lincoln and Douglas, despite their years of animosity, had joined in common cause

WORLD PERSPECTIVE

The Cotton Famine

"Y ou do not dare make war on cotton," South Carolina senator James Henry Hammond had declared in 1858. "No power on Earth dares to make war upon it. Cotton is king." In the mid-19th century, the senator spoke truth.

Since the introduction of short-staple cotton in the 1820s, cotton cultivation spread like wildfire throughout the Deep South. This courser cousin to long-staple cotton had the great advantage of adapting to the variable southern climate. Its seeds were more difficult to remove, but the invention of the cotton gin in the 1790s had taken care of that. The rise of textile mills in New England and western Europe had taken care of demand. In a few short decades the Deep South had become the Cotton Kingdom, and King Cotton accounted for nearly two-thirds of U.S. exports.

Cotton was both a blessing and a curse. It encouraged slavery and discouraged economic diversity. When war came and Lincoln imposed a blockade on southern ports, the South had few resources to fall back on to support itself. But it did have cotton in abundance and could have purchased European-manufactured weapons with its surplus.

Instead, the Confederacy put great stock in its own cotton and held onto supplies, expecting demand and prices to escalate abroad. The Confederacy reasoned that in time Europe would support the South in order to procure cotton for its own mills. But unbeknownst to the South, France and England, with their vast mills,

In South Carolina, slaves continued to prepare cotton for the gin even as war raged.

particularly in the world's "cottonopolis" of Manchester, had stockpiled cotton, and the South lost a critical opportunity to arm itself. As the war continued, though, Britain and France felt the sting of the northern blockade. Some historians contend that Europe declined to help the South because they did not want to support people who clung to slavery. Without cotton, European textile mills lay idle and the workers went hungry.

As a French diplomat observed to an American minister, "We are nearly out of cotton, and cotton we must have." Desperate for more, Europeans looked abroad for other sources.

Increasingly, Britain came to rely on India, imposing tariffs and other restrictions on cloth from the colony to keep the raw fiber flowing to its textile mills. But Indian cotton was deemed inferior, and soon both Britain and France turned their eyes toward Egypt. Cotton had been introduced there in the 1820s, and the finer, much coveted long-staple variety grew well. With European demand swelling, Egyptian farmers abandoned other crops to plant more cotton, and British and French traders began to invest heavily in Egyptian cotton plantations.

Cotton is a fickle master, and the cotton curse soon wreaked havoc on Egypt as well. Egypt lost its market edge when the Civil War ended and the South reentered the cotton business. Working those southern lands were black sharecroppers, who had escaped bondage only to be enslaved once again by a life of toil in the cotton fields.

Gen. Winfield Scott (above) was enormous both in girth and reputation. His "Anaconda Plan" (top) called for squeezing the Confederacy in a vise, but the plan required patience, and the North, eager for a quick victory, had none to spare.

to save the Union, and Douglas's death was a blow. It only added to the grief the President had experienced a month before, when the dashing young Zouave colonel Elmer Ellsworth had been killed. Ellsworth had studied law in Lincoln's Springfield office, becoming such a close friend of the family that he accompanied the Lincolns on the Inaugural train. When Virginia seceded and Lincoln ordered Federal troops to occupy Alexandria and Arlington Heights, the site of Lee's home, Ellsworth's Zouaves were among the Union soldiers who marched into Virginia.

Ellsworth knew that Lincoln was aggravated by the sight of a secessionist flag he could spot with his spyglass flying atop the Marshall House hotel in Alexandria. Determined to relieve Lincoln of the sight, the young officer went to the hotel himself and took the flag down. On his way back downstairs, he was shot by the hotelkeeper. In his letter of condolence to Ellsworth's parents, a devastated Lincoln wrote, "So much of promised usefulness to one's country, and of bright hopes for one's self and friends, have rarely been so suddenly dashed, as in his fall."

Lincoln's call for troops to fight for the preservation of the Union had resounded through the North, and several governors proudly told him that more regiments could be filled than had been requested. By early summer, 186,000 men had volunteered to defend their country. The problem that confronted the army was a lack of training and leadership. The professional army had only 13,000 men to deal with all the green recruits. At the helm of this problem was Gen. Winfield Scott. An enormous man who

Federal cavalrymen cross Bull Run at Sudley Ford, as onlookers watch. Expectations for a Union victory were so high—and the understanding of what warfare truly entailed so low—that picnickers gathered to watch the first major battle of the war here.

actually towered over Lincoln by an inch, Scott had been a warrior in every conflict since the War of 1812, as well as the Whig candidate for President in 1852. Now the venerated general, a Virginian by birth, was 75. While he was still a strong tactician, he could no longer command troops in the field and had to oversee operations from Washington. Early in the war, Scott came up with a strategy dubbed the "Anaconda Plan," because it would place a stranglehold around the Confederacy from the sea to the Mississippi—but it would take time to implement. The public and the press were clamoring for action.

Lincoln understood how woefully unprepared the army was, but Ellsworth's death had inflamed him. By midsummer, he was pushing

for decisive action. Gen. Irvin McDowell, a distinguished veteran of the Mexican-American War, had come up with an obvious plan—to cross the Potomac River into Northern Virginia and attack the Confederates under Gen. P.G.T. Beauregard, encamped at the Manassas railroad junction, about 30 miles west of Washington. Over Scott's objections, Lincoln and his Cabinet adopted the plan and insisted that McDowell launch the attack sooner than he was prepared to do.

Though McDowell knew he needed more time to train his raw troops, he dutifully marched 30,000 men toward Manassas on July 16. The battle cry from the men, who were uniformed in everything from kilts to Zouave pantaloons to fezzes, was "Forward to Richmond." Planning to revel in a sure and swift victory, a handful of senators and congressmen, a cadre of newspapermen, and an excited crowd of spectators, picnic baskets in hand, followed the army into battle.

> "WHAT A COMPANY!
> THE OFFICERS PRESENT WERE
> COMPOSED AS FOLLOWS:
> FIVE SPANIARDS, SIX POLES
> AND HUNGARIANS,
> TWO FRENCHMEN ... ONE
> AMERICAN, FOUR ITALIANS,
> AND NINE TEUTONS."
>
> WILLIAM RUSSELL,
> BRITISH JOURNALIST,
> ON THE 39TH NY INFANTRY

On July 21, a Sunday, McDowell's forces reached Manassas and the North awaited news of an imminent victory. Lincoln went to church, then in the afternoon called on Scott at his office and found the old commander napping. Once awakened, he assured Lincoln that all would be well.

News from the front was slow to reach Washington, but in the early evening, Seward rushed to the President's House with "a terribly frightened and excited look" on his face, telling Nicolay that "Tell no one … The battle is lost … Find the President and tell him to come immediately to Gen. Scott's."

As the evening progressed, Lincoln and his Cabinet gathered in Scott's office. Lincoln stayed up through the night, talking to those who witnessed the battle, absorbing their appalling accounts, and wondering if an attack on Washington was imminent.

As the South crowed over its victory and Confederate politicians claimed Manassas had virtually "secured our independence," Lincoln calmly assessed the damages. Militarily, the victory was not so catastrophic. The North had suffered some 2,600 casualties and the

South almost 2,000. But to Union morale, the injury was severe. Former war hawk Horace Greeley wrote the President that "On every brow sits sullen, scorching, black despair." He counseled, "If it is best for the country and for mankind that we make peace with the rebels, and on their own terms, do not shrink even from that."

Sadly, the poor military planning that had cost the North Manassas would not improve in coming battles. Delays in McDowell's advance had given the Rebels time to reinforce Beauregard. Among the reinforcements, was Brig. Gen. Thomas Jackson. Standing firm in the face of enemy fire, Jackson had been spotted by a fellow Confederate officer, who yelled to his men, "There is Jackson standing like a stone wall! Rally behind the Virginians." In future battles, "Stonewall" Jackson would be a great rallying point for the South and a terror to the North.

Reporting on the battle for the London *Times*, English journalist William Russell described the Union retreat in detail. "Men literally screamed with rage and fright when their way was blocked up," he wrote. "Faces black and dusty, tongues out in the heat, eyes staring—it was a most wonderful sight." And one that did not impress the British with the Union's military prowess.

Russell had established his reputation as one of the first war correspondents by using the newly invented telegraph to wire in reports on the Crimean War. He was never allowed to accompany Federal forces again after Manassas, but his classic, *My Diary North and South*, captures the first year of the war through the eyes of Confederate and Union soldiers and citizens.

Ellen McClellan offered her husband, George, the support and praise he craved as a commander of Union forces. The egotistical young general became known as the "Little Napoleon" and often struck the French general's classic hand-in-coat pose. Pages 110-111: The southern front of the White House was called the President's House in the mid-19th century.

After the humiliating Virginia defeat, Lincoln understood that Union troops, many thousands of whom were encamped around Washington, were too green for battle. They needed time and support. The President began to visit the fortifications around Washington, encouraging the men. And he brought in a new commander to train them, the glamorous young George McClellan, who had already bested the Confederates in western Virginia. The press had made much of his small victories, as had McClellan. Lincoln hoped he could turn the raw troops, now joining to serve three years rather than a mere 90 days, into an army. Fatally confident, McClellan arrived in the capital to great fanfare. "By some strange operation of magic, I seem to have become the power of the land," he wrote his young wife.

As the summer progressed, Lincoln's problems mounted. The press and his own party kept up a constant call to action. One senator purportedly said that he "did not wonder that people desert to Jeff. Davis, as he shows brains; I may desert myself." Other Republicans, including Vice President Hamlin and Union military commanders, wanted a stronger statement on slavery. The President must announce the emancipation of all the slaves, many insisted.

At Fort Monroe, a Union-held bastion on the Virginia coast, Gen. Benjamin Butler had taken in escaped slaves and refused to return them to their

An official model for a ship's howitzer was given as a toy to Tad when its pin broke. Always fascinated by weapons technology, Lincoln often visited Captain Dahlgren, who designed cannons and other ordnance and headed the Washington Navy Yard.

Confederate owners, even when the owners invoked the Fugitive Slave Act. Butler, a lawyer by training, argued that, if Virginia considered itself no longer part of the U.S., then American laws did not apply to the state's citizens. Butler called the escaped bondsmen "contraband of war," and allowed them to stay, working in the Union camp. The administration made no public comment, but northern papers applauded Butler. Word of Butler's actions spread quickly through the slave community and more "contraband" found their way to Fort Monroe.

More worrisome for Lincoln was Gen. John C. Frémont, head of the Union's Western Department. Frémont had taken it upon himself to proclaim martial law in the border state of Missouri and freedom for the slaves of anyone assisting the Confederacy. Hearing of Frémont's rash orders, Lincoln mildly admonished him in a letter, and soon found the redoubtable Mrs. Frémont on his doorstep, arguing her husband's cause. He responded that this "was a war for a great national idea, the union. General Frémont should not have dragged the Negro into it."

Throughout his campaign and the early Presidency, Lincoln reiterated this time and again. The war was not being waged to free the slaves but to preserve the Union. He clearly believed this at the time, but his reasoning also had a strategic benefit—it did not offend the crucial border slave states of Kentucky and Missouri, which the Union desperately needed in its ranks. That summer of 1861, Congress had passed the Crittenden Resolution, echoing the same sentiment. But the northern press and much of the public saw the abolition of slavery as part and parcel of the war. And over time, so would Lincoln.

The Home Front

Even with the constant pressures on him, Lincoln still took time to see a phalanx of daily visitors, from members of Congress to office seekers to the voluble public. He insisted that his meetings with citizens who came to the President's House invigorated him, and he called them his "public-opinion baths." His secretaries Nicolay and Hay tried to regulate Lincoln's schedule, but with little success.

The two young men affectionately referred to their boss as the "Tycoon," after the Japanese shogun, but they wasted no terms of endearment on Mary. She was the "Hell-cat." In the midst of war she had begun redecorating the President's House. Former Presidents had been allocated $20,000 as an allowance to refurbish the executive mansion, but there wasn't much evidence of their efforts amid the broken furniture and peeling wallpaper

> "SHE IS A SMART, INTELLIGENT WOMAN WHO LIKES TO HAVE HER WAY PRETTY MUCH. I WAS DELIGHTED WITH HER INDEPENDENCE."
>
> BENJAMIN FRENCH, COMMISSIONER OF BUILDINGS, ON MARY LINCOLN

that the Lincolns found when they arrived.

Mary had received the same allowance for the Lincolns' four-year tenure. In May, despite the uncertain times, she set off for Philadelphia and New York on a buying expedition. She ordered expensive and tasteful furniture, rugs, draperies, Parisian wallpaper, then returned again in the fall for china and glassware. William Wood, the Interim Commissioner of Public Buildings, went with her on these trips, causing Washington tongues to wag.

When the bills arrived, Mary realized she had spent more than the four-year allowance. Panicked, she devised ways to cover the expenses, even putting herself on the payroll of the President's House as the steward. But Lincoln discoverd the enormous cost overruns. He was furious. He would pay for them

out of his own pocket, he said, before asking for more money. "It would stink in the land," he said, for Congress to make an additional allocation "*for flub dubs for that damned old house … when the poor freezing soldiers have not blankets.*" In the end, Congress quietly paid Mary's bills.

The overruns were only one part of the embarrassment Mary's behavior caused Lincoln. Rumors mounted that her relationship with her travel partner, Wood, was more than

Playful and mischievous, Tad Lincoln (above, on his pony) and his older brother, Willie, delighted their parents but often shocked White House guests with their antics. Wanting to participate in the war, they accompanied Lincoln on visits to troops stationed around the capital city.

a friendship. One anonymous letter writer brought the "scandal of your wife and Wood" to the President's attention in June, warning that "If he continues as commissioner, he will stab you in your most vital part." Through the summer and early fall of 1861, the Lincolns' relationship was strained.

His young sons offered Lincoln one of the few escapes from his worries. Mischievous and undisciplined, Willie and Tad amused their father—and he doted on them, playing or reading with them whenever he could find a moment to spare. The boys kept pet goats and a pony on the White House grounds, and sometimes in the White House, and thought nothing of intruding on official meetings.

Eager to play a part in the war, they often accompanied their father when he reviewed the troops encamped around the city. They even set up their own fort on the White

WORLD PERSPECTIVE

Freeing Russia's Serfs

Called by Divine Providence and by the sacred right of inheritance to the Russian throne of our ancestors, we vowed in our heart to respond to the mission which is entrusted to us and to surround with our affection and our Imperial solicitude all our faithful subjects ... from the soldier who nobly defends the country to the humble artisan who works in industry; from the career official of the state to the plowman who tills the soil." Thus begins the Emancipation Manifesto issued by Tsar Alexander II, Emperor of Russia, in February 1861. With this document, some 22 million serfs across the empire were freed from the shackles that had bound them for generations to the noble class, and it "granted [them] the right to purchase their household plots" as well as additional land, if their former masters agreed.

Despite the lofty rhetoric of the emancipation proclamation, the freeing of the serfs was based largely on political calculations. Russia had fared badly as a result of the Crimean War, losing its influence in the Middle East, and liberal reformers in the government understood that if Russia persisted as a feudal state, it would continue Ito lose prestige as a world power. Freeing the serfs was to be a step toward modern reform, free enterprise, and a market economy. And, as the tsar himself had observed several years earlier, "It is better to abolish serfdom from above than to wait until the serfs begin to liberate themselves from below."

One of the last of the Romanov dynasty to rule Russia, Alexander II, the Tsar Liberator, reigned from 1855 until 1881.

Anxious not to destablilize the social order nor to offend the 100,000 noble families who relied on the serfs' labor, Alexander's government conceived the emancipation as a gradual evolution: Serfs would continue to work for their masters for two years, and the state would pay landowners compensation for the property the peasants received. But the freed peasants then had to repay the state in annual "redemption payments." These were often inordinately high, and the peasants struggled to survive, just as they had as serfs. In 1907 the redemption payments were finally canceled. In the intervening decades between emancipation and the final cancellation of their debts, the peasant class was granted other rights: the right to assemble, to vote, and to their day in court, though little was done to educate them. During this time the bureaucracy of state grew quickly, extending into the far reaches of the empire. Fifty years after emancipation, the peasant class, if no longer "owned" by their overlords, still found life hard and the old Slavic proverb true: "God is high above and the tsar is far away."

Though somewhat inept himself, Tsar Alexander II is credited with leaving an expansive legacy that profoundly affected Russian history. Chiefly remembered for freeing the serfs and expanding the Russian rail infrastructure, he is also credited with a series of reforms that propelled the country forward into the modern era.

House roof. Its sentry, a stuffed bunny, was frequently arrested as a spy, court martialed, and executed. At one point, the boys decided to bring the bunny's case before the President and his Cabinet. As the children solemnly entered the conference room, silence fell. The President somberly received the boys and the accused rabbit. The boys told their story, the President pardoned the rabbit, wrote and signed an official statement, and his satisfied sons returned to the roof.

Lincoln indulged the boys proudly and often. According to Herndon, his Springfield law partner, "Had they [the boys] s--t on his hat and rubbed it on his boots, he would have laughed and thought it smart."

Lincoln had little else to laugh about his first year in office. The public cry for military action grew louder, as McClellan drilled and trained the army around Washington. Lincoln had learned his lesson at Manassas and backed McClellan's cautious pace. Never one to accept any blame, McClellan countered his loud and insistent critics by blaming his commander, Gen. Scott, whose age and infirmity were leaving him more and more debilitated. To his wife, McClellan wrote, "I hear that off[icer]s & men all declare that they will fight under no one but 'our George,' as the scamps … call me."

In November, Lincoln accepted Gen. Scott's resignation "with sadness and deep emotion." Predictably, Lincoln placed McClellan as general-in-chief of all the Union armies. When Lincoln worried that the position was too much for even the confident McClellan, the general replied, "I can do it all."

As McClellan organized the forces under him, Lincoln was faced with another crisis, this one international. Secretary of State Seward had been monitoring the pulse of Europe since the war began, and he knew that the Europeans were doing the same with America. Seeing the powerful young republic weakened by war and disunion suited all

of them for different reasons. But none of the them were going to make a precipitous move until the conflict played itself out further.

On May 14, Britain, the world's greatest naval power, declared its neutrality in the American war and recognized the Confederacy as a belligerent, which gave it the status of a political entity separate from the Union—a status Lincoln had never accorded it. Other European powers soon followed suit. Under international law, the belligerent status allowed the South to purchase arms from neutral nations and to commission cruisers on the high seas with the power to search and seize foreign vessels. The British announcement caused Seward to rage "like a caged tiger," and he drafted a written response warning Britain against intervening in the war. His language was so harsh and undiplomatic that Lincoln tempered it before allowing it to be sent.

Meanwhile, the Confederacy was courting recognition and assistance from Britain and France. In the fall, it dispatched two diplomats to Britain. James Mason and John Slidell ran the Union blockade and took ship from Cuba; however, Union naval Capt. Charles Wilkes boarded their mail packet, the

Willie, Lincoln's third son, was a smart, studious boy and Mary's favorite. She kept a lock of his baby hair beside his picture. His indulgent father truly believed that "Love is the chain, whereby to bind a child to its parents."

MARY TODD LINCOLN REVEALED

She may rank as America's most controversial First Lady, a term newly in vogue when she moved into the White House. Wily, vain, arrogant, and a pathological spendthrift; intelligent, charming, energetic, and well educated—historians agree that Mary Todd Lincoln was all those things. They do not agree on whether she was emotionally imbalanced or simply difficult, whether she was Lincoln's great helpmate or hindrance; whether her hardships excuse her behavior or not.

Certainly she did suffer. Motherless from a young age and often emotionally unsupported, she learned to be both charming and demanding. Her ambitions no doubt fueled Lincoln's own and probably pushed him forward. She was an ardent patriot committed to the war and abolition, and yet she was accused of being a southern sympathizer and even a spy by some. She also lost three of her four sons and became estranged from Robert, the only surviving one.

There is no doubt about Mary's need for "things." In an 1857 letter, she wrote that "poverty was my portion … I often laugh and tell Mr. Lincoln that I am determined my next husband shall be rich." Apparently, she felt entitled to act as if she were rich. She spent profligately, buying far beyond her needs or means. She cajoled and bullied shopkeepers into giving her special treatment and ran up debts, expecting creditors to defer to her. Her creditors turned on her, and yet she survived the assault. In all, it could be said that that may be the greatest truth about Mary Todd Lincoln—she was a survivor. ■

Mary Lincoln (top) was criticized by Washington gossips for favoring the white ball gowns with revealing necklines generally worn by younger women. She also often loved to twine flowers in her hair on formal occasions.

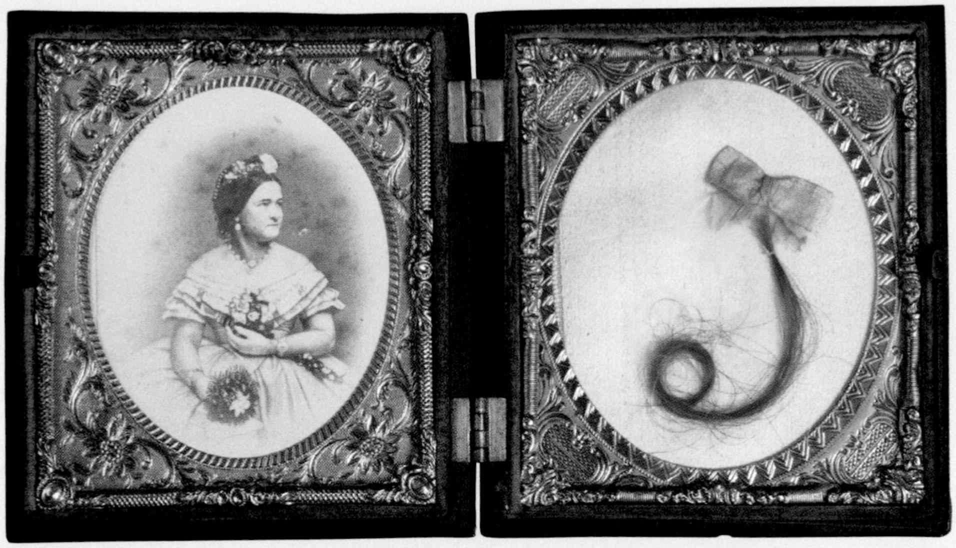

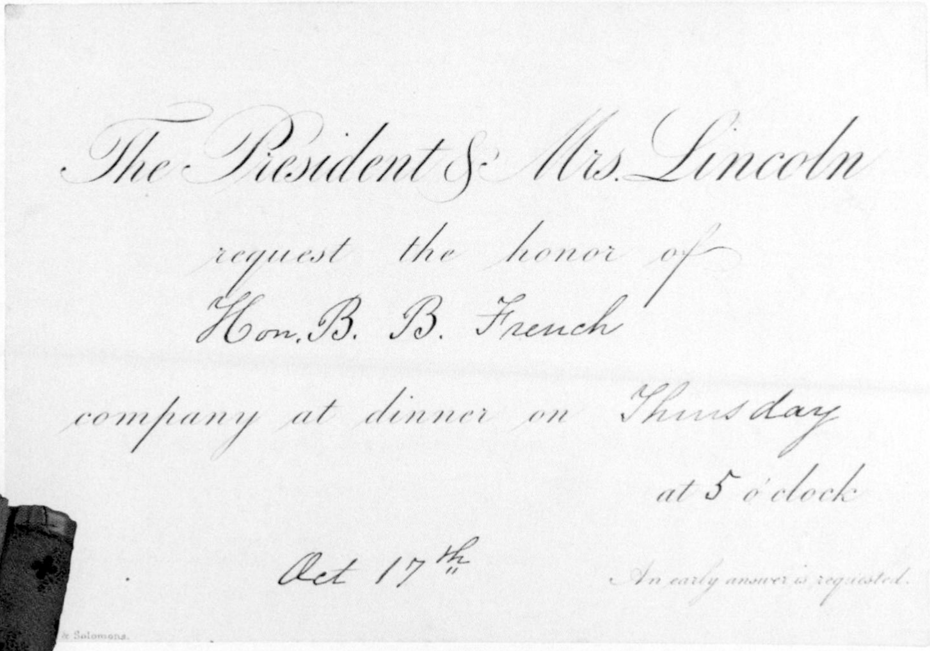

The President & Mrs. Lincoln

request the honor of

Hon. B. B. French

company at dinner on Thursday

at 5 o'clock

Oct 17th   *An early answer is requested.*

Surviving personal items from Mrs. President Lincoln's White House years include her leather letter box (opposite, far left); a copy (opposite) of Philp's Washington Described: A Complete View of the District of Columbia; *her night cap (top, left); a photographic case with images of her, her family, and a framed locket of Willie Lincoln's hair (top, right); a strip of cloth with Lincoln's image sewn among the colored squares (above, middle) found in her red "needle safe" (left); and a formal invitation written in her hand to a White House dinner (above).*

Trent, in an unauthorized search and seizure operation, and apprehended the two envoys. When word reached Lincoln and his Cabinet, they were exultant. Finally, a victory. The northern press joined in. "We don't believe the American heart ever thrilled with more genuine delight than it did yesterday, at the intelligence of the capture of Messrs. Slidell and Mason," the *New York Times* reported.

Britain was furious. The apprehension violated international law and was an insult to British naval power. Britain demanded an apology and a release of the Confederates.

An accomplished horseman, Ulysses S. Grant preferred his war horse, Cincinnati, to all others. The animal was given to him after the Battle of Chattanooga. Late in the war, Lincoln, on a visit to Grant's headquarters, rode Cincinnati—one of the few besides Grant who ever did.

After deliberation, Lincoln accepted that he couldn't have "two wars on his hands at a time." The men were released.

Despite British equivocation, Lincoln had foreign support in unexpected places. The King of Siam, Somdetch Phra Paramendr Maha Mongut—celebrated in the musical *The King and I*—sent Lincoln gifts, including an exquisite sword and an offer to breed elephants. "This Government would not hesitate to avail itself of so generous an offer," Lincoln replied. "Our political jurisdiction, however, does not reach a latitude so low as to favor the multiplication of the elephant."

A Year of Loss

As 1862 dawned, Lincoln faced one of his ongoing Cabinet crises. Simon Cameron's War Department, like the man himself, had been accused of corruption and profligate spending. Some spending could have been the result of Cameron's own disorganization.

> "WHAT SHALL I DO? THE PEOPLE ARE IMPATIENT; CHASE HAS NO MONEY ... THE GENERAL OF THE ARMY HAS TYPHOID FEVER. THE BOTTOM IS OUT OF THE TUB."
>
> ABRAHAM LINCOLN

He had no capacity for handling the plethora of documents that came before him—his personal filing system consisted of hastily scribbled notes. Realizing that the secretary must go, Lincoln eased him out with an offer of the post of minister to Russia. Lincoln then appointed Edward Stanton, a no-nonsense lawyer noted for his integrity and arrogance. Another former Democrat, Stanton's politics had evolved over the years and he now leaned toward an abolitionist stance.

With the capital's mood generally bleak that winter, Mary Lincoln resolved to lift the spirits of official Washington by hosting an invitation-only dinner party in February. This broke with the norm of official—and expensive—state dinners that the Lincolns had to pay for themselves and with the public receptions to which anyone could come.

Mrs. President Lincoln's first blush of popularity in the press had given way to the tedious criticisms of Washington society. Now, she would invite 500 selected guests and show them the miracles she had wrought on the President's House. At the gala, the Lincolns dispensed with dancing, but the Marine Band did play a new composition, "The Mary

Lincoln Polka," written for the occasion. It was after midnight when the guests entered the dining room for a sumptuous buffet that went on for three hours. Reaction to the evening was generally positive. "The most superb affair of its kind ever seen," the *Washington Star* wrote admiringly.

Mary had been distracted during her triumphant evening by worries over her favorite son, Willie. As the revelry went on downstairs, he lay upstairs ill with "bilious fever." Both parents escaped frequently from their guests to sit by the boy's side. Soon Tad, too, was ill, and Mary ministered to both her sons virtually round the clock. Willie showed no improvement, despite his doctor's original reassurances that he was "in no immediate danger." On February 20 the boy died, probably of typhoid fever caused by the contaminated Potomac River water that ran through most Washington pipes. "He was too good for this earth," Lincoln lamented, devastated by the boy's death.

Mary was literally prostrate with grief at losing another son and did not leave her bed for three weeks. She never fully recovered from the loss and came to see Willie's death as punishment for her own sin of pride.

The Union's U.S.S. Monitor *(above) took on the Confederacy's* Virginia *(the former U.S.S.* Merrimack*) in the inconclusive duel of the ironclads in Virginia's Hampton Roads harbor on March 9, 1862. The following December, the* Monitor *sank in a storm off Cape Hatteras, North Carolina. The wreck, discovered in 1973, became the nation's first marine sanctuary. Page 120: A sheet of 12 uncut cards traces the life of a Civil War–era slave, from the southern cotton fields to death on the battlefield for the Union cause.*

"I had become, so wrapped up in the world, so devoted to our own political advancement," she believed, "that I thought of little else." After Eddie's death, she had turned to religion. Now, encouraged by her dressmaker and confidante, Elizabeth Keckley, a mulatto and former slave, the President's wife sought solace in spiritualism. For the rest of her days in the White House, Mary held periodic séances, hoping to contact her lost son.

To overcome his own grief, Lincoln buried himself in work, of which there was an endless amount. McClellan himself had contracted typhoid fever in December and his illness only added to his inaction. Since taking over command in August, he had spent a good deal of his time training the Army of the Potomac, but he had done little else. The only military foray he had allowed ended in defeat, when, in October 1862, a Union contingent lost 1,700 men at Ball's Bluff, in Northern Virginia. Since then, he had made no move; his critics became vocal. "Nobody knows his plans," Attorney General Bates had complained. "I … told the President that *he* was commander-in-chief, and that it was not his *privilege* but his *duty* to command. … I greatly fear he, has not the *power to command.*" In truth, McClellan refused to be commanded, even by the President.

His ego was so immense that it bowed to no one. On one particular evening, he had arrived in his home to be told that Lincoln, Seward, and Hay were waiting to see him. McClellan left them waiting and went to bed. Lincoln made no comment, feeling that it was "better at this time not to be making points of etiquette and personal dignity."

With spring approaching, McClellan had had seven months to ready his troops for an assault on the South and still he equivocated. Lincoln had been losing patience since January and had told a group of Union commanders that if McClellan did not plan to use the army, "he would like to borrow it."

In time, it became clear that McClellan would never wage an all-out war on the South. Politically a Democrat, McClellan held no serious objection to slavery in the South, and he wasn't planning or hoping for decisive battlefield victories. He hoped to wear his opponent down and bring the rebellious states back into the Union with as little carnage on either side as possible. His war was one of attrition.

Not so the general in the western theater. Ulysses S. Grant had had an unremarkable career before the war, but he had now proved himself an aggressive fighter. He had scored a decisive victory in February, taking Forts Henry and Donelson in Tennessee and 14,000 prisoners. In a skirmish in Missouri, Grant said he realized the enemy commander "had been as much afraid of me as I had been of him…. The lesson was valuable." It was one that McClellan apparently never learned.

By early March, the South had begun to make its own decisive moves, withdrawing from Manassas to Richmond and launching a new weapon, the ironclad C.S.S. *Virginia*, a retrofitted U.S. naval vessel that had been called the *Merrimack*. The North countered with its own ironclad—the U.S.S. *Monitor*. Off Fort Monroe in Hampton Roads Harbor, the duel of the ironclads ended in a draw, but the fort was about to see more action. McClellan had convinced a skeptical Lincoln that the North should ferry the Army of the Potomac downriver to the fort. From there, it would march up the Virginia peninsula to Richmond.

Military matters consumed most of Lincoln's time in early March, but he was also pondering the gnawing question of slavery. For years, Lincoln had supported the idea of colonization—sending free slaves to a colony on foreign soil but under America's protection. Africa had long been one solution and it had a precedent—in the early 19th century the West African colony of Liberia had been

MARY LINCOLN'S WHITE HOUSE "FLUB DUBS"

A Limoges custard cup bearing the Lincoln "L," part of the family's private dinner service.

Also Limoges, the official state dinner service featured the presidential seal.

A stemmed glass of sought-after Dorflinger cut crystal.

A crystal relish dish.

founded as a haven for freed American slaves. The possibility of a new colony in Central America had been raised as well. Even his Cabinet's most ardent abolitionist, Secretary of the Treasury Chase, was a colonizationist. Blacks and whites could not live together because they were "adapted to different latitudes and countries," he argued, overlooking the fact that most slaves had a long pedigree as Americans and knew it as their home.

To Lincoln the essential dilemma of American slavery revolved around the struggle between human and property rights. Black humans deserved to be free, but white slave owners had rights to their property, even if it were other human beings. Trying to resolve this problem, Lincoln now put before Congress the idea of compensated emanci-

pation: For "any state which may adopt the gradual abolishment of slavery," the federal government would give "pecuniary aid … to compensate for the inconveniences public and private, produced by such change of system." While most of Congress and the press applauded the idea, the border states rejected it, and Congress did not act. Still, Lincoln's message had laid critical groundwork.

The spring of 1862 was no less trying for Lincoln than the previous winter had been. In Tennessee, Grant had been caught off guard by a southern attack near Shiloh Church. By the end of the bloody Battle of Shiloh, the Union had lost 13,000 men to the Confederates' 10,700. Even though Grant had forced the Rebels to withdraw, he was lacerated in the northern press, and Lincoln was strongly

In the winter months of 1862, Grant's forces moved south along the Tennessee River, advancing toward Corinth, Mississippi. By early April, they were encamped around Shiloh Church when Rebels launched a surprise attack. The Battle of Shiloh became the bloodiest yet fought in the war, with more than 10,000 casualties on either side.

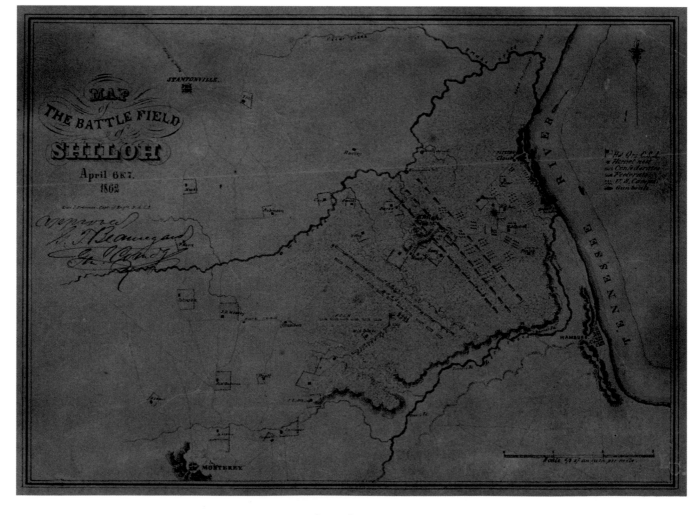

pressured to remove him. "I can't spare this man," Lincoln declared, "he fights."

> "I CANNOT HELP BUT
> FEEL THAT ALL THESE
> GOVERNMENTS ARE
> DISPOSED TO TAKE
> ADVANTAGE OF THE PRESENT
> DISTRACTED CONDITION
> OF THE UNITED STATES."
>
> WILLIAM L. DAYTON,
> U.S. MINISTER TO FRANCE

To counter the Union forces in Tennessee, the Confederacy had sent troops from New Orleans and eight gunboats, which the Federals had destroyed at Memphis. That left the port of New Orleans vulnerable. U.S. naval commander David Farragut took advantage of the situation, and by late April, the mouth of the Mississippi was in Union hands.

The victories in the West vindicated Lincoln's own belief that the Union Army should be attacking simultaneously on several fronts. Lincoln had no military background, but he had talent as a strategist and his instincts were borne out in battle after battle. Still, his suggestions made no headway with McClellan. In command of an army 100,000-men strong now gathered on the Virginia peninsula, "Little Napoleon" was again refusing to fight, despite Lincoln's urgings. Finally, McClellan began to inch up the peninsula toward Richmond, and by May 4, he had his guns pointed at the Confederate troops in Yorktown.

As McClellan began his advance, Lincoln ventured down to Fort Monroe. The trip invigorated both him and the troops stationed at the fort. At Lincoln's suggestion, a Union contingent crossed Hampton Roads and took the city of Norfolk. In order to keep the ironclad *Virginia* out of Union hands, the South scuttled their revolutionary weapon.

McClellan hesitated at Yorktown, believing the Rebels had a much greater army than they did. It was to become a classic mistake for a general who over and over seemed loathe to do battle. After a month, the Confederates extricated themselves from Yorktown and moved farther north on the peninsula.

As the two armies edged closer to Richmond, McClellan kept up a steady stream of telegrams to Washington, complaining that he did not have the forces he needed. In fact, some of the requested reinforcements were being kept at bay in western Virginia by Stonewall Jackson. From late March through early June, Jackson's "foot cavalry" moved up and down the Shenandoah Valley, outmaneuvering larger Union forces and preventing some 50,000 troops from reinforcing McClellan. Jackson's unpredictable movements also played to Lincoln's fears that the U.S. capital was vulnerable to attack.

That attack did not materialize, but outside Richmond on May 31, the South's commanding general, Joe Johnston, attacked

At Seven Pines, outside the Confederate capital in Richmond, Union artillerymen guard their howitzers, which pounded Rebel forces during two days of fighting there during the summer of 1862.

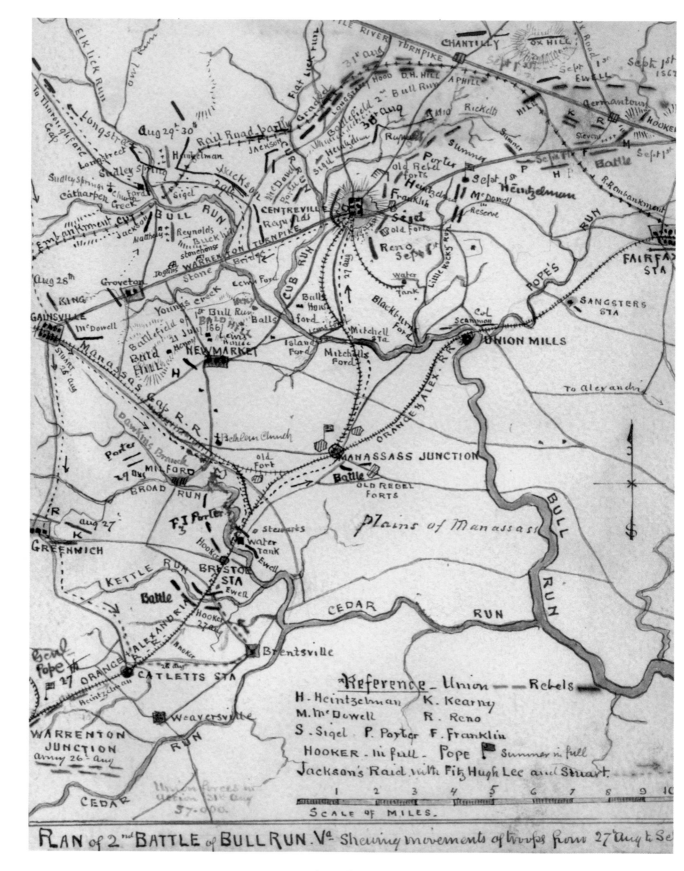

two Union divisions mired in the rain-swollen Chickahominy River. An anxious Lincoln dispatched advice to McClellan—"Stand well your guard." The Battle of Seven Pines was a Union victory, but like so many other ironies of this war, it had an unexpected outcome. Johnston, wounded in the battle, was replaced by Robert E. Lee.

As Lincoln watched, waited, and sent reinforcements, McClellan too waited, this time for the rains to end. Though Winfield Scott had offered Lee command of Union forces, McClellan had low expectations of the new southern commander, predicting that he would prove "timid and irresolute in action." But Lee quickly took the offensive. On June 25, his army sprang at the Union forces. For the next week, the two armies were locked in combat, the battlefield moving across the landscape encircling Richmond. At the end of the Seven Days' Battle, McClellan retreated from Richmond to Harrison's Landing, on the James River.

Despondent at the defeat, Lincoln again left Washington to inspect the army. The troops greeted him with enthusiastic applause. McClellan, oblivious to his own failures, presented Lincoln a letter offering to serve as commander-in-chief of the army. Lincoln thanked the general for his opinions. When he returned to Washington, he appointed Henry Halleck to the position, and McClellan was ordered to abandon the campaign.

All together, Lee had suffered 20,000 casualties, twice as many as McClellan, and he could ill afford to lose a quarter of his army. But McClellan had lost face completely. Even Lincoln, his most patient defender, was now out of patience with the arrogant Little Napoleon. As McClellan waited on the banks of the James River, the President put John Pope in charge of the newly constituted Army of Virginia. Pope's orders on how to treat the enemy, both military and civilian, were so harsh that

Lee called him the "miscreant Pope" and declared he must be suppressed.

McClellan's failures had cost Lincoln emotionally, physically, and politically. The President's friend and adviser, Orville Hickman Browning, whom he'd known since the Black Hawk War, expressed concern to Lincoln at seeing him so "weary, care-worn and troubled." Lincoln replied, "Browning I must die sometime." He confessed that he was "as nearly inconsolable as I could be and live."

No End in Sight

The northern failure to achieve a decisive victory was closely marked by the European powers. Intervention was in the air, as one northern defeat after another seemed to signal that the war for the Union could not be won.

Britain and France also understood that the longer the war lasted, the more impact it would have on their economies. Their textile mills needed southern cotton, blockaded by northern ships, and intervention in the war was the way to get it. Meanwhile, Napoleon III, nephew of Bonaparte, was also agitating for greater European involvement in Mexico, where France had already established a presence. He had formed a tripartite alliance with Britain and Spain and by the spring of 1862, the alliance was occupying Veracruz, Mexico.

Seward viewed this as an act of territorial aggression, directly counter to the Monroe Doctrine. Rumors flew on both sides of the Atlantic that Napoleon planned to put his nephew Maximilian on the Mexican throne.

Napoleon III, nephew of Napoleon I, hoped to regain France's imperial standing in the world. His "grand design" for America envisioned French dominion over Mexico and Latin America. Opposite, the North's loss at the Second Battle of Bull Run made European powers skeptical that it would ever win the war with the South.

Seward saw this as "the beginning of a permanent policy of armed European intervention, injurious and practically hostile to the most general system of government on the continent." America would not stand for it, he warned. But he and Lincoln knew that they were powerless to take on Europe so long as their own war raged, and so they held their breaths. Would Europe intervene in Mexico, or worse, in America, on the South's side?

Certainly, the Confederates were working hard to make that happen. In France, their envoy, John Slidell, appealed directly to Napoleon III, hoping to convince him to intervene and end the war. The French emperor was encouraging. "I have committed a great error, which I now deeply regret. France should never have respected the blockade." But Napoleon also clearly understood the drawback to intervention: If Europe were to intercede and

WORLD PERSPECTIVE

Germ Warfare

The Civil War was waged, according to Union surgeon general William Hammond," at the end of the medical middle ages." Few doctors who treated battlefield wounds understood one of the basic tenets of modern medicine—that germs cause disease and infection and that they can be passed from person to person, as well as in water and in human and animal waste. Even the fundamental notion that surgeons should wash their hands and disinfect their instruments between patients was largely unknown at the time.

During the decade before the war, a British physician named John Snow had traced a London cholera outbreak to contaminated water, but prior to Snow's discovery, most scientists and physicians believed in the miasma theory of disease, which explained epidemics like cholera as the result of "bad air." Snow's findings were a major contribution to what later came to be called the germ theory of disease and also to the field of public health.

Another step forward came in the early 1860s, when French chemist Louis Pasteur began to experiment with fermentation. What Pasteur discovered was that the fermentation process was not a simple chemical reaction but rather was caused by the growth of live microorganisms and that these microorganisms did not spontaneously generate themselves, as had been previously believed. They appeared through a process called biogenesis, and their detri-

mental effects in some liquids could be controlled by heating the liquids to just below the boiling point. The process of pasteurization, named for Pasteur's discovery, radically changed the transmission of many microbial

A contemporary artist's rendering shows the groundbreaking chemist Louis Pasteur at work in his laboratory.

diseases and came to revolutionize the dairy and food industries. Crowned the "father of bacteriology," Pasteur later contributed to the first vaccines for rabies and anthrax and was a pioneer in the field of immunology.

Pasteur's research is credited with spawning the emergence of several new branches of science—stereochemistry, microbiology, virology, immunology, and molecular biology, among them. An inquiring and disciplined researcher and habitual problem-solver, he was singlehandedly responsible for some of the most important theoretical concepts and practical applications in modern medical science.

Pasteur's germ theory of disease struck a responsive chord with English surgeon Joseph Lister, inspiring him to investigate the microbial cause of gangrene, a frequent cause of death among soldiers wounded on the battlefield. Lister discovered that hygiene and antiseptics—specifically, carbolic acid—could help prevent conditions causing gangrene. But by then, the Civil War was over, and thousands of soldiers had returned home missing arms and legs, because at that time amputation, not antiseptics, was the battlefield cure for gangrene.

Of the soldiers who never returned from the Civil War, many had succumbed not to their wounds but to disease and infection. The overcrowded conditions in the military camps, the lack of facilities for sanitation, and the lack of understanding as to how diseases were transmitted encouraged dysentery, diarrhea, typhoid, pneumonia, and malaria to thrive. In the end, approximately twice as many soldiers died of disease than of the wounds of war.

end the war, what then? What new boundaries would be established to divide the two new American republics? Also, Britain and France were antislavery. How could they legitimately back the South's slaveocracry?

From Britain, the U.S. minister Charles Frances Adams expressed his own concerns that intervention could be imminent. To stop it, he said, required a statement from Lincoln that the war was being fought for freedom—for all Americans. "The effect," he wrote, "would be to concentrate in a degree the moral sense of the civilized nations of Europe."

In Washington, Lincoln was hearing a similar chorus, lead by Sumner and Chase, calling for a federal decree freeing the slaves. But Lincoln had already arrived independently at that decision. During the late spring, as he had waited in the War Department cipher room for dispatches from McClellan, he had quietly worked on an emancipation proclamation. In mid-July, he told Seward and Welles that he "had about come to the conclusion that we must free the slaves or be ourselves subdued." At a Cabinet meeting a week later, he shared the proclamation draft. He drew on his privilege as Commander in Chief to issue such a decree "as a fit and necessary military measure," but his Cabinet members warned against it. It was too incendiary. Their arguments convinced him to wait. "We *mustn't issue it*," he declared, "till after a victory."

To pursue that victory, the military needed more men. In early July, the President called for 300,000 new three-year volunteers. A month later, Congress enacted the Militia Act, which allowed the federal government to draft state militias for nine-month tours of duty in the U.S. military. To fulfill the national requirement, some states instituted their own military drafts—a move so unpopular that rioting and arrests ensued.

Some of the unrest that summer was aimed against Blacks, who, if freed, would compete,

it was feared for northern jobs. Already contrabands—former slaves—were "invading" northern cities. The Irish particularly, who did the most menial work, protested in the streets of New York and Cincinnati.

By the end of August, preserving the Union came to feel like an increasingly futile goal, even to Lincoln. Pope's Army of the Potomac had been bested at the Second Battle of Manassas, and when the conflict

The "Iron Chancellor," Otto von Bismarck, engineered the unification of Germany in the mid-19th century. A social reformer and a militarist, he managed to subdue the once great Austro-Hungarian Empire as well as other European kingdoms, making Germany a world power.

ended, Lee's forces were poised within striking distance of Washington. The loss only served to increase European doubts about the Union's ability to prosecute the war. Though McClellan had refused to send reinforcements to Pope, Lincoln concluded that he "must have McClellan to reorganize the army and bring it out of chaos." "McClellan," he conceded, "has the army with him." His Cabinet loudly protested, but by now, Lincoln was in such despair that he admitted "he felt almost ready to hang himself."

He got no sympathy from his fellow countrymen, particularly the Democratic press.

The outspoken Horace Greeley of the *New York Tribune* had written to Charles Sumner, "Do you remember the old theological book containing this: 'Chapter One—Hell; Chapter Two—Hell Continued?' Well, that gives a hint of the way Old Abe *ought to be* talked to in this crisis." Abolitionists were equally fulsome, attacking Lincoln for equivocation on emancipating the slaves. William Lloyd Garrison called him "nothing better than a wet

> "NOT THROUGH SPEECHES
> AND MAJORITY DECISIONS
> WILL THE GREAT QUESTIONS
> OF THE DAY BE DECIDED—
> THAT WAS THE GREAT MISTAKE
> OF 1848 AND 1849—BUT
> BY IRON AND BLOOD."
>
> OTTO VON BISMARCK,
> CHIEF MINISTER OF PRUSSIA

rag." Northern Democrats, particularly the "Copperheads," kept up a steady drumbeat of vitriol. They had always favored restoring the slave-holding South to the Union rather than launching a destructive war. Even the Republicans provided Lincoln little solace.

Lee was fully aware of the pressures on Lincoln and the low morale of the North. With victories shoring up the spirits of his own men, he decided to strike at the Union. In early September 1862, he crossed the Potomac River 35 miles northwest of Washington and marched into Maryland toward Pennsylvania.

Unafraid, Lincoln and McClellan believed an opportunity awaited. For once, fate assisted the Union side: Two northern soldiers found Lee's orders for army movements written on a paper wrapped around three cigars, mistakenly left in a Maryland field. McClellan crowed, "Here is a paper with which if I cannot whip 'Bobbie Lee,' I will … go home."

4

FRESHMAN CLASS. 1860-61.

Annual Scale.

	Per cent.			Per cent.		
1	94	Brackett		77	C. C. Read	29
2	92	Binney		76	Robins	30
3	89	Atwood		76	Page	31
4	89	Pierce		76	Bowers	32
5	87	Appleton		75	Bellows	33
6	86	Sprague		74	Morris	34
7 8	85	Greenough		74	Chase	35
	84	Graves		74	C. F. Davis	36
9	84	Bush		73	Hare	37
10	84	Sinclair				
11	84	Bixby		72	Horton	38
				72	Richardson	39
12	83	Hodges		72	Chapin	40
13	83	Lawrence		72	Hagar	41
14	83	Ward				
15	83	McFadon		71	Braman	42
				71	Lincoln	43
16	82	Dillon		71	J. A. Blanchard	44
				71	Wells	45
17 8	81	Munroe				
18	81	Paull		70	King	46
19	81	Beckwith		70	Hildreth	47
20	80	Crocker		69	Barrett	48
21	80	Cutter		69	Derby	49
22	80	Kennedy				
23	80	Thayer		68	Palmer	50
				68	Washburn	51
24	79	Flagg		68	Hedges	52
25	79	E. S. Abbot		68	Huntington	53
26	78	Fisk		67	C. L. Howe	54
27 8	78	Gove		67	Wing	55
28	78	French		67	Elliot	66

The rank of Shaw does not appear, on account of absence, from sickness.

On September 17, near the small town of Sharpsburg on the banks of Antietam Creek, the armies clashed in the bloodiest single day of fighting in the war. The relentless slaughter continued into the next night, when Lee retreated back into Virginia. The retreat gave the North a tactical victory, but McClellan's army had lost 12,400 men to Lee's 10,300. McClellan's halfhearted pursuit let the Confederates escape to the Shenandoah Valley.

The Battle of Antietam was another lost opportunity for the North, but it gave Lincoln the victory he had been waiting for—and perhaps the sign from Providence he had sought to announce emancipation.

The week after Antietam, he called his Cabinet together and told them, "I think the time has come," though, he added, "I wish it were a better time." Once again his advisers were asked to contemplate the emancipation document, whose purpose was "restoring the constitutional relation between the United States, and each of the states, and the people thereof." In the summer, after presenting the proclamation to his Cabinet, he had met with Black leaders at the White House, to pursue his idea of colonization. "Your race are suffering the greatest wrong inflicted on any people," he had told them. "On this broad continent, not a single man of your race is made the equal of a single man of ours," and for that reason, he believed removing freed Blacks to their own colony was the best course. None of this was addressed in the Emancipation Proclamation that he issued on September 22, 1862. Its language was uninspiring—except for the opening statement: "That on the 1st day of January, A.D. 1863, all persons held as slaves within any State or designated part of a State … in rebellion against the United States shall be then, thenceforward, and forever free." As Lincoln signed the document, he told Seward, "I never, in my life, felt more certain that I was doing right, than I do in signing this paper."

As Lincoln knew it would, the Emancipation Proclamation drew fire from all sides. Northern Democrats predicted it would spur a social revolution. Abolitionists embraced it but wished for a bigger statement, as it did not abolish slavery in the five Union border states where some 425,000 humans were still in bondage. The border states, fearing that it was the first step toward complete abolition, railed against it as expected. But the antislavery Republicans celebrated. Joseph Medill of the *Chicago Tribune* called it the "grandest proclamation ever issued by man."

European reaction was mixed. Seward anticipated the French and British would

Despite the many pressures, Lincoln frequently read to Tad (above) and even slept beside his young son when the boy needed company. Eldest son Robert (opposite, top) never lived full-time in the White House. As a Harvard freshman, he ranked only 43rd in a class of 56, but he would become a successful lawyer, like his father. Pages 130-131: The Battle of Antietam, remains the single bloodiest day of war ever fought by the United States.

Lincoln and Secretary of State William Seward signed the Emancipation Proclamation, ending slavery in the "states in rebellion against the United States" as of January 1, 1863. It would take the passage of the 13th Amendment almost two years later to put a final end to slavery in the U.S.

worry that the proclamation might further interfere with their cotton supply. Hoping to put the war on a moral footing, he issued a circular explaining that the American objective had changed from "Union and not abolition" to "Union and abolition." The Paris *Presse* retorted, "In place of a principle, it is only a bomb thrown into the midst of the population of the South." But since France and England were ardently antislavery, Lincoln's proclamation effectively tied their hands. And they were becoming less dependent on southern trade as they began to develop other sources in Egypt and India.

Soon after releasing his document, Lincoln issued another proclamation—this time curtailing freedom. Under the War Powers Act, he suspended the writ of habeas corpus: "All Rebels and Insurgents, their aiders and abettors within the United States, and all persons discouraging volunteer enlistments, resisting militia drafts, or guilty of any disloyal practice, affording aid and comfort to Rebels … shall be subject to martial law and liable to trial and punishment by Courts Martial or Military Commission…The Writ of Habeas Corpus is suspended in respect to all persons arrested by any military authority of by the sentence of any Court Martial or Military Commission."

> "[THE SOUTHERN SLAVES] HAVE NEVER BEEN MORE QUIET AND MORE RESPECTFUL AND NO BETTER EVIDENCE CAN BE GIVEN OF THEIR BEING CONTENT."
> CONFEDERATE ENVOY JOHN SLIDELL TO NAPOLEON III

In the elections of 1862, the two proclamations and the continued war cost the Republicans votes, though they managed to retain control of the House of Representatives. Prominent members of Lincoln's party blamed voter dissatisfaction on the Union's incompetent and irresolute generals. Only Grant seemed able to fight, wresting another victory from the South, at Corinth, Mississippi, in October. More and more Lincoln had come to distrust McClellan and the officers under his command, who were undyingly loyal to their general. He had personally overseen a court-martial for Maj. John Key, when he heard of Key's explanation as to why Lee's army was not pursued after Antietam. "The object," Key had explained, "is that neither army shall get much advantage of the other, that both shall be kept in the field till they are exhausted, when we will make a compromise and save slavery."

On a visit to McClellan at Antietam in the fall after the battle, Lincoln climbed a hill with a colleague, looked down on the Union Army, and declared that rather than it being the Army of the Potomac, it was "*General McClellan's body-guard.*"

As the fall progressed, Lincoln accepted what he had long suspected, that McClellan must go if the North wanted victory. The President was, he admitted, weary of trying to "bore with an auger too dull to take hold." On November 5, McClellan was relieved of his duties, and Gen. Ambrose Burnside, a hero of Antietam, was named to replace him. On the western front, Don Carlos Buell, like McClellan a foot dragger, was replaced with W. S. Rosecrans, who had been winning Union victories there since the war began.

Burnside protested that he was unqualified to command the Army of the Potomac, but he accepted the post out of a sense of duty and immediately planned an overland attack on Richmond, over Lincoln's objections. Moving his army, now 110,000-men strong, to the north bank of the Rappahannock about 40 miles south of Washington, Burnside planned to cross the river on pontoons and continue south. His strategy might have worked, but the pontoons necessary for the crossing were delayed by a week. In that window, Lee amassed his army of 75,000 on the far bank of the river, dug in, and waited. One Confederate corps occupied Marye's Heights above the town, with an open sight line to anything crossing the river.

Before dawn on December 13, 1862, the Union began laying its pontoon bridges across the river. By the time the fog lifted in mid-morning, Union soldiers were crossing the open plain below Marye's Heights with nothing to protect them from the Rebel forces on the high ground above. "It can hardly be in human nature for men to show

more valor, or a general to manifest less judgment," journalist Henry Villard observed as Rebel fire raked the advancing Union troops. Hurrying to Washington, Villard was greeted by the President, wanting news of the battle. "I hope it is not so bad as all that," Lincoln lamented. But Villard's impressions were confirmed. The Union had suffered 13,000 casualties, almost as many as at Antietam; the Confederates had lost only 5,400 men.

Within days of the defeat, a caucus of Republican senators, incited in part by Secretary of the Treasury Chase met and voted among themselves to reorganize Lincoln's Cabinet. Chase's sworn enemy, Seward, ever accused of being a southern sympathizer and

Years after the war ended, printmakers continued to produce lithographs of famous battles. This one of the Battle of Fredericksburg depicts the Army of the Potomac crossing the Rappahannock toward the city on the fateful morning of December 13, 1862.

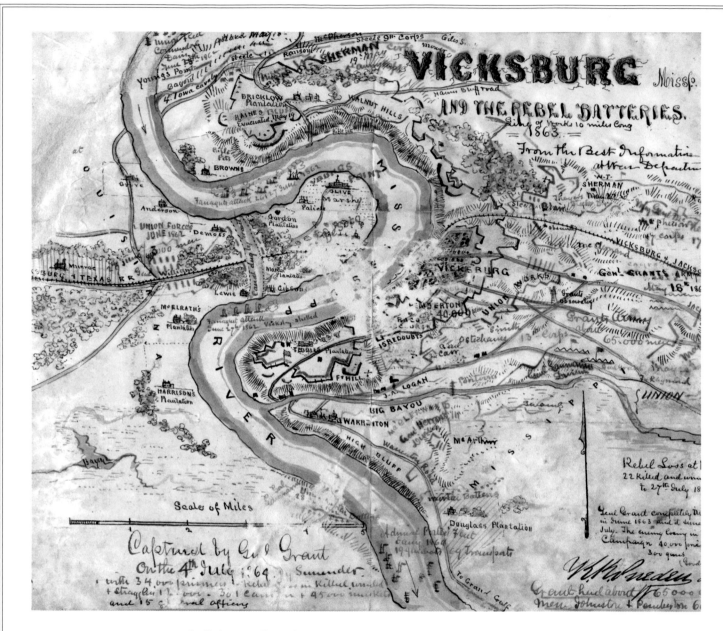

Occupying the bluffs above a prominent bend in the Mississippi, Vicksburg was strategic to all shipping moving up and down the river. From October 1862 until the following summer, Grant attempted to approach the city from various directions and failed. Finally, on July 4, 1863, after a prolonged siege, the city surrendered to the Union.

"lukewarm" on the war, had to be removed. He was "a paralyzing influence on the army and the President." The group voted in favor of a resolution declaring "a want of confidence in the Secretary of State."

Only when Seward tendered his resignation to Lincoln did the President learn of the senators' machinations. Reading the resignation, Lincoln was distraught. He had come to trust and rely on Seward and could not afford to lose him. Seward and the President also understood that, with no end to the war in sight, Lincoln was the true target of Repub-

lican vengeance. "They wish to get rid of me," he said, "and sometimes I am more than half disposed to gratify them." The situation, Lincoln admitted, distressed him more "than … any event of my life." In his despair, he even concluded "that the Almighty is against us."

Yet, when a committee of senators arrived to present the resolution, Lincoln assumed his usual open and affable manner. The senators expressed their concern that Lincoln had put Democratic generals who were sympathetic to the South and slavery in charge of the war, while abolitionist commanders like John Frémont "had been disgraced." All of this, they believed, could be attributed to Seward's influence over the President. Lincoln listened respectfully and came away feeling the conversation had gone well.

Lincoln's resolution to the problem was masterful. He invited the senators to a meeting with all of his Cabinet—except Seward. After five hours of frank discussion, it became clear that Chase had misled the senators. The Cabinet, with the exception of Chase, generally agreed with Postmaster General Blair, that Seward, despite his arrogance, was "as earnest as any one in the war" and "it would be injurious to the public service to have him leave the Cabinet." Yet again, Lincoln had reined in his fractious team of rivals.

Leadership is a lonely business, particularly during a war Presidency, and while Lincoln was rarely alone, no one could share the weight of his office. Nicolay and Hay were his most constant companions, and they in turn considered him "a backwoods Jupiter" who had learned to handle both war and government "with a hand equally steady and equally firm." Seward, too, was a trusted friend and confidante, and Lincoln's old Illinois friend, Orville Hickman Browning, was often at the President's House. But all of these men understood that Lincoln kept his own counsel.

The person he took the greatest delight in was his rambunctious, affectionate young son Tad, who turned nine in 1862. Lincoln read to him, played with him, and was generally unconcerned that the boy could not read and that a speech impediment made him hard to understand. Robert, away at Harvard, did not have the same close relationship with his father that the younger sons had enjoyed.

In the summer and early fall, the family moved to a Victorian "cottage" on the shaded grounds of the Soldiers' Home, three miles north of the White House. Tad became an honorary member of the company of Pennsylvania Bucktails who guarded the family during their stays. The bucolic setting gave the Lincolns respite from the incessant clamor of the city and a place where they could relax and spend occasional evenings together. "How dearly I loved the Soldiers' Home," Mary wrote in 1865. But family time was brief. Every morning, Lincoln would return to the city.

The Lincolns did not offer much comfort to each other during these hard years. His preoccupation with the war and her grief

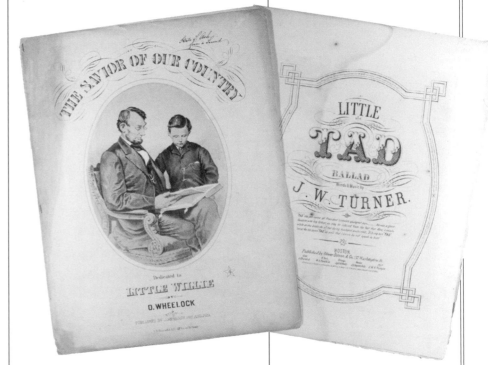

over Willie's death left them less close than formerly. Mary sought solace in séances, hoping to contact Willie, and she socialized with the capital ladies, as her position required. She took delight in her "beau monde friends of the Blue Room." These evening salons were attended by those who "could talk of love, law, literature and war … could gossip of courts and cabinets … of commerce and the church, of Dickens and Thackeray," the great writers of the day. Ever one to indulge those he loved, Lincoln made no objection to these evening salons. They occupied and consoled her, while he himself tended, often into the night, to the demands of a nation gripped by war.

Sheet music from the Civil War sometimes featured the First Family; the piece on the left is dedicated to the Lincolns' lost "Little Willie."

A Watershed Year

In late January 1863, General Burnside made another attempt to cross the Rappahannock River at Fredericksburg, but the weather this time proved his foe. Driving rain made the crossing impossible, turning the whole operation into a "mud march," humiliating the general and his troops. As Burnside's army lost all confidence in their commander, desertion became rampant. By the end of January, some 25,000 men had deserted.

> "IT IS WELL THAT WAR IS SO TERRIBLE—[OR] WE SHOULD GROW TOO FOND OF IT."
> ROBERT E. LEE

Lincoln was faced again with an ineffectual general who had to be replaced. This time, he chose a commander who took the offensive—Joseph "Fighting Joe" Hooker. His last name was as telling as his nickname. The term "hooker" had already become synonymous with ladies of the night—and the general's headquarters were often described as both "barroom and brothel."

Lincoln had strong doubts about Hooker's moral fiber and cockiness and said so in a letter to him. But Hooker would not be deflated and declared that it was not a question of whether he would take Richmond but when. To this, Lincoln coolly replied, "The hen is the wisest of all the animal creation because she never cackles until the egg is laid."

As Hooker readied his troops for a spring campaign in the East, Grant in the West continued to look for a way to capture the port of Vicksburg, on the Mississippi. His critics charged him with everything from ineptitude

A Union artillery unit rolls across Morris Island, South Carolina, in the summer of 1863, preparing to bombard nearby Charleston. Among the 6,000 Federal troops who occupied the island was the 54th Massachusetts, the first black unit to serve in the war.

to drunkenness, but his men respected and trusted him. Lincoln reiterated what he had said the previous year. "What I want … is a general who will fight battles and win victories. Grant has done this, and I propose to stand by him."

In March, the 37th Congress adjourned. Despite the war, it left behind a remarkably fruitful legacy, the repercussions of which are still felt. Early in its term, Congress passed the Revenue Act that put into force the first U.S. income tax ever. The following year, 1862, it passed the Homestead Act, allowing any citizen over 21 to file for 160 acres of free land; the Pacific Railway Act, "to aid in the construction of a railroad and telegraph line from the Missouri river to the Pacific ocean, and to secure … government … use of the same for postal, military, and other purposes"; the Morrill Land-Grant Act, which gave the states federal lands to establish land-grant colleges "in order to promote the liberal and practical education of the industrial classes"; the Militia Act that called for a draft of 300,000 eligible soldiers and allowed African Americans to join the military; and the Legal Tender Act, resulting

A Civil War board game mirrors the reality at sea. Lincoln's order to blockade southern ports early in the war became more and more enforceable as the conflict continued and the North brought new ships into service.

in "greenbacks"—paper notes issued as the first national currency. It also passed a controversial National Banking Act that established a national charter for banks and allowed the federal government to raise money for the war by selling war bonds.

When Congress adjourned, Lincoln took the opportunity to leave Washington and take stock of the Army of the Potomac for himself. Mary and Tad went with him as he sailed down the Potomac into Northern Virginia. A late season snowstorm forced their boat to shelter in a cove overnight before they continued to Aquia Creek, then took a train to Hooker's camp. The general's talk, again of imminent victory, left Lincoln worried. "That is the most depressing thing about Hooker. It seems to me that he is over-confident."

Lincoln had the same misgivings about the naval commander Samuel F. Du Pont, and they proved right. While Lincoln was with Hooker, Du Pont led a fleet of ironclads in an attack on Fort Sumter, in the largest naval operation of the war. But the Union ships were so badly damaged in battle that they were forced to withdraw. With yet another humiliating defeat, Lincoln could only hope Hooker would deliver more than bravado.

Weather had delayed the Union advance, but on April 28, Hooker moved his forces across the Rappahannock, despite the rains. "My plans are perfect," he had gloated, "and when I start to carry them out, may God have mercy on General Lee, for I will have none."

Lee was waiting for Hooker on the south side of the river, just as he had been for Burnside. The Union forces outnumbered the Confederates by two to one, and Hooker planned to squeeze the enemy in a vast pincer. But when the armies met at Chancellorsville, a farm outside Fredericksburg, Hooker's bravado inexplicably evaporated, and he ordered his men into defensive positions. Characteristically, Lee took the offensive, and he and his ever daring general, Stone-wall Jackson, conceived "one of the biggest gambles in American military history." After a night march, Jackson managed a surprise attack on Hooker's flank. Chancellorsville was a resounding southern victory, though it had come at great cost. Jackson, mistakenly shot by his own men, was lost to the South.

WORLD PERSPECTIVE

Bermuda's Boom

The American Civil War resounded worldwide, but it was perhaps heard most loudly on the Atlantic island of Bermuda, a British colony of some 11,000 residents. "There is nothing to talk of here but war," one resident wrote in 1861, even before Lincoln declared a blockade of southern ports.

After the blockade, Bermuda became a lifeline for the South. With scant industry of its own, the Confederacy relied on Europe for manufactured goods, but Lincoln's blockade threatened to stop that flow. Early in the war, the North lacked ships to enforce the blockade, but as new Union ships were built, the South resorted to shallow-draft "blockade runners" to bypass them. The runners at first operated from nearby Caribbean ports, especially Nassau, where they took on imported European goods from larger ships. But the Caribbean ports were crowded, and the South soon looked to St. George, Bermuda, with its strong British naval presence. Here, safe from Union vessels, the South could bring in its own larger ships, offloading war matériel and other goods onto runners.

Though Britain was officially neutral in the Civil War, its sympathies leaned toward the South, as did those of many Bermudians. The *Trent* affair in 1861 encouraged. that leaning. U.S. naval captain Charles Wilkes, who had set off the affair, created new animosity a year later, when he steamed into St. George Harbor on the tail of two blockade runners. Wilkes's ship stayed for six days, in violation of a British ban. Bermuda held its breath, fearful that Britain would be forced into the American conflict on the side of the Confederacy, and their island would be engulfed in war.

Events never came to that; instead, Bermuda flourished during wartime, its docks bustling, its chandlers busy, its merchants, pubs, and prostitutes prospering.

Shallow-draft blockade runners like the Teaser *kept limited commerce moving between the Confederacy and Europe during the war.*

As the battle raged, Lincoln had been hovering at the War Department, in a "feverish anxiety to get facts." When he received the telegram reporting yet another defeat, he returned to the President's House, to two waiting friends. "Never as long as I knew him," said Noah Brooks, "did he seem so broken, so dispirited, and so ghostlike. Clasping his hands behind his back, he walked up and down the room, saying 'My God! My god! What will the country say!' "

As the war effort stalled and wavered, the Peace Democrats made unrelenting attacks on the President, the "hellish war," and "the Constitution-breaking, law-defying, negro-loving Phariseeism of New England." At a rally in Ohio in May, state congressman Clement L. Vallandigham spoke forcefully against the "wicked, cruel and unnecessary war," and was promptly arrested by General Burnside, now in charge of the army's Department of the Ohio. Vallandigham had sought this outcome. He knew his arrest would result in protests, and it did. When he filed for a writ of habeas corpus, it was denied because Lincoln had earlier suspended the writ in such cases. By a military tribunal the congressman was sentenced to imprisonment for the rest of the war.

Lincoln understood the firestorm created by Vallandigham, and he commuted the sentence, instead banishing the prisoner to the South. He answered critics of the affair with a letter to the *New York Tribune*, in which he argued with lawyerly eloquence, "Must I shoot a simple-minded soldier boy who deserts, while I must not touch a hair of a wiley agitator who induces him to desert?"

Lee understood as well as Lincoln that the Union cause was now at a breaking-point. If the North continued to lose, the Peace Democrats would prevail over the Republicans in the coming fall election, and the Europeans might finally grant the Confederacy recognition as a sovereign nation. Hoping to push the war to that conclusion, Lee again decided to invade the North, to make a quick move into Pennsylvania, where a decisive victory could end the war. Also Pennsylvania's fertile fields would feed his troops. By early June, Lee's army was crossing the Potomac, leaving war-torn Virginia behind. Hooker wanted to follow, but Lincoln was leery of another river crossing. Then Hooker changed his tune, deciding the army should march on Richmond. Lincoln had heard these stratagems before. "I think *Lee's* Army, and not *Richmond,* is your true objective," he shot back. "Fight him when opportunity offers." But Hooker complained of too few forces. Lincoln had learned his lesson with McClellan; this time he didn't hesitate. In late June, he replaced Hooker with one of the general's own commanders, Gen. George Meade. Of the appointment, Meade said, "Well, I've been tried and convicted without a hearing. I suppose I shall have to go to execution."

As the summer wore on, the opposing armies drew closer together until at last they converged near the small Pennsylvania town of Gettysburg.

Will Senator Sumner please come to breakfast with Gen, Hooker this morning, half past 8, ?

May 14. 1863,

A Lincoln

GETTYSBURG

BATTLE-FIELD.

25

"WAR AT THE BEST IS TERRIBLE, AND THIS WAR OF OURS, IN ITS MAGNITUDE AND IN ITS DURATION, IS ONE OF THE MOST TERRIBLE."

ABRAHAM LINCOLN

[CHAPTER FIVE]

WE CANNOT ESCAPE HISTORY
1863-1865

GEORGE MEADE, THE LATEST IN LINCOLN'S COMMANDERS OF THE ARMY of the Potomac, never wanted the job. But he vowed to his wife to "settle this thing one way or the other." The way he chose was the way Lincoln had so often advised—to go after Lee's army, now strung out through the countryside of Pennsylvania. On the last day of June 1863, Meade's cavalry division under John Buford reached Gettysburg, Pennsylvania, and found it quiet. But Buford "had gained positive information of the enemy's position and movements and my arrangements were for entertaining him." When a Confederate advance column reached the town, on an expedition to find shoes for the ill-shorn feet of Lee's army, Buford took them by storm. It was the opening salvo in what would become a titanic, four-day battle.

The enlisted men of both armies were spoiling for a fight, and Gettysburg gave them what they wanted. Through oppressive summer heat and across the rocky ground and now famous rises surrounding the town—Little Round Top, Cemetery Hill, Culps Hill, the Peach Orchard—the fighting roared. Even at night, "the carnage wore on," one soldier recalled. "There seemed to be a viciousness in the very air we breathed."

By the third day of the battle, the Union held the high ground and Lee was determined to take it. Over the strong objections of his trusted general James Longstreet, he ordered a charge on the Union central position, atop Cemetery Ridge. "My brave Virginians are to attack in front," Confederate commander George Pickett wrote

In 1864, the small Virginia port of City Point on the James River was transformed into a major staging ground for the Federal Army (opposite). Above, a leather case holding the presidential seal embossed with Lincoln's signature.

Gen. George C. Meade, the bearded man at center, poses with his staff. Born in Spain, Meade spent his early years there until his father, a naval agent for the United States government, lost his fortune in the Napoleonic Wars.

his wife moments before the attack. "Oh, may God in mercy help me as He never helped before." The general's plea was in vain. What became known as Pickett's Charge was a needless bloodbath of historic proportions. Over half of the 13,000 Southerners who charged were killed, wounded, or captured.

When the exhausted armies finally gave up the Gettysburg fight, the casualties totaled 51,000 men—28,000 for the South and 23,000 for the North. Lee took all blame for the southern defeat. "All this has been my fault. It is I that have lost this fight." As Lee retreated toward Virginia, Meade was slow to follow, knowing how battle-weary his own forces were.

In Washington, Lincoln learned of the victory after the fact, and now he waited expectantly to hear that Meade had dealt a final blow to Lee's army, whose retreat had been thwarted by the Potomac River, swollen by heavy rains. But that word never came, and Lincoln's frustration grew. "We had them within our grasp," he railed. "We had only to stretch forth our hands and they were ours."

Still, Gettysburg was the victory Lincoln had so long wanted, and there was more good news from the West. During the spring, Grant had managed, after countless tries, to maneuver his men into a position to take Vicksburg, the much coveted Mississippi port. In the third week of May, his forces had tried twice to storm the fortified town, on high bluffs above the river. Both attempts had failed, but Grant at last had laid siege to the town. Little word had gotten through to Lincoln of the general's movements, and Lincoln spent May waiting for news of Grant's intentions. When at last Lincoln did understand Grant's campaign, he was in awe, calling it "one of the most brilliant in the world."

Throughout an anxious June, the citizens of Vicksburg and the Confederate troops under General Pemberton who had been forced back into the town held out against federal bombardments, famine, and want. "Dogs howled through the streets at night, cats screamed … an army of rats, seeking food, would scamper around your feet," one Confederate soldier later recalled. As the siege wore on, people consumed rats, mules, dogs, and cats. At last it became too much. On June 28, Pemberton received a letter from "Many Soldiers." "If you can't feed us, you had better surrender," it advised. "This army is now ripe for mutiny, unless it can be fed." On July 4, as Lee retreated at Gettysburg, Vicksburg surrendered, and with it 30,000 Rebel soldiers. Realizing he had no effective way to deal with so many prisoners of war,

> "IN THE PRESENT CIVIL WAR
> IT IS QUITE POSSIBLE
> THAT GOD'S PURPOSE
> IS SOMETHING DIFFERENT
> FROM THE PURPOSE OF
> EITHER PARTY."
>
> ABRAHAM LINCOLN

Grant paroled them. They were so dispirited from the ordeal that he believed they would never fight again. The real prize, long in coming, was the port itself. Later, Grant would state, "The fate of the Confederacy was sealed when Vicksburg fell." For his part, Lincoln declared, "Grant is my man, and I am his the rest of the war."

Jubilation greeted the two monumental Union victories, and throughout the North throngs took to the streets in celebration. In Europe, talk of intervention in the war finally came to an end. But the high spirits gave way almost immediately. On July 11, the first lottery of the new conscription law, passed the previous spring, was held. The law favored the well off—anyone who could afford $300 for an "exception" could opt out of national service. Otherwise, male citizens between the ages of 20 and 35 were subject to the draft.

Antiwar papers were quick to couple conscription with the Emancipation Proc-

lamation. Black men were not subject to conscription, and they would soon be flooding northern cities, taking jobs that white, mostly immigrant, men now held. The stage was set for trouble by the time the July lottery was held, but at first all was quiet. Then in the early morning of July 13, New York City erupted in riots. Initially, only government and military buildings were attacked, but soon the anger spread to Black people on the street. Black establishments, like the Colored Orphan Asylum, were set on fire. The mayhem went on for five days, overwhelming the

Best known for his ill-fated charge at Gettysburg, Gen. George Pickett was a dapper man, who perfumed his long curls. He never forgave Robert E. Lee for ordering the charge, which resulted in the slaughter of his men.

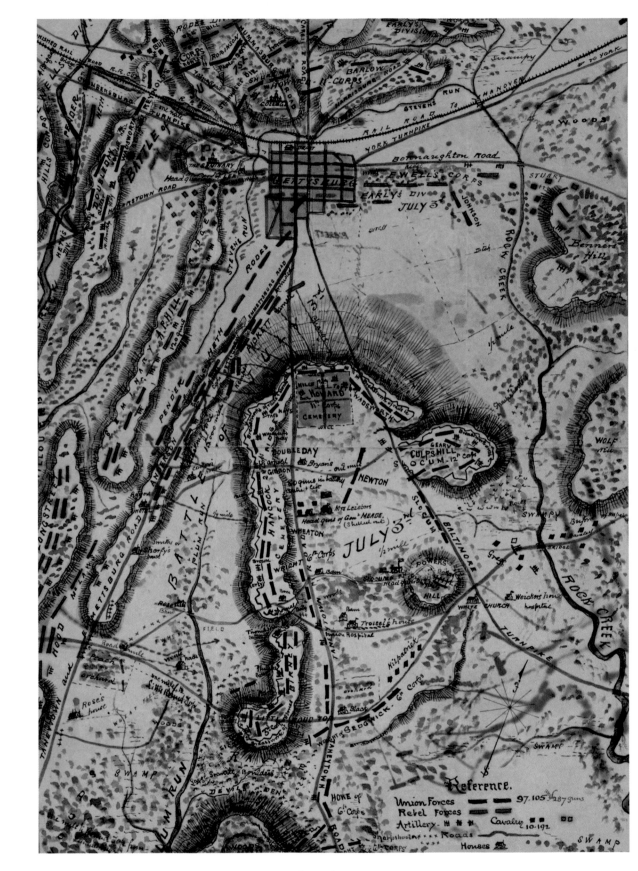

police force. Only when the U.S. military was called in was the rioting quelled; by then 11 Black men had been lynched and hundreds of others, men and women, attacked.

Except for the riots, the summer of 1863 was a relatively peaceful one for Lincoln. He, Mary, and Tad had moved to the Soldiers' Home cottage, where Mary recuperated from

> "THE FULL AND EQUAL RIGHT
> OF THE COLORED MAN
> TO WORK FOR WHOEVER
> CHOOSES TO EMPLOY HIM,
> AND THE… RIGHT OF ANY
> CITIZEN TO EMPLOY WHOEVER
> HE WILL, IS TOO MANIFEST
> TO NEED PROOF."
>
> THE NEW YORK
> MERCHANTS' COMMITTEE

a carriage accident, a result of maliciousness. The intended victim had no doubt been Lincoln himself. The bolts securing the driver's seat to the carriage had been loosened and they came undone as the carriage wound downhill. The driver was thrown off his seat, and as the horses bolted, Mary jumped from the carriage. She suffered a head wound that seemed inconsequential, but it became infected, and her headaches increased in ferocity. Robert came to believe that the head trauma did lasting damage to his mother.

When the family was at the cottage, Lincoln followed the same route every morning and evening between the Soldiers' Home and his offices in the city. He always had an armed contingent, but there were ample opportunities for harm from potential assailants, and his advisers warned him against keeping a predictable routine. As always, Lincoln refused to change his behavior out of fear. Once, a guard found his stovepipe hat along the route, with a bullet hole through it. When

he gave it to the President, Lincoln merely took it and asked that Mrs. Lincoln not be told about the incident.

In August 1863, taking advantage of the triumphs of Gettysburg and Vicksburg, Seward made a characteristically bold diplo-

matic move. He invited the foreign ministers of Great Britain, France, Spain, Germany, and Russia to tour the North with him for two weeks. With a Union victory now more feasible, talk of intervention in the American war was fading in the councils of Europe. Seward wanted the ministers to see for themselves the power and prosperity of the North. As his son and the assistant secretary of state, Fred Seward, wrote, the dignitaries were shown "hundreds of factories with whirring wheels, thousands of acres of golden harvest fields, miles of railway trains, laden with freight, busy fleets." They were also shown a more congenial, less strident Seward than the one who had warned them brusquely time and again not to interfere in America's war. Socially, Seward could be a charming

Above, Confederate soldiers in the "slaughter pen" at the foot of Little Round Top were caught in the deadly fire between opposing forces. For three days in July 1863, the armies of the North and South moved back and forth (map, opposite) as they positioned and repositioned themselves on the hills, gullies, and farmland outside the little town of Gettysburg.

conversationalist, and he worked his magic on the ministers.

An Interminable War

As the Union's triumphant summer of 1863 drew to a close, it seemed increasingly unlikely that European powers would intervene for the Confederacy or press for a mediation between the North and South that would give the South its independence. "We are now in the darkest hour of our political existence," Jefferson Davis admitted.

The cloud over the Confederacy lifted briefly in the third week of September, when the armies of the North and South clashed in the tangled Tennessee woods and thickets along Chickamauga Creek. When the smoke cleared on the bloodiest battle ever to be fought in the western theater, the Confederate forces under Gen. Braxton Bragg had suffered 20,000 casualties, including ten generals, but most of Gen. W. S. Rosecrans's Union forces had suffered disgrace, as they fled in panic before the southern wave. His Army of the Cumberland had retreated to Chattanooga and now were pinned down by the Confederates, with no way for further food or supplies to reach them. As to Rosecrans himself, Lincoln characterized him best as "confused and stunned like a duck hit on the head." To lose the Army of the Cumberland would be a catastrophe, and Secretary of War Stanton convinced Lincoln that enforcements had to be sent west. When Lincoln reluctantly agreed, two corps totaling some 20,000 men under the command of Joe Hooker were quickly dispatched by train on a 1,200-mile trip from Virginia to a railhead near Chattanooga.

A Union line advances through the thick, smoke-filled Tennessee forests near Chickamauga Creek in this drawing by famous Civil War artist Alfred Waud. Drawings like his were the only depictions of war seen in newspapers, as there was no way to quickly reproduce photographs at the time.

Not satisfied that the reinforcements would be enough, Lincoln fell back on his one sure bet in the western theater—Ulysses S. Grant. Creating the new Division of the Mississippi to encompass almost all of that theater, he put Grant in charge and soon Grant, too, was on his way to Chattanooga. By the final week of November, Grant and Hooker had engineered an impossible victory. Much later, when Grant was told the southern commanders had considered their position impregnable, the phlegmatic general replied, "Well, it was impregnable."

On the last Thursday in November, the North celebrated the first official Thanksgiving Day. In October, Lincoln had issued a Proclamation of Thanksgiving that seemed to sum up his own apprehensions and elations concerning the war:

"The year that is drawing towards its close, has been filled with the blessings of fruitful fields and healthful skies … In the midst of a civil war of unequalled magnitude and severity, which has sometimes seemed to foreign States to invite and to provoke their aggression, peace has been preserved with all nations, order has been maintained, the laws have been respected and obeyed, and harmony has prevailed everywhere except in the theatre of military conflict; while that theatre has been greatly contracted by the advancing armies and navies of the Union …

"I do therefore invite my fellow citizens to set apart and observe the last Thursday of November next, as a day of Thanksgiving and Praise to our beneficent Father …"

November had been a month notable for another event whose significance even Lincoln did not fully realize. A week before Thanksgiving, he had taken a special four-car train to Gettysburg, to attend the dedication of a national cemetery on the battlegrounds. The featured speaker was to be Edward Everett, a former politician, now president of Harvard, and perhaps the most famous orator of the day. The events committee had decided, just a few weeks before the dedication, to invite the President as well. "It is the desire that, after the Oration, you, as Chief Executive of the nation, formally set apart these grounds to their sacred use by a few appropriate remarks," the letter of invitation read.

Lincoln worked on his "few appropriate remarks" off and on before the appointed day, but he "greatly feared he would not be able to acquit himself with credit, much less fill the measure of public expectation" surrounding the event. Apparently he finished his speech the night before the dedication.

The town was filled with "people from all parts of the country," wrote a *New York Times* reporter, who had "taken this opportunity to pay a visit to the battlefields which are hereafter to make the name Gettysburg immortal." That night, from his room in the home of the cemetery's founder, David Wills, Lincoln could hear the crowds singing and cheering. Among the songs was the then popular "We are coming Father Abraham, three hundred thousand more."

On the morning of the dedication, 9,000 people gathered for the ceremony, including Lincoln and three of his Cabinet members. The chaplain of the House of Representatives began with a prayer so lengthy that John Hay called it "a prayer that thought it was an oration." Next, Everett stood to talk and devoted the next two hours to an account of the battle so stirring that the audience was often moved to tears. When he had finished, Lincoln grasped his hand, saying, "I am more than gratified, I am grateful to you."

Known as "Old Rosy" to his troops, Gen. William S. Rosecrans, commanded the Army of the Cumberland for a year beginning in October 1862. He forfeited his command after the Confederate victory at Chickamauga.

A hymn was sung before Lincoln rose to speak, the audience settling in for another long speech. But Lincoln took them by surprise. In two minutes and only 270 words, beginning with the unforgettably cadenced "Four score and seven years ago," he explained what America could mean for human history, why the war was worth fighting, and what was owed those whose lives had been lost. He ended with "We here highly resolve that these dead shall not have died in vain—that this nation, under God, shall have a new birth of freedom—and that government of the people, by the people, for the people, shall not perish from the earth."

> "WE CANNOT HALLOW THIS GROUND. THE BRAVE MEN, LIVING AND DEAD, WHO STRUGGLED HERE HAVE CONSECRATED IT FAR ABOVE OUR POOR POWER TO ADD OR DETRACT."
>
> LINCOLN'S GETTYSBURG ADDRESS

Taken aback by such an abrupt finish, the audience waited for more in silence, but Lincoln took his seat and applause slowly followed. To Lincoln the delayed audience response might have indicated disapproval. Speaking to his old friend, Ward Hill Lamon, afterwards, Lincoln confessed that his speech had been "a flat failure, and the people are disappointed." But Everett, the skilled orator, knew better and the next day wrote to congratulate Lincoln on capturing "the central idea of the occasion." Lincoln had successfully communicated the concept

Lincoln delivers his brief but immortal Gettysburg Address in this Mathew Brady photograph that captures a blurry image of the President on stage. Lincoln had refused to address a group who came to serenade him the night before, explaining that "I have no speech to make. In my position it is somewhat important that I should not say any foolish things."

of war and its role in America in a way comprehensible to Americans.

Lincoln had preached this idea since the Douglas debates—that America was an experiment in democracy and equality for all men, and that it must not fail. About that he was right, but he was wrong in another respect. In his "remarks," he had said that "The world will little note, nor long remember, what we say here ..." More than seven score years later, his Gettysburg Address is the high point of American oratory.

World Reaction

Even as Lincoln delivered his speech, he had not felt well. In fact, he was coming down with varioloid, a mild case of smallpox that kept him in bed for several weeks after. Despite his isolation, or maybe because of it, his mood was jubilant. "Yes, it is a bad disease, but it has its advantages," he quipped to visitors. "For the first time since I have been in office, I have something now to give to everybody that calls." His high spirits were understandable. The Union had scored major victories

---

WORLD PERSPECTIVE

What Hath God Wrought

For most of human history, news had trailed no faster than human feet, pack animal, or ship could carry it, but in the mid-19th century that changed irrevocably and dramatically. In 1837 two inventors—Charles Wheatstone and W. F. Cooke—were successful in transmitting messages electromagnetically along a telegraph line in England. That same year, an American artist named Samuel Morse failed to receive a commission from the U.S. Congress to paint a mural for the Capitol Rotunda. So despondent was Morse at the rejection that he gave up painting and turned his attention to the new technology of electromagnetic telegraphy. Six years later, Congress appropriated $30,000 for Morse to lay a telegraph line between Washington, D.C., and Baltimore, Maryland.

Morse tried an underground line first, but when insulating proved a problem, he put up poles and strung wire between them. On May 24, 1844, a group of prominent Americans gathered in the chambers of the U.S. Supreme Court to watch Morse tap out in the code he had developed the words "What Hath God Wrought." The message, with its biblical echo (it was a quote from Numbers 23:23) was successfully received in Baltimore. It is no exaggeration to say that Morse's prophetic message heralded the age of information.

In its first days the telegraph, in Morse's hands, received information of goings-on

Telegraph battery wagons accompanied armies into the field to relay news quickly from the front. Their operators, often at great risk, were civilian employees, not members of the military.

at the Democratic presidential convention taking place in Baltimore, where Polk was ultimately nominated. But telegraph lines, which shot up so fast that jokesters claimed the wires were carried on "beanpoles and cornstalks," soon carried commercial and international news. Protestant America had high hopes for the telegraph's moral implications: "This noble invention is to be the means of extending civilization, republicanism, and Christianity over the earth," a Methodist women's magazine proclaimed. But Morse's new technology also deepened schisms, particularly between the telegraph-connected industrial North and Midwestern heartland and the agrarian South, where far fewer lines operated. Transcendentalist Henry David Thoreau quipped, "We are in great haste to build a magnetic line from Maine to Texas, but Maine and Texas, it may be, have nothing important to communicate."

By 1861, a transcontinental line linked New York and San Francisco, and the many thousands of miles of lines across the country had been linked under one entity, the Western Union Telegraph Company. By 1866, after a number of failed attempts, a transatlantic cable was completed between the U.S. and Britain. The first message transmitted read: "A treaty of peace has been signed between Austria and Prussia." That was soon followed by a message from Queen Victoria to the President, saying she hoped the cable would "serve as an additional bond of Union between the United States and England."

in the last half of 1863; his Republican Party had emerged victorious in the recent fall elections; the Copperhead Democrats—northern sympathizers with the South—had been quelled. The victories and the Emancipation Proclamation had served to reinvigorate the North and give the war a new cause.

Over the course of a lifetime, Lincoln had become an astute politician. The ordeal of a war Presidency and a cantankerous Cabinet had only served to burnish his skills. Before him in that fall of 1863 lay the two great issues of the day—slavery and reconstruction. The South, it was now clear, would go down in defeat, and already Lincoln and Congress were considering the implications of that.

> "THE BEST INTERESTS AND PRESENT AND FUTURE PROSPERITY OF BRITISH NORTH AMERICA WILL BE PROMOTED BY A FEDERAL UNION UNDER THE CROWN OF GREAT BRITAIN."
>
> QUEBEC RESOLUTIONS OF 1864, FRAMING THE FUTURE OF CANADA

As always, his advisers and members of his party, as well as the Democrats, clamored to have their views on both issues heard and acted on. The Radical Republicans wanted more than just emancipation—they wanted equality under the law for all—something most southern whites would see as a flagrant break with the natural order. The Conservative Republicans did not want to alienate southern whites further by insulting their way of life. At war's end, they favored leniency toward the Confederacy, and readmission of southern representatives to Congress.

Lincoln threaded a course between the various factions in his annual message to

Confederate prisoners of war wait at a train depot in Chattanooga, Tennessee, a vital southern rail juncture that fell to Union forces in November 1863. After its fall, Sherman began his drive to capture Atlanta, Georgia.

Congress in December 1863. He wrote of the recent successes in Gettysburg and of the hundred thousand slaves then in the military, whose presence gave "the double advantage of taking so much labor from the insurgent cause, and supplying the places which otherwise must be filled with so many white men." He went on to speak of "the resumption of national authority within the States wherein that authority has been suspended"—that is, the states in rebellion—and he said he had affixed to his message a proclamation regarding "what is called reconstruction … in the hope that it may do good without danger of harm … and avoid great confusion." The proclamation read in part:

"I, Abraham Lincoln, President of the United States, do proclaim … to all persons who have, directly or by implication, participated in the existing rebellion … that a full pardon is hereby granted to them … with restoration of all rights of property, except as to slaves…on condition that every such person shall take and subscribe an oath … [to]

A map by a London publisher darkens the southern areas under Union control by January 1864. Sympathetic to the Confederacy, Britain made no overt move to support the South militarily, choosing instead to watch and wait.

henceforth faithfully support, protect and defend the Constitution of the United States, and the union of the States thereunder."

International Reaction

As Christmas approached, the Lincolns relaxed a bit from the endless strain they had been under, and Mary's younger half-sister Emilie Helm was to spend the holidays with them. Given that she was a staunch Confederate and her husband had died as a southern soldier, the invitation was a large-hearted one, and the Lincolns welcomed her "with the warmest affection." It did Mary good to confide in a female relative. She told Emilie of her spiritualist beliefs. Willie, she assured her sister, "comes to me every night with the same sweet, adorable smile he has always had … little Eddie is sometimes with him." And

she turned to her sister for support. "Kiss me, Emilie, and tell me you love me," she said one morning, after reading more criticisms of herself in the newspapers. "I seem to be the scape-goat for both North and South."

The Lincolns had kept Emilie's visit quiet, knowing the furor it would cause to have a Confederate widow in their home. Too often, the press had accused Mary of being wedded to the southern cause. But one evening they entertained two of Mary's beau monde friends, Senator Ira Harris and Gen. Daniel Sickles. When talk turned to the war, a subject Emilie and Mary avoided, Emilie would not give ground, and the evening grew increasingly tense. Then the senator turned on Mary, asking why Robert was not in the military. Her face "turned white as death" as she took all blame. "Robert is making his preparations now to enter the Army; he is not a shirker—if fault there be it is mine, I have insisted that he should stay in college a little longer as I think an educated man can serve his country with more intelligent purpose than an ignoramus."

When Sickles, who had lost a leg at Gettysburg, turned to Lincoln and insisted loudly, "You should not have that rebel in your house," Lincoln was just as emphatic. "Excuse me, General Sickles, my wife and I are in the habit of choosing our own guests."

Lincoln's controlled response reflected the skill he had cultivated in dealing with Washington sniping. On the cold, blustery New Year's Day of 1864, the *National Republic* crowed over Lincoln's leadership. "We have had a rebellious storm, and … the political horizon is somewhat muggy; but our gallant old ship of State, with Abraham Lincoln at the helm, has weathered the gale."

The political horizon was in fact muggy, and soon to become muggier. Secretary of the Treasury Salmon Chase, ever ambitious for the Presidency himself, had stumped through his home state of Ohio in the previous fall's elections and had drawn enthusiastic crowds. "That visit to the west is generally understood as [his] opening campaign" for the Presidency," Secretary Bates, who had long resented and mistrusted Chase's ambition, noted. Lincoln was well aware of Chase's desire to be President, but he did not stifle the secretary's machinations. "I suppose he will, like the bluebottle fly, lay his eggs in every rotten spot he can find," Lincoln told Hay.

Though Seward, Stanton, and most other members of his Cabinet had come to a deep respect of Lincoln's leadership, Chase never shared their view. His own gnawing desire for the office, and his vanity, wouldn't let him. Despite the fact that his maneuverings the year before to have Lincoln's Cabinet "reorganized" had ended in his own humiliation and a show of party confidence for the President, he still felt certain that he could make a strong showing against the awkward prairie lawyer in a presidential election. And after all, there had not been a two-term President since Andrew Jackson, in the 1830s.

In early 1864 a "Chase for President" committee was announced, headed by Kansas senator Samuel Pomeroy. The committee's strongest financial backer, however, was Chase's new son-in-law, William Sprague. Sprague had married Chase's much admired daughter Kate in a wedding that had been the highlight of the Washington social season that fall. In late February a confidential document that came to be called the Pomeroy circular was sent to influential Republicans throughout the North. It explained why a second Lincoln term would lead the country to ruin and that, in any case, the President's reelection was "practically impossible." It went on to assure its audience that Salmon P. Chase should be the Republican candidate. The circular made its way into the press, creating a furor and weakening the Republican Party. Chase denied any knowledge of it in a carefully worded letter to Lincoln that included an oblique offer to resign. "I do not wish to administer the Treasury Department one day without your entire confidence."

Lincoln's reply was cool, calculated, and noncommittal. He said that he had received Chase's letter and would "answer a little more fully when I can find time to do so." While Chase waited, Lincoln had the gratification of watching the backlash against his secretary grow. Across the North, even in Chase's home

The New York wedding of "General" and Mrs. Tom Thumb helped lift the wartime mood. Mary Lincoln later held a reception for the couple (below). Lincoln was presented with a "royal album" (bottom) from the Prince of Wales's 1860 American visit. Pages 158-59: The Chain Bridge linked Northern Virginia with the capital.

Federal soldiers dreaded capture and confinement at the South's notorious Andersonville prison in southwestern Georgia. Of the 45,000 prisoners held there over the course of the Civil War, some 13,000 died of malnutrition, disease, or exposure.

state of Ohio, Republican loyalists passed resolutions for the renomination of Lincoln. With the tide in his favor, Lincoln magnanimously wrote Chase that he saw no "occasion for a change" at Treasury. On March 5, Chase withdrew as a contender for the presidential nomination. But Lincoln advisers believed the move was "a mere sham." The President's old friend David Davis was sure that at the convention, the secretary's supporters would "present Chase again."

Total War

Lincoln well understood that both his political future and the future of the nation hinged more than ever on a swift conclusion to the war. After three years of watching his generals hesitate and fail, he was no longer tolerant of military misadventures and lost opportunity. Since Gettysburg, Meade and Lee had danced around one another without the armies ever really engaging. Time and time again, Lincoln bluntly urged Meade to "be sure to fight, the people demand it of the Army of the Potomac." But Meade had lost his confidence at Gettysburg and made no decisive move. Meanwhile Lincoln had been forced to order the draft of an additional half million men. In March, he would have to add 200,000 more.

Late in February, perhaps out of desperation, Lincoln conceded to a wild scheme suggested by the son of his ordnance chief and friend, John Dahlgren. An enthusiastic proponent of the new Machine Age, Lincoln loved the hardware of the military, and Dahlgren reported that "the President often comes to see the [Navy] Yard and treats me without reserve." Dahlgren's son Ulric had lost a foot at Gettysburg but that did not deter the young colonel from his enthusiasm to fight. He conceived a plan for an expeditionary raid on Richmond to liberate Union prisoners of war held in the notorious Belle Isle prison. The raid failed before it reached Richmond, and Dahlgren was killed in another thwarted attempt to penetrate the Confederate capital.

None of these unsuccessful strategies and half measures would help either Lincoln's electability or the national cause, but victory would ensure both. There was one general who had consistently delivered victory, at whatever cost, and that was Grant. Not only had Grant, with the help of Sherman, virtually destroyed the Confederate threat in the western theater, but his policy to free slaves as he took territory had left the South further weakened.

Grant seemed the obvious choice to bring Lee at last to his knees, but Lincoln was hesitant. Grant had become a popular hero. Was he, like Chase and others, afflicted with what Lincoln called the "presidential grub … gnawing at him"? Through indirect channels, Lincoln set about to find out and was rewarded with a letter from Grant assuring him he was not. Lincoln worked to have Congress reinstitute the rank of lieutenant general, held once by George Washington, and Grant took the helm of the Union Army.

Grant had hoped to stay in the western theater and oversee the military from there, free from Washington's meddling. But Lincoln was adamant that he come East to bring the Army of the Potomac to victory. So on March 8, 1864, the unobtrusive general arrived with his teenage son, Fred. After dinner at Willard's Hotel, he walked to the President's House to join the weekly reception then in progress. Grant was expected, and Lincoln caught sight of him "walking along modestly with the rest of the crowd." The President came quickly to Grant's side, and towering eight inches above him, extended his hand. "Why here is General Grant!" he exclaimed warmly. "Well this is a great pleasure."

The next day, with Grant ceremoniously installed as lieutenant general, Lincoln took him to his office and told his new commander that he would have "all the power of the government" behind him. He also assured Grant, "I wish not to obtrude any constraints or restraints upon you."

Grant did however place constraints on himself, and almost immediately he went by train to visit General Meade in Northern Virginia. His orders to Meade were simple— "Wherever Lee goes, there you will go also." His plan now was total war, and Lincoln approved. He would lead the Army of the

Potomac in a relentless assault on Lee's Army of Northern Virginia.

Grant planned a three-pronged attack on the Confederacy: As Meade pursued Lee, Grant's trusted comrade-in-arms General Sherman would march from the west across Georgia and attack Atlanta. Benjamin Butler,

still on the Virginia peninsula, would follow the James River northwest to assault Richmond. Throughout his Presidency, Lincoln had advised his generals to make coordinated attacks. Here at last was one who would.

One Washington observer had characterized Grant as a man with "a slightly seedy look," but "a clear blue eye," whose expression looked "as if he had determined to drive his head through a brick wall." Lee was Grant's brick wall, and his determination did not flag.

Lincoln understood only too well that if Grant moved into Virginia, Lee would choose his own ground for the fight, and that had always signaled disaster for the Union. Still he watched with anxious hope as the wheels

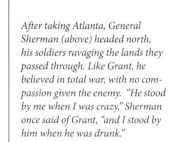

After taking Atlanta, General Sherman (above) headed north, his soldiers ravaging the lands they passed through. Like Grant, he believed in total war, with no compassion given the enemy. "He stood by me when I was crazy," Sherman once said of Grant, "and I stood by him when he was drunk."

of Grant's three-pronged attack were set in motion in early May. Butler landed his 30,000 troops on the James between Richmond and Petersburg, and Grant moved the Army of the Potomac across the Rapidan River. Both northern and southern armies had spent the winter close by each other on the banks of the river; now they would face off again.

> ## "HE'S A BUTCHER AND IS NOT FIT TO BE AT THE HEAD OF AN ARMY."
>
> MARY LINCOLN, ON GRANT

Lee patiently let Grant advance, waiting until the northern army was deep in the tangled thickets of the Wilderness, where Hooker's men had been trapped a year before. Grant's organized army fared much better, and by mid-morning on May 6, the Union advance had swept the Confederate Army into a retreat that looked as though it would be a rout. But when the Rebels launched an unexpected assault, they managed to drive the Federal flank back and capture two generals. Union commanders panicked. Grant would have none of it. "I am heartily sick of hearing what Lee is going to do," he snapped. "Go back to your command, and try to think what we are going to do ourselves."

For his part, Grant was going to continue the pursuit, despite heavy casualties: In the bloody, two-day battle in the Wilderness, he lost close to 18,000 men. Many had died as the conflagration turned the dense, dry thicket into a fiery tomb. Yet in his report to Lincoln, who had haunted the War Department for two days waiting for news, Grant said simply, "Everything pushing along favorably."

Grant's message may not have reflected his losses, but it did reflect his attitude. Unlike other Union commanders who had gone up against Lee, he did not take time to lick his wounds. After the Wilderness, he surprised his troops by ordering a night march forward, following Lee south. Elated to find themselves with a general who was not afraid to go after Lee, Grant's soldiers cheered him as he rode alongside them through the night. "Men swung their hats, tossed up their arms, and pressed forward to within touch of their chief, clapping hands, and speaking to him with the familiarity of comrades," Grant's aide remembered.

Lee, too, was an offensive general, and he lay in wait again for the Army of the Potomac, just southeast of the Wilderness, at Spotsylvania Courthouse. In two battles waged on and off for a week in spring rains, the armies suffered carnage that accomplished little. "The fighting was horrible," one Confederate soldier wrote. "The breastworks were slippery with blood and rain, dead bodies lying underneath half trampled out of sight."

In two weeks, the Army of the Potomac had suffered 32,000 casualties, including one of Grant's few trusted generals, John Sedgewick. Lee had lost his eyes and ears, the cavalry commander Jeb Stuart, wounded in a battle near Richmond. "I can scarcely think of him without weeping," Lee said. Each army had lost about a third of its strength. But Grant, more easily able to accommodate his losses, had vowed to Lincoln, "Whatever happens, there will be no turning back."

As the bloody month of May closed, Grant trailed Lee as he retreated south. The Confederates understood that they at last faced a general who would keep at Lee, regardless of losses or public opinion. "That man will fight us every day and every hour till the end of this war," Gen. Longstreet warned Lee.

Opposite, in his typical, bruised battle uniform, Grant (far left) leans forward to confer with Gen. Meade during a "council of war" at Massaponax Church, convened between battles in the spring of 1864. Above, a rare glass campaign lantern bearing Lincoln's image lit the way for its carrier.

That was exactly what Lincoln himself believed and hoped. "It is the dogged pertinacity of Grant that wins," Lincoln said to John Hay. The President was in no mood to compromise on any level and no longer showed leniency to deserters. He also would not broker interference from the press. In May, when two northern papers erroneously and deliberately printed a proclamation purportedly from Lincoln calling up another 400,000 draftees, Lincoln ordered the arrest of the editors. In fact, another 300,000 draftees were needed, but Lincoln would not allow the press to meddle maliciously with public opinion. Initial press reports in May were jubilant, heralding "Glorious Successes" and "The End Draws Near." But very soon the grim truth became known, and in early June, it turned from grim to horrific.

Since Grant had begun his pursuit of Lee, the two armies were rarely out of contact. The toll taken was enormous. "Many a man has gone crazy since this campaign began from the terrible pressure on mind & body," Capt. Oliver Wendell Holmes, Jr., wrote. Both armies had called in reinforcements, and when they engaged again on June 3, they were at fighting strength, though the Confederates were ill clothed and fed. Grant thought the Confederates' condition would help him, but it did not. The next encounter was at Cold Harbor, ten miles northeast of Richmond. It was the most horrendous of the war, for its brief duration. In less than an hour, Grant lost 7,000 men who fell before a Confederate wall of fire. "The dreadful storm of lead and iron seemed more like a volcanic blast than a battle," a Union captain reported.

For another nine days, the armies confronted each other. "The world has never seen

On June 3, ten miles northeast of Richmond, Grant ordered 50,000 men to attack Lee's forces, dug in at Cold Harbor, Virginia. The North took horrific casualties, losing 7,000 men in less than an hour. "It was not war; it was murder," declared one Union general.

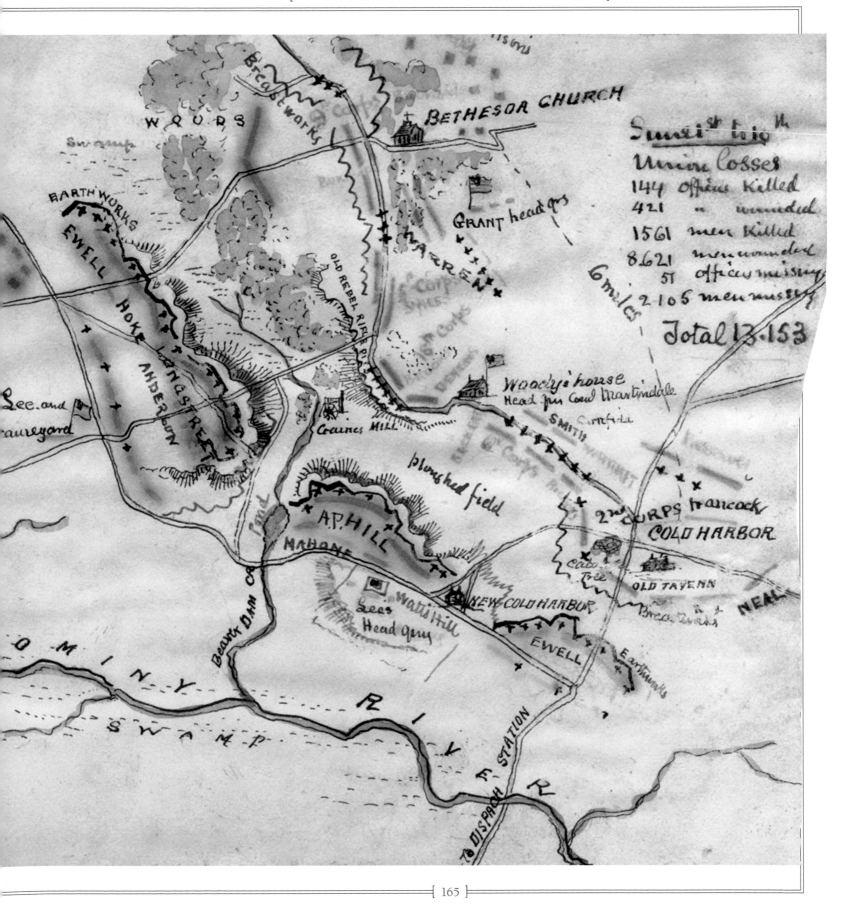

Union Losses
144 Officers Killed
421 " wounded
1561 men Killed
8621 men wounded
51 Officers missing
2105 men missing
Total 13.153

so bloody and so protracted a battle as the one being fought," Grant wrote to his wife. He had lost 13,000 men, while Lee suffered only between 1,500 and 2,500 casualties. Throughout his life, Grant would regret ordering the assault at Cold Harbor, and he came to realize the foe he was up against. In a month he had lost more than 50,000 men. "Without a greater sacrifice of human life than I am willing to make, all cannot be accomplished as I had designed," he admitted.

In Washington, steamers filled with the wounded docked at city wharves. In the War Department, Gideon Welles reported that "the intense anxiety is oppressive and almost unfits the mind for mental activity." The losses in Grant's campaign did nothing to help Lincoln's political standing. All spring, his own party had "harassed [him] with petty faultfinding and criticisms," observed one congressman, "until he had turned at bay, like an old stag pursued and hunted by a cowardly rabble of men and dogs." The Chase and Blair factions had been loudly and publicly at each other's throats, exchanging accusations of political and fiscal corruption. Lincoln had quelled the rift with his usual deft aplomb, but that did not keep both Radical and Conservative factions of the party from quietly voicing their doubts

Washing off the war, soldiers bathe in Virginia's North Anna River. The ruins of the Richmond and Fredericksburg railroad bridge, burned by Union troops during a battle here, stand in the river behind them.

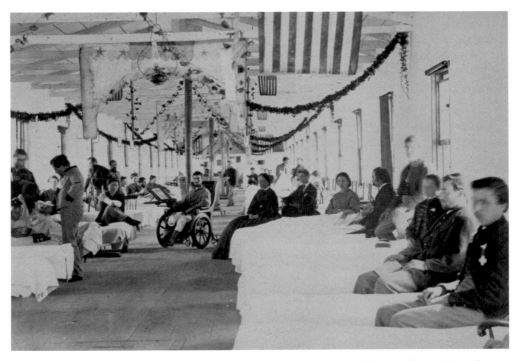

Built in 1862 to take in wounded soldiers, the thousand-bed Armory Square was one of the capital's largest hospitals.
As Grant and Lee tangled through the spring and early summer of 1864, Washington's hospitals overflowed with casualties.

PRESIDENTIAL ARTIFACTS

Lincoln's personal photo album with images of White House visitors.

A walking stick given to Lincoln by California senator John Conness.

The ivory-handled Presidential Seal for Lincoln's second administration.

Lincoln's leather briefcase, in which he carried important papers.

about Lincoln's electability in the coming race; some operatives looked for another candidate. Chase was often mentioned, and in Cleveland, a convention of party defectors nominated John C. Frémont, the abolitionist general who had caused Lincoln problems earlier, as an alternative candidate for President.

Yet by the time the Republican convention, or as it was called that year, the National Union convention, opened in the early June heat of Baltimore, it was clear that Honest Old Abe easily had the nomination. Even his often vocal detractor, *New York Tribune* editor Horace Greeley, who had hoped that a strong alternative to Lincoln might become apparent, conceded that "The People think of him by night & by day & pray for him & their hearts are where they have made so heavy investments." Lackluster Vice President Hannibal Hamlin, a Radical Republican, was replaced on the ticket with Andrew Johnson, a War Democrat who had served in Congress before being appointed by Lincoln in 1862

as military governor of his home state, Tennessee. There, he had begun testing some of the policies Lincoln had formulated for reconstruction. The convention also passed a resolution for a constitutional amendment abolishing slavery, something that would stand after the war, which the Emancipation Proclamation, enforcible only under the War Powers Act, would not.

Waiting for a telegraph of the convention results, a nonplussed Lincoln learned of Johnson's nomination before his own. But the next day, a delegation arrived in person with the news. Lincoln told them he doubted they had found him "the best man in the country; but I am reminded, in this connection, of a story of an old Dutch farmer," who contended that "it was not best to swap horses when crossing streams." There were many streams yet to cross.

After the slaughter at Cold Harbor, Grant had attempted to take Petersburg, a town just south of Richmond. Threaded with rail lines and with easy access to the James River, it was

In an 1864 campaign chart (opposite), Lincoln and running mate Andrew Johnson face off against their opponents, Democrats George McClellan and George Pendleton. The yellow swath on the map shows Union-held territory. Pages 170-71: The Union's "Dictator," a 13-inch seacoast mortar mounted on a railroad flatcar could be pointed at different locations in the Confederate defenses during the Siege of Petersburg in April 1865.

a major supply center for the Confederacy. Lee again had gotten in front of Grant and held the town, but Grant dug in, as he had in Vicksburg, and prepared for a siege. A siege did not augur well for the predicted defeat of the Confederacy by the fall. Meade had written to his wife earlier in the spring, "Grant has had his eyes opened and is willing to admit now that Virginia and Lee's army is not Tennessee and Bragg's army." Meade was right.

WORLD PERSPECTIVE

Red Cross Relief

In 1859, as saber-rattling between North and South grew louder in America, European powers were again readying for battle, as they had so often in the past. In June of that year, the forces of Napoleon III and Austria's Franz Josef squared off at the bloody Battle of Solferino in northern Italy. Swiss businessman Henri Dunant witnessed the carnage and wrote of it his in short but powerful *Memory of Solferino*. In it he argued that nations should form relief societies to care for the battlefield sick and wounded.

Dunant's writing and crusading inspired the Geneva Public Welfare Society in Switzerland to press for an international relief effort. In August 1864, delegates from 12 nations met and signed the Geneva Convention for the Amelioration of the Condition of the Wounded and Sick in Armed Forces in the Field. They also adopted a red cross on a field of white—the reverse of the Swiss national flag—as the symbol of their new organization, the International Red Cross, headed by Dunant. The convention was a turning point, marking the first treaty to establish international humanitarian law. From then on, when signatories to the treaty went to war, they guaranteed neutrality for medical personnel and equipment on the battlefield. By 1870, medical teams flying the Red Cross flag were ministering to troops on the killing fields of the Franco-Prussian War. Among the Red Cross volunteers was an American

Focused on humanitarian causes, Red Cross founder and businessman Henri Dunant later found himself homeless in the 1870s.

and former patent clerk named Clara Barton. During the American Civil War, Barton had distinguished herself as the "Angel of the Battlefield," courageously tending the wounded on the front lines. Barton soon lobbied American Presidents for U.S. involvement in the International Red Cross, but she didn't succeed until 1881, when Chester Arthur signed the Geneva Convention treaty. For 20 years Barton herself headed the American Red Cross, offering disaster relief and organizing volunteers for international relief efforts.

With the war weighing so heavily on the nation and on his own thoughts, Lincoln decided to leave the confines of the capital. In June, with Mary and Tad, he went by train to Philadelphia, where the Great Central Fair was in progress. The fair was being held to benefit the U.S. Sanitary Commission, a volunteer civilian organization that helped with the medical and health needs of Union soldiers. Along the route to Philadelphia, crowds cheered the President. Supporters filled the streets of Philadelphia to greet him. That evening, Lincoln spoke solemnly to an assembled crowd: "We accepted this war for an object, a worthy object, and the war will end when that object is attained."

> "I MAY BE COMPELLED
> TO FACE DANGER, BUT NEVER
> FEAR IT, AND WHILE OUR
> SOLDIERS CAN STAND AND
> FIGHT, I CAN STAND AND
> FEED AND NURSE THEM."
>
> CLARA BARTON

After Philadelphia, Lincoln set out to see the person he hoped could end the war. Returning to Washington, he took a riverboat down the Potomac, then up the James to Grant's headquarters at City Point, Virginia. Overnight, the quiet riverside spot had become an enormous port facility, supplying 125,000 Union troops and 65,000 animals. Again Lincoln was greeted with affection by the troops, who didn't seem to mind that, as he sat on Grant's horse, his pants hiked up above his ankles, he looked like "a country farmer riding into town wearing his Sunday clothes." Always dauntless in the face of danger, he ventured out to the front lines with Grant to reconnoiter the virtually impregnable earthworks that encased Petersburg and Lee's army. On his way back, he was moved

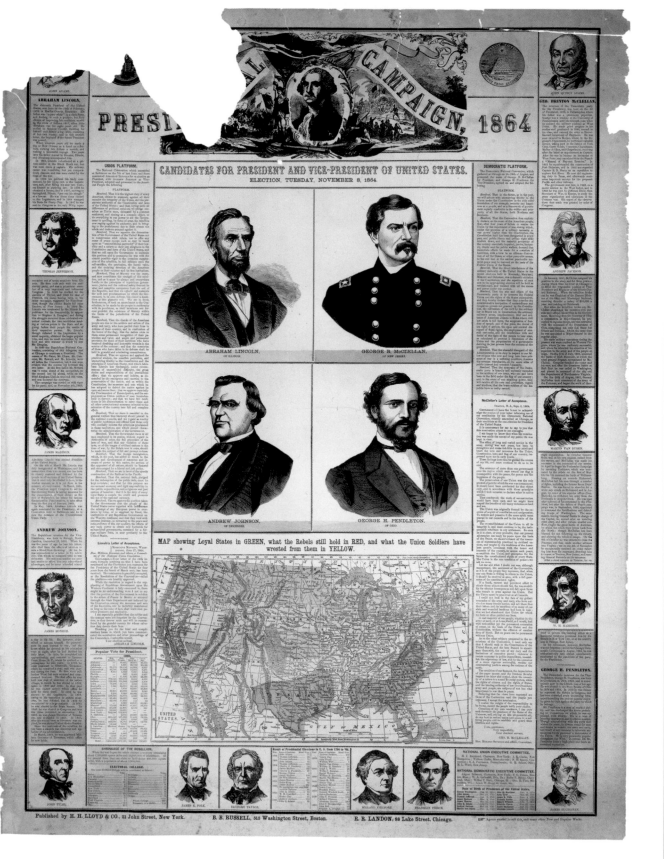

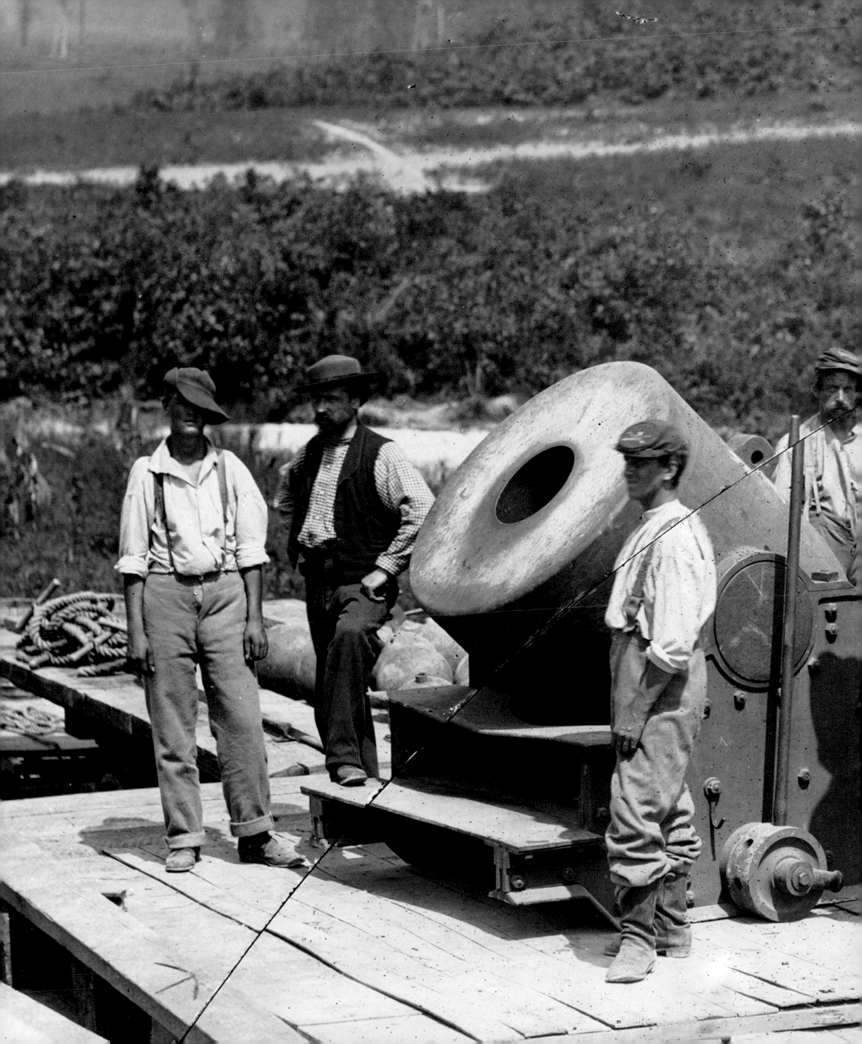

Union Avenue functioned as a covered thoroughfare connecting a vast complex of temporary structures built for Philadelphia's Great Central Fair. Organized by the United States Sanitary Commission, such fairs were held in large cities to raise money for military medical supplies.

War and Politics

After four years at Harvard, Robert Todd Lincoln graduated in early July 1864. To his bitter disappointment, he learned by telegram that "The President will not be at commencement." Mary and Tad did attend, but that did little to assuage Bob's feelings. Lincoln had always treated his eldest son with a reserved, almost formal cordiality, and when Bob saw him again in Washington, Lincoln chatted for a brief few minutes. According to Bob, Lincoln asked, "Son, what are you going to do now?" to which Bob replied, "As long as you object to my joining the army, I'm going back to Harvard to study law." To that Lincoln retorted, "If you do, you will learn more than I ever did, but you will never have so good a time."

Lincoln's—and particularly Mary's—reluctance to let their son join the Union cause no doubt stemmed in part from having lost two sons already. Lincoln apparently also believed that his wife's mental stability was too precarious to endure the loss of another child. But it nonetheless seems out of character for Lincoln to have made this personal exception. Four of his Cabinet members—Seward, Blair, Bates, and Welles—had sons serving in the military, and their apprehension for their children's safety only grew as the war drew on. They were just a handful of the thousands of families who feared their sons would never return, or if they did, would be wounded for life. Yet the President's son, despite his own protestations, was headed for more schooling in the midst of war.

While the rest of the family was away for Robert's graduation, Lincoln was grappling as always with his unwieldy treasury secretary. Once again, Chase had tried to impose his will on the President, and when he could not, took offense. Lincoln had been through this before and paid little mind when a messenger brought him correspondence from Chase. After a conciliatory opening, Chase

to tears when a brigade of Black soldiers ran toward him, yelling, "God Bless Master Lincoln! The Lord save Father Abraham!"

The visit with Grant and the army refreshed and reinvigorated Lincoln, as he knew it would. When he took leave of City Point, Grant pledged to him, "You will never hear of me farther from Richmond than now, till I have taken it…. It may take a long summer day, but I will go in." Even with Grant's resolve, the long summer day would roll into winter, and Lincoln would return to City Point again.

went on to offer, for the fourth time since his appointment, his resignation: "I cannot help feeling that my position here is not altogether agreeable to you." Other Cabinet members may have doubted Lincoln's abilities as he took office, but they had come to be staunch loyalists, and, in the case of Seward and Stanton, true confidantes. Chase had never let go of his own arrogant ambitions, and Lincoln was at last weary of his obstreperousness and scheming. This was, Lincoln admitted,

"the last straw." He accepted the resignation, writing, "you and I have reached a point of mutual embarrassment in our official relation which seems can not be overcome."

The following morning, Lincoln dispatched his secretary John Hay to the Senate to announce Chase's resignation, which had been accepted this time. Chase had expected Lincoln's usual attempt at conciliation, and when he learned the President had already recommended a successor to his position,

---

WORLD PERSPECTIVE

Mexico's Emperor Maximilian

The American Civil War presented some tantalizing opportunities to the monarchies of Europe. The American Republic and its experiment in democracy had previously been a threat to them, and now that experiment seemed to be imploding of its own accord. The European monarchies were happy to help the implosion along—or at least to take advantage of it.

Throughout the war, Britain and France had considered overt intervention in support of the Confederacy. While they had decided to refrain from intervening, they had concocted a tripartite expedition, in conjunction with Spain, to invade Mexico in 1862. They called it a "debt collection" mission, but Lincoln and Seward were not taken in by this attempted European subterfuge. In March 1862, Seward wrote officially to warn against "a permanent policy of armed European monarchical intervention ... hostile to the most general system of government on the continent of America."

Having overthrown Mexico's republican government of President Benito Juárez, Britain and Spain eventually withdrew from the tripartite arrangement, but the ambitions of Napoleon III were not easily deflected. Forging a new alliance with Austria's Emperor Franz Joseph, Napoleon hatched a scheme to install an impe-

From 1864 until 1867, Archduke Ferdinand of Austria ruled as Emperor Maximilian of Mexico.

rial ally on the throne of Mexico. Emperor Franz Joseph then offered up a candidate for the position—his exasperatingly liberal younger brother, Ferdinand Maximilian.

In May 1864, Maximilian and his wife, Carlotta, landed at Vera Cruz and made their way to Mexico City to claim the throne, greeted by cheering crowds waving flowers and flags. The pro-monarchist Confederate States applauded, while the pro-Juárez U.S. reacted by dispatching troops to Texas to head off any foreign intervention from across the border.

In almost every way, the imperial experiment was doomed from the very beginning. The new emperor antagonized some groups and remained unpopular. He was never able to solidify the grass-roots support of the Mexican people, and local forces frequently opposed the French troops who were bent on shoring up the monarchy. The once-esteemed, deposed president, Benito Juárez, a Zapotec Indian and Mexican cultural hero, led the opposition against Maximilian's rule, despite the liberal policies the Emperor sometimes put forward.

With the conclusion of the American Civil War, the United States wanted the French out of Mexico and at last had the resources to come to Juárez's aid. Meanwhile, Napoleon III began returning his troops to Europe, to counteract the growing threat of Bismarck's Prussian army. In May 1867, the star-crossed Maximilian was captured by Juárez's fighters. A month later he was executed by firing squad, ending all hopes of an imperial Mexico.

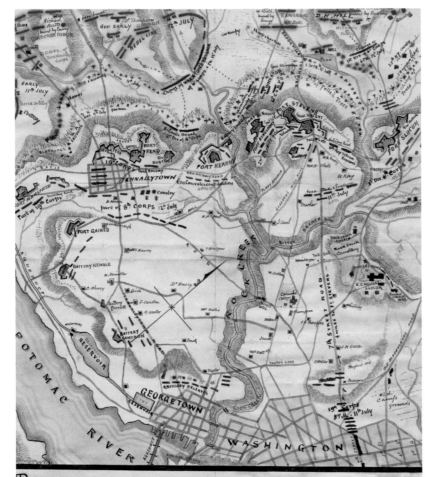

PLAN of the REBEL ATTACK on WASHINGTON. D.C. JULY 11ᵗʰ and 12ᵗʰ 1864.
Maj Genl H.G. Wright. Union Forces 20,000 —— Rebel Force 12000 under Genl Early & Breckinridge
Union Loss 140 Killed 220 wounded. Rebels unknown.
Union for... Artillery Batteries ❘❘❘ ❘❘ Rebel Forces— Infantry .... Cavalry ⚊⚊ Guns ❘❘❘

Jubal Early (above) launched his July attack on the nation's capital during Grant's Siege of Petersburg (top), forcing the general to send his most accomplished unit, the Army Sixth Corps, to defend Washington.

he was amazed, as was the Senate. Various factions approached Lincoln to reconsider, but he held fast. "Chase has fallen into two bad habits," Lincoln replied. "He thinks he has become indispensable to the country…. He also thinks he ought to be President."

Chase's replacement, Senator William Fessenden of Maine, only learned of his position after Congress had confirmed him. He knew what lay ahead and told Secretary Welles that he believed the job would kill him. Welles, who had survived four years as Secretary of the Navy in a time of war, had no sympathy. "You cannot die better than in trying to save your country," he told Fessenden.

Lincoln was not a man to hold grudges, and he recognized in Chase, for all his disloy-

alty, a man of skill who the country could ill afford to lose. When the troublesome Chief Justice Taney died in October 1864, Lincoln appointed Chase to head the nation's highest court, saying, "I should despise myself if I allowed personal differences to affect my judgement of his fitness for the office."

Hard on the heels of the Chase Cabinet resignation had come another political standoff. In early July, as the 38th Congress prepared to adjourn for the summer, its Republican members realized in alarm that they had passed no substantive legislation. Hoping to do so, the radicals in the party resurrected the proposed Wade-Davis bill, which dealt with issues of slavery and reconstruction. In it the southern states would receive harsher treatment than Lincoln had proposed. Lincoln understood that the bill was a direct assault on his authority, and that it would cost him in the upcoming presidential election. He made no move when it landed on his desk, then literally turned his back on a delegation that came to his office to plead for his signature. He explained, "This bill was placed before me a few minutes before Congress adjourned. It is a matter of too much importance to be swallowed this way." Lincoln chose to pocket veto the bill, telling Hay, "I must keep some consciousness of being somewhere near right: I must keep some standard of principle fixed within myself."

While Lincoln was distracted by Wade-Davis, the Confederate forces of Jubal Early had been inching closer to the capital. Much of the Union manpower that had defended Washington had been diverted to Grant's campaign, and now, in a feeble response to the possible threat, clerks and recovering soldiers were given rifles. In Petersburg, Grant did not take the threat seriously, but he magnanimously offered to come to the defense of the capital himself. Lincoln wrote back, requesting but not ordering that he come with most of the army and "make a vigorous effort to destroy the enemy's forces in this vicinity." Instead, Grant dispatched the seasoned troops of the Sixth Corps.

By July 11, Early's force of 15,000 was on the outskirts of Washington, poised to attack nearby Fort Stevens. From his Soldiers' Home cottage, Lincoln rode out to the fort several times, Mary at one point joining him. Even though she had been counseled to abandon the capital, she refused. Throughout Early's advance, Lincoln himself had been "in a pleasant and confident humor," apparently not concerned that the capital would fall. "With him the only concern seems to be whether we can bag or destroy this force in our front," one adviser noted.

Once at Fort Stevens, the President watched the action from a parapet, the tall, unmistakable figure in a stovepipe hat directly in the line of fire. At one point, it is alleged that the young Capt. Oliver Wendell Holmes, Jr., had shouted, "Get down you fool!" But Lincoln seemed elated to experience battle firsthand.

In the end, the battle wasn't much of one. When the Sixth Corps arrived, Early knew his advance was doomed and he retreated. But he had enjoyed letting the Federals know he could get within five miles of their Capitol. In London, the *Times* viewed Early's raid as proof that "the Confederacy is more formidable than ever." It was not a view shared by Prime Minister Palmerston, however. Of the

European powers, only Napoleon III held out any lingering hope for a Confederate victory.

No definitive good had yet come of Grant's three-pronged attack on the South. Butler's forces had been pinned down by the Confederates south of Grant on a neck between the James and Appomattox Rivers. Sherman had battled across Georgia. In late June, resolved to show that "his men could fight as well as Grant's," Sherman ordered an assault on Kennesaw Mountain, where Joe Johnston's Rebel army was dug in. Like Grant's attack at Cold Harbor, Kennesaw proved to be a northern bloodbath, with 3,000 men lost. In a letter to his wife, Sherman wrote, "I begin to regard the death and mangling of a couple thousand men as a small affair, a kind of morning dash, and it may be well that we become so hardened."

By mid-July his army was in sight of heavily fortified Atlanta, but Johnston's army had gotten there before him. A linchpin in the south, the Gate City connected the southern coast with the interior, and the South could not afford to lose it. Despite Johnston's successes, Jefferson Davis, desperate for a battlefield victory, replaced him with Gen. John Bell Hood, ignoring the adage Lincoln had so recently cited about himself, that "it was not best to swap horses when crossing streams." On July 20, Hood attacked the northern forces and lost 2,500 men. On July

A lithograph from the 1864 campaign features an image of presidential candidate George McClellan, the popular Union commander and son of a prominent Philadelphia family. His running mate, Ohio congressman George Hunt Pendleton, was a noted antiwar Democrat.

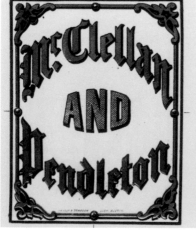

Born in 1818 as a Maryland slave, Frederick Douglass escaped to the North when he was 20. He became an eloquent, internationally recognized spokesman for the rights of Blacks and women and an adviser to Lincoln, though the two did not always agree. In 1872, he ran for Vice President on Victoria Woodhull's Equal Rights Party ticket.

was hatched by men of the 48th Pennsylvania, many of them coal miners. By digging a tunnel—the equivalent of a mine shaft—underneath the fortifications, they could plant a mine and blow a hole in the Confederate defenses, through which Federal troops would then pour. Neither Grant nor Meade put much stock in the plan but they let it proceed, and on July 30, the explosion blew a crater 170 feet long in the fortifications, taking down an entire Rebel regiment.

> "[NAPOLEON III IS] HOVERING OVER US, LIKE THE CARRION CROW OVER THE BODY OF THE SINKING TRAVELER, WAITING UNTIL WE ARE TOO WEAK TO RESIST HIS PREDATORY INSTINCTS."
>
> JOHN BIGELOW, U.S. GENERAL CONSUL TO FRANCE

The follow-up by the Union forces, though, was leaderless and disorganized, and the Confederates soon regrouped. The Battle of the Crater was, Grant reported, "the saddest affair I have witnessed in the war. Such opportunity for carrying fortifications I have never seen and do not expect again to have."

The only good news during the interminable days of summer came from the Deep South, where Adm. David Farragut had taken Mobile Bay with a battle cry, perhaps apocryphal, that would echo through history, "Damn the torpedoes! Full speed ahead!" As helpful as closing Alabama's port of Mobile was, it was not a significant turning point.

21, the opening salvos in the two-day Battle of Atlanta were fired. When the fighting ended, the South had not yet lost the city but Hood had lost altogether 8,000 men in three days. Rather than storm the city, Sherman now bombarded it, much as Grant had done to Vicksburg. Cutting off the supply lines feeding it, he drew a noose around the city that tightened as the summer drew to a close.

Grant was hoping to do the same thing with Richmond, by besieging Petersburg and cutting the lines feeding through there to the Confederate capital. But very little progress had been made by late July, when, without much enthusiasm, he approved an ingenious plan to break through Lee's formidable entrenched defenses in Petersburg. The plan

With no end to the war in sight and a presidential election at hand, Lincoln was again attacked from all sides—by Radical Republicans, Peace Democrats, and even War Democrats, who objected to what seemed to be his support of abolition. So far, slavery had only been abolished in certain areas, and Lincoln had never avowed complete abolition. Now, with freedmen fighting for the Union cause, he couldn't conceive of returning "the black warriors … to their masters to conciliate the South." Frederick Douglass, the great Black orator and statesman who had advised Lincoln during his Presidency, naturally agreed. At the risk of losing the upcoming election, Lincoln held to his principles. "It seems exceedingly probable that this Administration will not be re-elected," he wrote in a memo that he asked his Cabinet to sign without reading. He added that it would be his, and their, "duty to so co-operate with the President elect, as to save the union between the election and the inauguration."

He fully expected that his opponent in the race would be his former general, George McClellan, a War Democrat, and he was right. But just days after McClellan's nomination, in early September, the tide of war finally turned with the fall of Atlanta. In the Shenandoah Valley, too, the new commander of Union forces, Phillip Sheridan, had finally triumphed over the troublesome Jubal Early. Suddenly, Lincoln's candidacy had grown so strong and viable that John Frémont bowed out of the race. In mid-October both the Democrats and Republicans anxiously watched the results of state elections in Ohio, Indiana, and Pennsylvania to gauge the electorate's leanings. In the two western states, the Republicans enjoyed strong victories, but Pennsylvania was a bare win, and Lincoln worried about how these populous states would vote the following month in the presidential race. He also recognized that without a decisive electoral win, "his power to prosecute the war and make peace would be greatly impaired."

When the votes were tallied in November, Lincoln got the endorsement he had hoped for, taking 212 electoral votes to McClellan's 21, though the candidates were separated by

only 400,000 popular votes. Most important to Lincoln was the soldiers' vote. "I would rather be defeated with the soldier vote behind me than to be elected without it," he had said before the election. But the troops fighting the protracted war stood solidly behind him in the election.

At Christmas there was more good news from the front. Rather than chase Hood's Confederate forces, Sherman had convinced Grant that, "If we can march a well-appointed army right through his territory, it is a demonstration to the World, foreign and domestic, that we have a power which Davis cannot resist. This may not be war but rather Statesmanship." Living off the farms and harvest of the South, Sherman's army of 60,000 had cut a swath through Georgia on their March to the Sea, and on December 25, the general sent Lincoln a historic telegram, "I beg to present you, as a Christmas gift, the city of Savannah."

The scars of war were left across Georgia from Atlanta to Savannah (above) as Sherman made his notorious March to the Sea in the fall of 1864. Abandoning supply lines, he instructed his men to forage off the land. His plan to break Confederate morale was successful. Pages 178-79: The South's Fort McAllister guarded the Ogeechee River, Savannah's "back door."

HARPER'S WEEKLY.

A
JOURNAL OF CIVILIZATION.

VOL. IX.—No. 425.]   NEW YORK, SATURDAY, FEBRUARY 18, 1865.   [SINGLE COPIES TEN CENTS.
[$4.00 PER YEAR IN ADVANCE.

Entered according to Act of Congress, in the Year 1865, by Harper & Brothers, in the Clerk's Office of the District Court for the Southern District of New York.

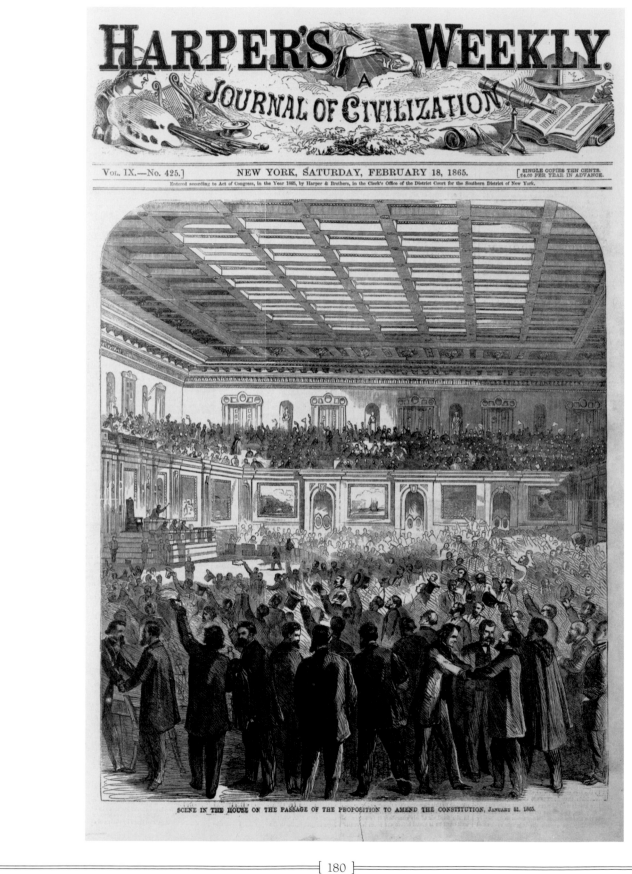

SCENE IN THE HOUSE ON THE PASSAGE OF THE PROPOSITION TO AMEND THE CONSTITUTION, January 31, 1865.

The Final Push

Mary Lincoln was both delighted and relieved at her husband's reelection. Contrary to press reports, she was a staunch supporter of the Union cause and had come to be an advocate of abolition as well. But she was still an uncontrollable spender, and with Lincoln entrenched as President for another term, her debts would not come back to haunt her so soon. The pressures of office would distract Lincoln—and keep her creditors at bay. "I owe altogether about twenty-seven thousand dollars," she had told Elizabeth Keckley. Lincoln had no idea of her debts, and now, continuing on as Mrs. President Lincoln, she could probably continue to hide them.

Mary unquestionably enjoyed her shopping trips—within Washington and to northern cities—but she had also spent the past year raising money for the Contraband Relief Association, a cause far less popular than other aid efforts. Elizabeth Keckley, the former slave and friend who probably exerted more influence on Mary than anyone else during the presidential years, had alerted her to the dire need of these newly freed slaves. "These immense number of Contrabands are suffering intensely …," Mary wrote, "many dying of want." What to do with the freedmen after the war was a question that plagued her husband also. After his election, Lincoln determined to settle the matter.

Lincoln's campaign platform had included support for a constitutional amendment to end slavery. He well understood that the Emancipation Proclamation was limited in scope and time frame. It would be abandoned when the war ended. He had tried to get an amendment abolishing slavery passed in the previous session of Congress and had gotten it through the Senate but not the House. Now, in January 1865, with victory behind him, he went back to Congress, claiming "It is the voice of the people now, for the first time, heard upon the question."

This time, with a big Republican majority in the House, he succeeded. On January 31, the 13th Amendment was passed, declaring that "Neither slavery nor involuntary servitude, except as a punishment for crime … shall exist within the United States, or any place subject to their jurisdiction."

The states still had to ratify the amendment, but "the passage of the resolution filled the President's heart with joy. He saw in it the complete consummation of his own great work, the emancipation proclamation." National jubilation greeted its passage, and in the North, abolitionist and frequent Lincoln critic William Lloyd Garrison made peace with the President at last. "And to whom is the country … indebted for this vital and saving amendment?" he asked a Boston crowd. "To the humble railsplitter of Illinois—to the President chainbreaker for millions of the oppressed—to Abraham Lincoln!"

Only a few days later, Lincoln was on a steamer "supposed to be the fastest in the world," to Fort Monroe, Virginia, where three envoys of the Confederacy waited for him. The Hampton Roads Peace Conference had been instigated by Francis Preston Blair, part of the powerful Blair clan that included Lincoln's former postmaster general (the pugnacious Montgomery Blair had resigned from the Cabinet after the election). Francis Blair proposed to Lincoln that the South be approached with an eye to postponing hostilities while North and South united to fight France. At last Napoleon III's ambitions to expand his empire to Mexico had

A Harper's Weekly *cover (opposite)* *celebrates the 13th Amendment by showing jubilation in the House when the legislation was passed. The accompanying article criticized those members who resisted the amendment "upon the incredible grounds that it is an inopportune time." Fort Monroe (above) was the site of many historic events during the war, including the Hampton Roads Peace Conference.*

been realized. In the spring of 1864, France had invaded the nation, and now Emperor Maximilian sat on Mexico's throne, in clear violation of America's Monroe Doctrine. But with civil war still consuming the U.S., Lincoln could make little response to the French incursion into North America.

Although he was highly skeptical of Blair's new plan, he agreed to allow to proceed, and Blair hurried off to present it to his

WORLD PERSPECTIVE

Charles Dickens

While Americans struggled to survive their protracted Civil War, the British reading public devoured the novels of their immensely popular tale-spinner and social commentator Charles Dickens. Dickens had an uncanny talent for capturing the essence of Victorian lives on many levels of the social ladder—no doubt because he himself had occupied rungs up and down that ladder.

As a boy, Dickens's family had been part of the "liquid middle class," whose fortunes changed often. In 1824, at age 12, his father was sent to debtor's prison. "In an evil hour for me," Dickens later wrote, he was sent to work in a shoe-blacking factory to help support the family. On his father's release, Dickens was able to go back to school, where he worked diligently to improve his lot. He eventually became a reporter, covering the courts, then began writing caricatures of Victorians and their manners, serialized as *Sketches by Boz* in 1836. *The Pickwick Papers* soon followed, and Dickens's literary career was launched.

In the next several years he wrote *Oliver Twist, Nicholas Nickleby,* and *The Old Curiosity Shop.* An 1842 trip to North America resulted in the controversial *American Notes,* in which Dickens both admired and castigated Americans. "They are, by nature, frank, brave, cordial, hospitable, and affectionate," he wrote. But he also called them distrustful, "dull and gloomy," "a trading people, [who] don't care for poetry." Ardently

Mr. Bumble, head of the orphanage in Oliver Twist, *ranks among Dickens's array of memorable villains.*

antislavery, he described the districts "where slavery sits brooding," as having "an air of ruin and decay abroad, which is inseparable from the system."

Dickens's views were not well received in America. Yet, after the war, he returned to the U.S. on a reading tour. Audiences embraced him, having forgiven earlier criticisms. In six months he made some 400 appearances and seemed to come to peace with America. While the trip profited him financially, it cost him physically. Two years later, the great novelist died suddenly at 58. He is buried with the other greats in Westminster Abbey.

old friend Jefferson Davis. Ultimately, Davis dispatched the three emissaries, who spent a night with Grant at City Point on their way. Like others, they were "instantly struck with the great simplicity and perfect naturalness of [Grant's] manners." For his part, Grant believed that "their intentions are good," and

"I CAN MAKE THIS MARCH AND MAKE GEORGIA HOWL!"
WILLIAM TECUMSEH SHERMAN

his opinion convinced a reluctant Lincoln to make the journey to meet with them.

The peace conference proceeded amicably and informally but accomplished nothing—except to assure the North that Lincoln would never give in to southern demands if they compromised the authority of the Union or the legal status of the 13th Amendment. In the South, the reaction was outrage at the North. "Every one thinks the Confederacy will at once gather up its military strength and strike such blows as will astonish the world," a clerk for the War Department recorded.

Such talk was mere bombast. Northern forces had ripped through Alabama, and Sherman's voracious army was about to "wreak vengeance upon South Carolina" for starting the war. "I almost tremble at her fate," Sherman admitted, adding, "but feel that she deserves all that is in store for her."

As Sherman's men took their vengeance, Lincoln was sworn in for his second term. Inauguration Day was cool, wet, windy, and exceedingly muddy, but that did not deter the crowds that gathered. As Lincoln rose to speak, the sun burst through the clouds, and the crowd cheered. His voice was calm this time, as he recalled that at his Inaugural tour four years before, "all thoughts were anxiously directed to an impending civil-war." He went on to infer that the war was God's

punishment for the offense of slavery. But he ended on a high and historic note: "With malice toward none; with charity for all … let us strive on to finish the work we are in; to bind up the nation's wounds … to do all which may achieve and cherish a just, and a lasting peace, among ourselves, and with all nations."

After his Inauguration, Lincoln's strength deserted him, and he spent two days in bed. "Poor Mr. Lincoln is looking so broken-hearted, so completely worn out," Mary confided to Elizabeth Keckley, "I fear he will not get through the next four years." Without telling her husband, she approached Grant and urged him to invite Lincoln to City Point. The President was frankly worried about his own health and endurance, and he knew that a trip away from Washington always helped restore his vigor. So in mid-May, he, Mary, and Tad boarded the steamboat *River Queen* for a visit with Grant and the troops still engaged, after nine months, in the Siege of Petersburg.

When the *River Queen* docked, the Lincolns were greeted by their son Robert, who

At Lincoln's Second Inaugural, he was sworn in by the chief justice he had earlier appointed, Salmon Chase. Behind him, the Capitol dome, under construction four years before, rose complete—a reflection of his own resolve that the Union would go on.

MATHEW B. BRADY'S STUDIO

T he dead of the battle-field come up to us very rarely, even in dreams. We see the list in the morning paper at breakfast, but dismiss its recollection with the coffee," the *New York Times* opined during the war. "Mr. Mathew Brady has done something to bring us the terrible reality . . . of the war. If he has not brought bodies and laid them in our door-yards and along our streets, he has done something very like it."

Photography was in its infancy then, and American portrait photographer Mathew B. Brady was one of its most recognized artists. Brady took his first portrait of Lincoln in 1860 before Lincoln gave his famous Cooper Union speech. The masterful portrait of the 51-year-old politician, touched up to disguise Lincoln's weak left eye, was distributed in engravings and lithographs throughout the Northeast, helping to cement Lincoln's national reputation.

When war engulfed the country, Brady and his cadre of 20 "photo-journalists" left the safety of the studio for the battlefields. The new wet-plate process required a wagon equipped for photo-processing. For the first time, the carnage and pathos of the battlefield were brought home in full force.

Brady's efforts to chronicle the war cost him his personal fortune. In the 1870s, he sold part of his massive glass-plate collection to the War Department. Fame and fortune deserted him, and he died penniless and in obscurity in 1896. No longer obscure, Brady today is hailed as the leading photographic documentor of the war. Most of his surviving images are preserved in the Library of Congress and the National Archives. ■

After the First Battle of Bull Run, Brady poses in his signature straw boater and long duster. Brady and his team used this wooden box (right) in the field to hold chemicals and lenses.

Brady's prewar New York studio was full of society portraits (above). In the field he captured scenes of daily life, including a shot of Gen. Burnside reading his newspaper (left), with Brady himself on the general's left. One of Brady's original team, Alexander Gardner (top, seated) went on to achieve his own fame.

With the fall of Richmond, former slaves (below), now homeless, piled their belongings into barges on the city's old canal. At the end of the war, nearby City Point, Virginia (opposite), became for a time one of the busiest harbors in the world.

had left law school in the fall and had at last been allowed to join the military. Lincoln, in an earlier letter to Grant, had explained that "my son … wishes to see something of the war before it ends," and asked whether Robert "could go into your Military family with some nominal rank, I, and not the public, furnishing his necessary means?" So Robert had been made a captain attached to Grant's personal staff.

Even with the Lincoln family briefly united, Mary became increasingly agitated on the trip. She was not receiving the attention she thought her due as the President's wife and she said so, loudly and publicly. Arriving late to a grand review of troops because her carriage was delayed, she found the proceedings had begun without her and that her husband was being escorted by the young and comely Mrs. General Ord, both on horseback. Climbing out of her carriage, Mrs. Lincoln repeatedly "attacked her husband in the presence of officers," one observer reported. "He bore it as Christ might have done with an expression of pain and sadness that cut one

to the heart … He called her mother, with his old-time plainness. He pleaded with eyes and tones, till she turned on him like a tigress." That night at dinner, she berated Grant's wife, Julia, for getting more attention than she did. A few days later, she returned to Washington on her own, no doubt to her family's relief.

Sherman had left his army in the field to travel to City Point and meet with Grant and the President. He would often recall the meeting with Lincoln later in life. "Of all the men I ever met, he seemed to posses more of the elements of greatness, combined with goodness, than any other." Both generals could not spare the President their belief that "one more bloody battle was likely to occur before the close of the war." The news only made Lincoln more haggard, but he told them that when defeat came to the Confederate Armies, "I want no one punished; treat them liberally all round. We want those people to return to their allegiance to the Union."

Lincoln saw Grant off for what both felt might be the last battle, the President's "voice broken by an emotion he could ill conceive." Lee had finally been forced out of his entrenched position in Petersburg, and he was moving west. As Grant went after the Confederates a final time, Lincoln stayed on in City Point. Stanton, sure that the fall of Richmond was imminent, had urged him to remain there. "I have strong faith that your presence will have great influence in inducing exertions that will bring Richmond."

The fighting moved back and forth for days, and Lincoln could hear the cannonades from the dock at City Point. As the North gained on the Confederate forces, Lee understood the demise of Richmond was inevitable.

On Sunday April 2, Jefferson Davis was attending church when a messenger interrupted the service to hand him a warning from Lee—Richmond must be abandoned. The President of the Confederate States

Fort Sumter (above), where the war began, was originally planned as one in a series of coastal defenses to protect the U.S. from foreign invaders; it was still under construction when fighting erupted. Pages 190-91: After four long years of war, Lee surrendered to Grant on April 9, 1865, at the home of Wilmer and Virginia McLean in the town of Appomattox Court House, Virginia. "I have done the best I could for you," Lee told his men. "My heart is too full to say more."

"walked hurriedly down the aisle, beneath the questionings of all eyes." The news soon spread through the city, and the race to vacate the capital was soon on. Rather than leave its stores to the enemy, the Confederates set fire to warehouses and industrial facilities, explosions shook the city, and looters made off with what had not gone up in the conflagration.

By April 3, Federal troops occupied Richmond. The following morning, Abraham Lincoln was ferried across the James to Richmond, with an escort of "vessels flying flags at every mast-head, hoping to enter the conquered capital in a manner befitting the rank of the President of the United States," Adm. David Porter recalled. But the tug escorting Lincoln's riverboat ran aground,

and he boarded instead a skiff to be rowed ashore. The lack of pomp probably suited Lincoln better. When he stepped ashore a group of freedmen greeted him with "Glory to God! … Bless the Lord! The great Messiah! I knowed him as soon as I seed him." Several reached forward to touch Lincoln, saying, "I know I am free, for I have seen Father Abraham and felt him." Choked with emotion himself, Lincoln told them not to kneel to him. "You must kneel to God only, and thank him for the liberty you will hereafter enjoy."

Walking through the streets of Richmond, the President's entourage proceeded to the home of the Confederate president, as bodyguards anxiously scanned buildings and windows for anyone planning harm to

Lincoln. Once at the Davis home, an older Black servant waited on the entourage, explaining that "Mrs. Davis had ordered him to have the house in good condition for the Yankees."

In Washington, a 900-gun salute, fireworks, and endless celebrations greeted the fall of Richmond. Lincoln, now ensconced on the riverboat *Malvern*, stayed in the Richmond area and was joined by Mary as Union forces pursued Lee into central Virginia. Sheridan, who had recently laid waste to the Shenandoah Valley, caught up to the rear of Lee's army at Saylers Creek, and the Rebels lost 8,000 men, a quarter of Lee's force. After the battle, Sheridan wrote Grant. "If the thing is pressed, I think Lee will surrender." Grant relayed the message to Lincoln, who responded: "Let the thing be pressed."

Lee had hoped to resupply his desperate army at the crossroads town of Appomattox in central Virginia, but Sheridan had arrived before him, with other Union corps close on his rear. "There is nothing left for me to do but go and see General Grant," Lee admitted, "and I would rather die a thousand deaths."

On April 9, in the Appomattox home of Wilmer McLean, Lee, in full dress uniform, met Grant, who came in his signature, battle-soiled boots, trousers, and private's blouse. As Lincoln had advised, Grant was magnanimous in victory. He had instructed his soldiers not to fire guns in celebration or exult over the Confederates' defeat in their presence. "The war is over," he said. "The Rebels are our countrymen again." Grant's terms of surrender were also generous—Lee's soldiers could "return to their homes, not to be disturbed by United States authority." Lee then asked a favor. His soldiers owned their own horses. Could they keep them, "to put in a crop to carry themselves and their families through the next winter"? When Grant agreed, Lee assured him, "this will have the best possible effect upon the men ... and will do much to conciliating our people."

Lincoln had been on his way back to Washington as the surrender was taking place and had gone directly to visit Seward, who had been badly wounded in a carriage accident. Lincoln only learned of Lee's capitulation when Stanton rushed to him with a telegram from Grant. "The President hugged me with joy," Stanton reported.

> "IT IS A GOOD FACE; IT IS THE FACE OF A NOBLE, BRAVE MAN. I AM GLAD THAT THE WAR IS OVER AT LAST."
>
> ABRAHAM LINCOLN, ON ROBERT E. LEE

Throughout the North, people hugged, celebrants filled the streets, bonfires blazed, and fireworks shrieked. In the Capitol, candles and lanterns illuminated the windows. Serenaders kept up a steady stream of music outside the President's House. Once Lincoln came to a window and requested "Dixie," saying it was "one of the best tunes I ever heard." The evening of April 11, he conceded to the crowds' incessant demands that he speak. Standing in a second-story window, below the portico of the President's House, he began, "We meet this evening, not in sorrow, but in gladness of heart." He then went on to speak of reconstruction, invoking the example of Louisiana, where 12,000 citizens "have sworn allegiance to the Union ... adopted a free-state constitution, giving the benefit of public schools equally to black and white, and ... confer[ring] the elective franchise upon the colored man." What he wanted, he said, was to get the "seceded States" back into "proper practical relation with the Union."

In the crowd listening to Lincoln was a pro-southern, proslavery actor of some fame, John Wilkes Booth. When the speech was over, Booth vowed to his companion "That is the last speech he will ever make."

"THE WAR IS NOW CLOSED, AND SOON WE WILL
LIVE IN PEACE WITH THE BRAVE MEN WHO HAVE
BEEN FIGHTING AGAINST US."

ABRAHAM LINCOLN, APRIL 14, 1865

[CHAPTER SIX]

HE BELONGS TO THE AGES
1865

THE NIGHT OF APRIL 13 LINCOLN HAD A DREAM THAT HAD RECURRED throughout the war. He was on a body of water "in some singular, indescribable vessel … moving with great rapidity towards an indefinite shore." He took it as a good omen, because in the past the dream had presaged news of a Union victory. The next day, Good Friday, he even shared it with his advisers at a Cabinet meeting that focused mostly on how to proceed with Reconstruction. Lincoln reiterated the need for leniency and aid for the defeated Confederate States. "No greater or more important [issue] could come before us, or any future Cabinet" than Reconstruction, he assured them.

The rest of the day was filled with more meetings, but in mid-afternoon, he took time out for his carriage ride with Mary. "I consider *this day,* the war has come to a close," he told her. It had cost both of them greatly, and he seemed anxious to restore the bond between them. "We must *both,* be more cheerful in the future—between the war and the loss of our darling Willie—we have both, been very miserable." When Mary later recalled the ride, she said, "I never saw him so supremely cheerful. His manner was even playful."

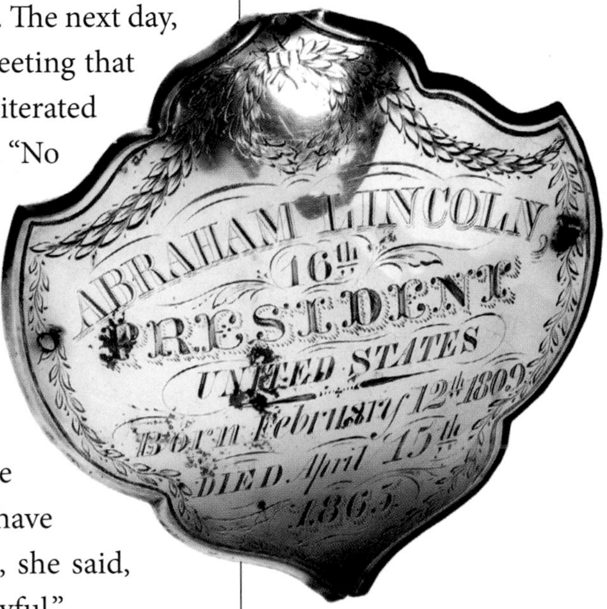

The Lincolns were scheduled to attend a benefit performance of *Our American Cousin* at Ford's Theatre that evening, but despite the enormous affection for him, the President had had a hard time finding other guests to make up their entourage. Over the course of four years in Washington, Mary Lincoln had managed to alienate a good many political wives, who now found excuses not to join the Lincolns at Ford's. Several of the men declined because they thought it dangerous for Lincoln

After Lincoln's assassination, the nation mourned. A funeral train carried the President's remains from city to city. In New York, thousands paid their respects at City Hall (opposite). The silver plate on Lincoln's casket (above) was eloquently simple, as he would have liked.

[193]

to appear at a public place, particularly since his longtime bodyguard, Ward Lamon, was in Richmond. But the press had announced Lincoln's attendance, and Ford's expected a record audience of some 1,700. Lincoln, as usual, refused to disappoint his public.

After asking 14 different people to make up the presidential party, Lincoln was finally accepted by Clara Harris, daughter of the New York senator, and her fiancé, Maj. Henry Rathbone. The presidential carriage picked the young couple up then proceeded through a spring night haloed by a chill fog. Lights along their route shone through the mist, in celebration of the Union victory. The farce was already in progress when the four took their places in the proscenium box reserved for them at Ford's.

When Lincoln arrived, the orchestra immediately struck up "Hail to the Chief," as the audience cheered long and enthusiastically. Lincoln bowed and smiled, then sank gratefully into the rocking chair provided for him in the box. Both Lincolns seemed to relax at last and enjoy the play, Mary snuggling affectionately into her husband to comment on the comedy. "What will Miss Harris think of my hanging on to you so?" she asked

Popular actor John Wilkes Booth appeared on playbills throughout the country, particularly in the South. Booth had theater in his blood. His father, Junius Brutus Booth—whose behavior was so erratic as to border on the insane—had been considered by many to be the greatest Shakespearean actor of his day. His brother Edwin was also a great stage celebrity, but ultimately, his fame would be eclipsed by John's acts.

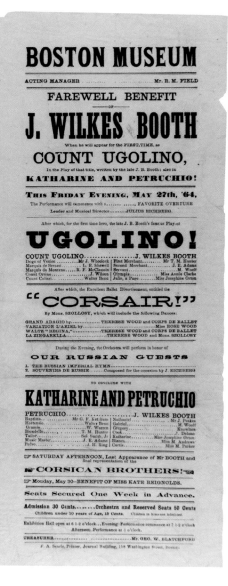

him coquettishly. "She won't think anything about it," Lincoln told her.

At about 10:15 p.m., in the second scene of the third act, the audience predictably reacted with laughter and applause when the male

> "OUR COUNTRY OWED
> ALL HER TROUBLES TO
> [LINCOLN], AND GOD SIMPLY
> MADE ME THE INSTRUMENT
> OF HIS PUNISHMENT."
>
> JOHN WILKES BOOTH

lead delivered a line about a "sockdologizing old man-trap." It was the moment another actor had been waiting for. John Wilkes Booth was a celebrated thespian who often appeared at Ford's—but not this night. Instead, he was standing outside Lincoln's box, where only a White House footman, Charles Forbes, guarded the door. Booth had presented his card to Forbes and been let into the box.

The President's Assassination

Once inside, Booth barred the door and moved quietly toward Lincoln, who was leaning forward, engrossed in the play. When he was within two feet of the President, Booth raised a derringer and shot Lincoln in the left side of the head. As the President fell forward, Mary caught and held him, his head slumping onto his chest as if he were sleeping. Rathbone leaped toward Booth, but the actor lunged at him with a seven-inch hunting knife and slashed his arm open. Booth then jumped from the box onto the stage, the kind of dramatic aerial gesture he was famous for. Only this time, he caught the spur of his boot on the bunting that had been draped outside the presidential box. He landed so hard on one leg that he broke it. He managed to shout *"Sic Semper Tyrannus—Thus Death Comes Ever to Tyrants"* before "hopping [like]

a bull frog" across the stage and out the rear of the theater. Shoving aside the guileless boy waiting in the alley with his horse, Booth galloped away into the night.

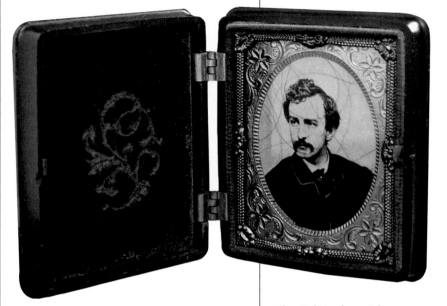

When Tad Lincoln saw John Wilkes Booth (above) perform, he declared, "He makes me thrill." Tad's father, the President, was himself an enthusiastic patron of the theater, frequently attending evening performances to take his mind off the war. Lincoln often invited actors to join him in his presidential box between acts, but Booth always refused invitations from the man he viewed as a traitor to the South.

Pandemonium erupted in the theater, as Mary screamed and sobbed, "Oh, my God, and have I given my husband to die?" The audience, suddenly aware of what had happened, began shouting "Booth! Booth!" A 23-year-old physician in the audience, Charles Leale, was the first to reach the stricken President. He stretched Lincoln on the floor, looked for a wound, and "soon discovered a large firm clot of blood" behind the left ear. "When I removed my finger which I used as a probe, an oozing of blood followed and he soon commenced to show signs of improvement." As Leale worked, a second doctor, no older than Leale, crawled over the box railing and helped Leale restore Lincoln's breathing. But Leale understood too well the damage that had been done by Booth's shot.

"It is impossible for him to recover," he admitted. As the doctors worked, the audience reached a hysterical pitch. "There will never be anything like it on earth," one woman who was present wrote. "The shouts, groans, curses, smashing of seats

On April 14, 1965, the benefit performance at Ford's Theatre featured the comedy Our American Cousin, *a popular satire that skewered both American and English stereotypes.*

… through all the ages will stand out in my memory as the hell of hells."

Leale knew that Lincoln would not survive a trip back to the President's House, so the decision was made to carry him across Tenth Street to the boardinghouse owned by William Petersen. It took several men, including two more doctors who had come to the President's side, to handle Lincoln's long, limp body. On the street, Mary became separated from her husband and screamed hysterically, "Where is my husband? Why didn't he kill me? Why was I not the one?" Once inside, Lincoln was taken to a small, dingy room at the back of the house and laid diagonally across a bed that was too short to accommodate his height. Mary covered him with kisses until she was taken into the front parlor, where she would wait out the long vigil, coming every hour to her husband's bedside. Crowds had swarmed into the unguarded house and the patient's room, but soldiers soon cleared them out.

As news of the attack spread, the entire Cabinet—save Seward—rushed to the President's bedside. Seward, injured in a carriage accident the week before, was bedridden in his own home, when, at 10:10 p.m. one of Booth's accomplices, Lewis Powell, appeared at his door, saying he had medicine for the secretary of state. Once inside, he attempted to shoot Seward's son Frederick, but the gun jammed and instead he brutally smashed the young man's skull with the butt of the pistol. When Powell reached his real target, Seward, he knifed the secretary so ferociously in the neck and cheeks that the wounds seemed fatal. Then he ran from the house. But Seward was not dead. Opening his eyes, he announced to the members of his household gathered round him, "I am not dead, send for a surgeon, send for the police, close the house!"

At the Petersen house, Lincoln was slowly expiring from his wound as ten physicians, his Cabinet, his wife, and his son Robert watched helplessly. Mary lamented, "Oh, that my Taddy might see his father before he died." In the early morning hours Lincoln's breathing took on the labored croak of a death rattle, and Mary cried out, "Oh have I given my husband to die?" and collapsed. Secretary Stanton, who had taken charge, ordered, "Take that woman out of here and do not let her in again."

Lincoln's "stertorous breathing subsided a couple of minutes after seven o'clock," one witness recorded. "From then til the end only the gentle rise and fall of his bosom gave indication that life remained…. At twenty-two minutes past seven … the Surgeon General gently crossed the pulseless hands of Lincoln across the motionless breast…. Mr. Stanton raised his head, the tears streaming down his face. A more agonized expression I never saw on a human countenance." The usually controlled Robert was sobbing as well. In farewell, Stanton put on his hat, then took it off in a gesture of honor. "Now," he proclaimed to those in the small, crowded room, "he belongs to the ages."

The Booth Tragedy

While so many mourned, Booth and other southern sympathizers rejoiced that Lincoln, the "false president," was gone. The 26-year-old actor had grown up on a slaveholding farm in Maryland, one of ten children of the well-known Shakespearean actor Junius Brutus Booth. While working in the theater in England, the older Booth had deserted his first wife for Mary Anne Holmes, who bore John Wilkes before the couple was married. The boy's illegitimacy and his father's drinking and mental instability, had made for a hard childhood, but when he took to the stage himself, Booth found a home. He also found an appreciative audience, both on stage and off, in the South, where he performed often and charmed social circles with his style and storytelling. During the war he even bought and smuggled medicines into the Confederacy to support the cause.

Histrionic and insecure, the young man entertained visions of his own gallantry and heroism, and in 1864 he hatched a plan to realize his dreams. Working with agents in the southern secret service, Booth began plotting to abduct Lincoln and hold him as ransom for southern soldiers. In the fall and winter of 1864, Booth recruited a motley group of young men in the capital to help him. By March the plot was fixed: On March 17, Lincoln was scheduled to attend a performance of a play at the Campbell Hospital, near the Soldiers' Home. While he was en route, the conspirators would waylay his carriage and kidnap the President. That plan dissolved when Lincoln fortuitously decided to review a regiment instead of seeing the performance.

The failure only heightened Booth's determination. Drinking more than ever and becoming increasingly delusional, the actor saw himself as the avenger of the now defeated South. On the evening of April 11, 1865, he went to the President's House with two of his fellow conspirators to hear Lincoln address the gathered crowd. Booth concentrated on the praise Lincoln gave Louisiana for agreeing to give "the benefit of public schools equally to black and white, and empowering the Legislature to confer the elective franchise upon the colored man." To Booth, that meant "nigger citizenship." "That is the last speech he will ever make," Booth had declared. Turning to one of the other conspirators, Lewis Powell, he urged him to shoot Lincoln then and there. When Powell refused, Booth vowed to bring the President down with his own hand.

The Ford's Theatre performance soon provided Booth with the perfect venue, and Booth didn't hesitate to act. Two of his co-conspirators—Powell, who made the attempt on Seward, and George Atzerodt, who was to have attacked Vice President Johnson but lost his nerve—were quickly apprehended, but not Booth. "I passed all … the pickets," he wrote in his journal. "Rode sixty miles that night, with the bone [in my leg] tearing the flesh at every jump."

Outside Washington, another conspirator, David Herold, caught up with Booth. Considered slow-witted, Herold had been brought into the conspiracy because he knew the Maryland countryside. The two

One of the leading lights of both the European and American stages, English-born Laura Keene was perhaps America's first female theater manager and owner. Our American Cousin debuted at her own New York theater years before it was performed at Ford's. Keene had played the coquettish female lead in the production more than a thousand times by that fateful April evening.

men now headed for Surrattsville, about a dozen miles south of Ford's Theatre in Maryland. There, they knew they could take refuge at Lloyd's tavern, where whiskey, field glasses, and a rifle were waiting for them. The whiskey didn't ease Booth's pain much, but the two rode on through the moonlit night. By 4 a.m. Booth could ride no more, and the fugitives stopped at the home of a physician Booth had met in the area. Dr. Samuel Mudd later claimed that he didn't recognize Booth, and in any case, had not yet heard of Lincoln's assassination, so he set the fracture and gave Booth a pair of handmade crutches. By late afternoon the following day, Booth and Herold were on the run once again. They soon managed to get lost in the marshes of southern Maryland and ironically had to pay a Black man to show them the way out. A Confederate sympathizer, Thomas A. Jones, then came to their rescue, providing them with food and news but no shelter for six rain-chilled days. The area was crawling with soldiers and policemen hunting for the assassin, and at one point, the searchers came within 200 yards of Booth and Herold without seeing them. Booth's leg was becoming more and more inflamed, and the two men were "wet, cold, and starving … and in despair."

Finally, conditions were right to cross the Potomac in Virginia, and they set out in a fishing boat they bought from Jones. Once on the other side, Booth grew increasingly despondent when the Virginians he had expected to greet him as a hero wanted nothing to do with the fugitives. With no plan now, Booth and Herold kept heading southeast, crossing the Rappahannock, then at last stopping at a tobacco barn owned by Richard Garrett. By now, they were calling themselves the Boyd brothers, but locals weren't fooled.

> "PA IS DEAD.
> I CAN HARDLY BELIEVE
> THAT I SHALL NEVER
> SEE HIM AGAIN.
> I MUST LEARN TO TAKE
> CARE OF MYSELF NOW."
>
> TAD LINCOLN

On the morning of April 26, a contingent of soldiers and Secret Service agents surrounded the barn where the two were holed up. Booth tried to get Herold to surrender and yelled out of the barn, "I declare before my maker that this man here is innocent of any crime whatever." Herold came out with his arms raised, and the barn was set fire, to force Booth out. Meanwhile, one of the posse, believing that he heard the voice of Providence, aimed through a chink in the barn wall and shot Booth fatally in the neck. "Tell Mother," Booth said in the hours he lay dying, "I die for my country."

A Nation Mourns

As word spread that Father Abraham was gone, people collected together in towns and cities across America, weeping openly. Telegraph offices were thronged with citizens waiting for further news, church bells tolled, and soldiers still in the field grieved their fallen commander. "What a hold Old Honest Abe Lincoln had on the hearts of the soldiers of the army could only be told by

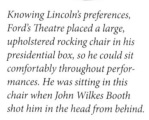

Knowing Lincoln's preferences, Ford's Theatre placed a large, upholstered rocking chair in his presidential box, so he could sit comfortably throughout performances. He was sitting in this chair when John Wilkes Booth shot him in the head from behind.

the way they showed their mourning for him," one soldier wrote in his journal. African Americans wore black armbands and their churches were decked in black, in honor of the Great Emancipator. A Republican opponent, Ignatius Donnelly, proclaimed, "He has carried a vast and discordant population safely and peacefully through the greatest of political revolutions." Now, that vast and discordant nation came together to honor Lincoln in death.

On the morning following the assassination, the nation had been briefly without a Vice President. Two senators had gone to collect Chief Justice Chase and take him to Kirkwood House, where Vice President Johnson boarded. Johnson at first could not be aroused from sleep, but at last, annoyed, he got up and came to the door of his rooms, half dressed and in his bare feet. When he heard the news, he immediately raised his right arm and said, "I'm ready." Chase administered the oath and Johnson became the 17th President of the United States.

At the White House, Lincoln's body, "all limp and warm," had been taken to a guest chamber on the second floor, opposite Mrs. Lincoln's room. Mrs. Gideon Welles had been sent for to comfort Mary Lincoln, but the two were not close friends and Mrs. Welles kindly asked if there were someone Mary wanted with her "in this terrible affliction." Mary requested her closest confidante, her dressmaker Elizabeth Keckley, who was soon at her side, as she grieved with "the wails of a broken heart, the earthly shrieks, the terrible convulsions." "Tad's grief at his father's death was as great as his mother," Keckley reported,

Lincoln's deathbed scene in the small, cramped room of the Petersen boardinghouse was depicted over and over by artists of the period, almost all taking liberties with the event. This 1868 painting by A. Kromer includes Secretary of State Seward, shown at Lincoln's head. Attacked in his own home, Seward was never at Lincoln's side at the end.

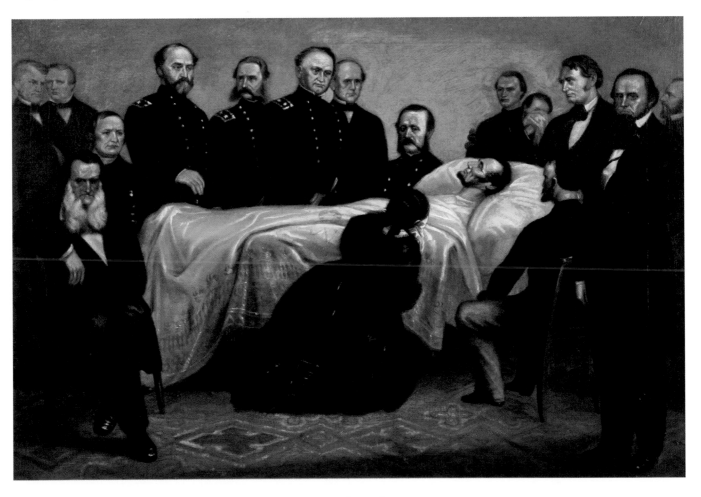

THE PRESIDENT'S WIDOW

After Lincoln's death, his family slowly dissolved. For almost two months, Mary was virtually bedridden and frequently hysterical with grief. Robert was forced to appeal to President Johnson, writing "my mother is so prostrated that I must beg your indulgence. Mother tells me that she cannot possibly be ready to leave here for 2½ weeks." And so Johnson remained in a small office in the Treasury Department until late May, when Mary and her two sons vacated the President's House, bound for Chicago.

Robert and family friends had tried to persuade Mary to return to Springfield, where she could afford to live. But because of her behavior regarding Lincoln's burial, she had few friends left there and no desire to return. For the next three years, the family lived in a succession of hotels and rented rooms. Tad finally began attending school, and Robert followed his father into the law, at last escaping Mary's emotional demands by taking rooms of his own.

Mary was again faced with financial ruin, as the merchants who had indulged her spending when she was Mrs. President Lincoln came to collect. She hatched a variety of schemes to raise money, including selling her old clothes and furniture and soliciting funds from Congress and from wealthy patrons—a custom not unusual at the time. Robert, always protective of his father's memory, became increasingly embarrassed by his mother's behavior.

In 1868, when Lincoln's estate was settled, Mary's money problems ended. She and Tad took passage for Europe and stayed for two and a half years. Even Europe could not quell

After Lincoln's death, Mary tried to contact her husband through séances. A strange and haunting photograph taken by "spirit photographer" William Mumler shows an aging Mary with Lincoln's ghostly image hovering behind, his hand placed protectively on her shoulder.

Mary's dissatisfaction—her youngest son was her one great joy. "Taddie is like some old woman with regard to his care of me," Mary wrote a friend. "His dark, loving eyes watching over me remind me so much of his dearly beloved father's." Soon after the two returned to Chicago, 18-year-old Tad developed "dropsy on the chest" and in July 1871 he succumbed. "Not one great sorrow," Mary moaned, "ever approached the agony of this."

She remained in Chicago, an eccentric figure prowling the shops and lamenting her life. In May 1875, Robert, now a respected lawyer, had his mother committed to a private asylum for the insane. She stayed four months before gaining her freedom. For the remaining years of her life, she lived mostly in Europe and in Springfield with her sister Elizabeth Edwards. In 1882, on the anniversary of Tad's death, she died in the Edwards's home of a sudden stroke. History has yet to come to terms with the extravagant and willful, clever and controversial Mrs. President Lincoln. ∎

Tad Lincoln (left) outlived his father by just six years. Only Lincoln's eldest son, Robert, lived to adulthood, serving as Secretary of War for Presidents Garfield and Arthur. In 1883, he accompanied Arthur on a trip to the first national park, Yellowstone, and brought back a leatherbound volume (below, left) with photographs, like that of Shoshone and Arapaho (above), along with a map (below, right).

F. Weisbrod phot.   Frankfurt a/M.

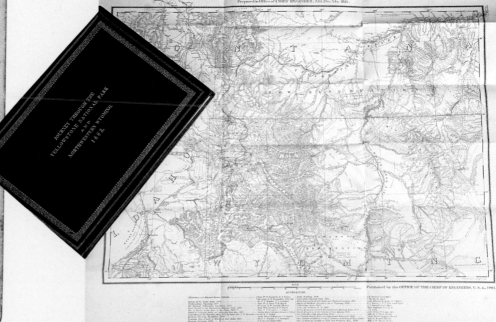

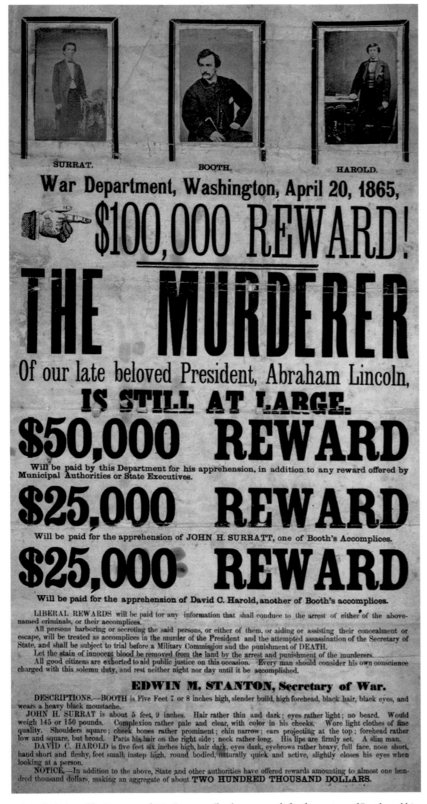

SURRAT. BOOTH. HAROLD.

War Department, Washington, April 20, 1865,

$100,000 REWARD!

THE MURDERER

Of our late beloved President, Abraham Lincoln,

IS STILL AT LARGE.

$50,000 REWARD

Will be paid by this Department for his apprehension, in addition to any reward offered by Municipal Authorities or State Executives.

$25,000 REWARD

Will be paid for the apprehension of JOHN H. SURRATT, one of Booth's Accomplices.

$25,000 REWARD

Will be paid for the apprehension of David C. Harold, another of Booth's accomplices.

LIBERAL REWARDS will be paid for any information that shall conduce to the arrest of either of the above-named criminals, or their accomplices.

All persons harboring or secreting the said persons, or either of them, or aiding or assisting their concealment or escape, will be treated as accomplices in the murder of the President and the attempted assassination of the Secretary of State, and shall be subject to trial before a Military Commission and the punishment of DEATH.

Let the stain of innocent blood be removed from the land by the arrest and punishment of the murderers.

All good citizens are exhorted to aid public justice on this occasion. Every man should consider his own conscience charged with this solemn duty, and rest neither night nor day until it be accomplished.

EDWIN M. STANTON, Secretary of War.

DESCRIPTIONS.—BOOTH is Five Feet 7 or 8 inches high, slender build, high forehead, black hair, black eyes, and wears a heavy black moustache.

JOHN H. SURRAT is about 5 feet, 9 inches. Hair rather thin and dark; eyes rather light; no beard. Would weigh 145 or 150 pounds. Complexion rather pale and clear, with color in his cheeks. Wore light clothes of fine quality. Shoulders square; cheek bones rather prominent; chin narrow; ears projecting at the top; forehead rather low and square, but broad. Parts his hair on the right side; neck rather long. His lips are firmly set. A slim man.

DAVID C. HAROLD is five feet six inches high, hair dark, eyes dark, eyebrows rather heavy, full face, nose short, hand short and fleshy, feet small, instep high, round bodied, naturally quick and active, slightly closes his eyes when looking at a person.

NOTICE.—In addition to the above, State and other authorities have offered rewards amounting to almost one hundred thousand dollars, making an aggregate of about TWO HUNDRED THOUSAND DOLLARS.

A broadside issued by Secretary of War Stanton offers huge rewards for the capture of Booth and his accomplices, John Surratt and David Harold. Booth was shot before he could be brought to justice, but four other conspirators were sentenced by a military court and hanged on July 7, 1865 (opposite).

"but her terrible outbursts awed the boy into silence. Sometimes he would throw his arms around her neck, and exclaim, between his broken sobs, 'Don't cry so, Mamma! Don't cry, or you will make me make me cry, too! You will break my heart.'"

> "ABRAHAM LINCOLN WAS NOT YOURS ONLY—HE WAS OURS … A BROTHER WHOSE GREAT MIND AND FEARLESS CONSCIENCE GUIDED A PEOPLE TO UNION AND COURAGEOUSLY UPROOTED SLAVERY."
>
> CITIZENS OF AN ITALIAN VILLAGE

Far from a day of resurrection, Easter Sunday dawned in bleak despair. In the East Room, construction on the coffin began, but the noise of hammering reminded Mary of Booth's shot and had to be muted.

On Tuesday, some 25,000 people filed past Lincoln's open casket in the East Room, where it lay beneath an 11-foot-high "Temple of Death" designed by Benjamin French, the commissioner of buildings. The President had been dressed in the blue suit he wore for his 1861 Inauguration and his face held an understanding smile. The following day, the funeral in the East Room was open only to invited guests, and 600 of them gathered. Robert sat at the foot of the coffin, Grant at its head. At the same time, services were held nationwide and 25 million people collected to mourn the slain hero. Mary remained upstairs in her bed, as she would for weeks, seeing only family and close friends.

After the funeral, in an elaborate two-hour-long procession down Pennsylvania Avenue, the body was taken by hearse to the Capitol and carried into the Rotunda. Robert and Tad rode in a carriage behind a

The kidskin gloves Lincoln carried in his coat pocket, stained with blood from his wounds.

A satin ribbon with Lincoln's image, one of the countless memorial items sold to commemorate him.

A chair from Ford's Theatre, which closed for more than 100 years after the assassination.

riderless horse, emblematic of the lost commander. The following day Lincoln's body lay in state again in an open casket, as thousands moved past.

Mary, Robert, and their longtime family friend David Davis, Associate Justice of the Supreme Court and executor of the estate, had insisted that Lincoln be laid to rest in Springfield, and plans had been made for a mighty final tribute to the martyred President. At dawn on Friday, his remains were taken to the B & O depot, where two Negro regiments were waiting to pay respects, "all weeping like children at the loss of a father." The bier was placed aboard a nine-car funeral train for the 1,700-mile journey. The route would approximate the one taken four years earlier, when the Lincolns had come to Washington as the young, energetic First Family. Now two coffins, one for the father and one for Willie, were aboard the *Lincoln Special*. Robert Lincoln would accompany them as far as Baltimore, but 300 other dignitaries would continue with the funeral entourage.

Lincoln's photograph had been attached to the engine above the cowcatcher.

The Long Way Home

The first stop was nearby Baltimore, the Union city that had given Lincoln more trouble than any other and the one he had had to circumvent four years earlier, under threat of assassination. Now, in the three hours his open coffin was on view, 10,000 people filed in to say good-bye. From there, the train moved on to even larger crowds in Harrisburg, Pennsylvania.

In Philadelphia on Saturday afternoon, the streets were jammed as the body was transported from the train station to Independence Hall, where Lincoln would again lie in state, this time through the following day, as some 300,000 people waited hours to see him. In the same hall in which his body now lay, Lincoln had declared four years earlier that he "would rather be assassinated on the spot than to surrender" the principle of freedom upon which the Union had been founded.

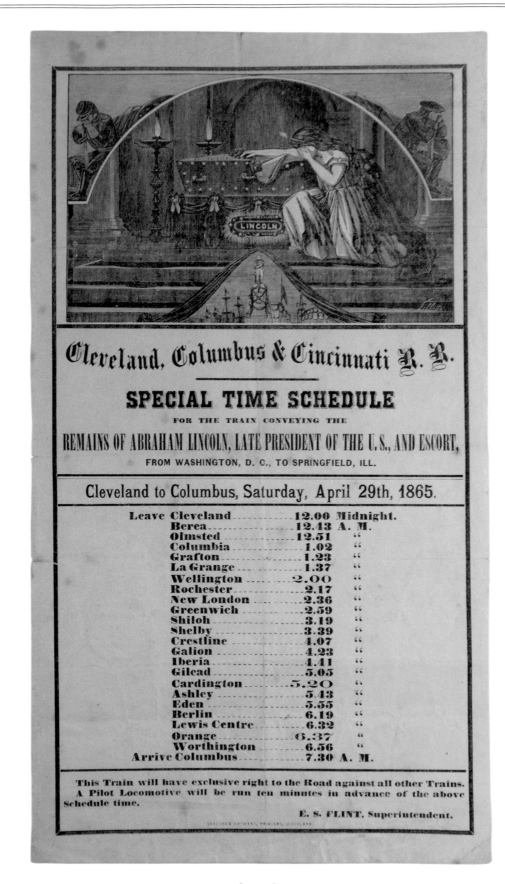

Cleveland, Columbus & Cincinnati R. R.

SPECIAL TIME SCHEDULE

FOR THE TRAIN CONVEYING THE

REMAINS OF ABRAHAM LINCOLN, LATE PRESIDENT OF THE U. S., AND ESCORT,

FROM WASHINGTON, D. C., TO SPRINGFIELD, ILL.

Cleveland to Columbus, Saturday, April 29th, 1865.

Leave Cleveland	12.00 Midnight.
Berea	12.43 A. M.
Olmsted	12.51 "
Columbia	1.02 "
Grafton	1.23 "
La Grange	1.37 "
Wellington	2.00 "
Rochester	2.17 "
New London	2.36 "
Greenwich	2.59 "
Shiloh	3.19 "
Shelby	3.39 "
Crestline	4.07 "
Galion	4.23 "
Iberia	4.41 "
Gilead	5.05 "
Cardington	5.20 "
Ashley	5.43 "
Eden	5.55 "
Berlin	6.19 "
Lewis Centre	6.32 "
Orange	6.37 "
Worthington	6.56 "
Arrive Columbus	7.30 A. M.

This Train will have exclusive right to the Road against all other Trains. A Pilot Locomotive will be run ten minutes in advance of the above Schedule time.

E. S. FLINT, Superintendent.

SANFORD & HAYWARD, PRINTERS, CLEVELAND.

Moving north, the train stopped in Jersey City, and the body was conveyed across the Hudson by ferry, then taken to City Hall. It was now ten days since his death, and the President's face had become sunken. Still, the city turned out to see him, with estimates ranging from 120,000 to half a million. After the viewing had ended, the city honored Lincoln with the largest parade it had ever held. Bizarrely, city officials had refused to allow Blacks to march in it, but at the last minute the police chief overturned the ruling.

From New York City, the *Lincoln Special* continued on to Albany before turning west toward the prairie from which Lincoln had come. In Buffalo, Cleveland, Columbus, and Indianapolis, town fathers planned elaborate pageants, torch lightings, and speechifying to honor the slain leader. In towns through which the train passed, people gathered along the tracks to pay their respects. As one member of the entourage observed, "The thing had become half circus, half heartbreak."

On May 1, the *Lincoln Special* reached the heartland capital, Chicago, and the President's remains were again put on view for many thousands to see. Finally, on May 3, Lincoln came home to Springfield. In his farewell to his fellow townspeople four years before, he had said, "Without the assistance of that Divine Being … I cannot succeed. With that assistance I cannot fail." Recognizing that success had cost him the ultimate price, Springfield made elaborate plans to offer tribute to their neighbor, friend, and local hero. Again the

Timetables listing when the funeral train bearing Lincoln's body would pass through various cities (opposite) were printed for each segment of the 1,700-mile route. The nine-car Lincoln Special *(above) held an image of the slain President on the engine's cowcatcher. A Guard of Honor accompanied the body the entire way, bearing it off and on the train at the ten cities where it stopped for separate funeral processions along the way.*

Lincoln's coffin lying in state at New York's City Hall (opposite). Pages 208-09: Mourners outside Chicago gather at the tracks to watch Lincoln's funeral train pass on the last leg of its journey back to Springfield.

President's body was put on view, this time in the State Capitol House's Representatives Hall, where Lincoln had earlier delivered his celebrated "House Divided" address. The Springfield town fathers had formed the Lincoln Monument Association and, without consulting Mary, had planned to

WORLD PERSPECTIVE

The World Mourns

Lincoln's assassination was not only an American tragedy. The world joined in mourning the Great Emancipator and savior of the republic. In his 1862 address to Congress, Lincoln had declared that America was "the last best hope of earth." With his death, he came to embody that hope.

Mourning was universal. In Chile, people wept in the streets and marched to honor Lincoln, "the incarnation of modern democracy," while Argentina proclaimed three days of mourning.

In England, "the whole people positively mourn," John Bright, a leading British Liberal, reported, "and it would seem as if again we were one nation with you, so universal is the grief." Queen Victoria reacted on a personal level. Having only recently lost her beloved Albert, she wrote a heartfelt note to Mary Lincoln as one widow to another. Albert, she said, had been "the light of my Life my stay my all." With his death, she was "utterly broken-hearted."

In France, expressions of grief surprised even the American minister, John Bigelow. Among them was a memorial medal fund to which 40,000 French citizens contributed. The boxed medal was given to Bigelow, with instructions that he present it to Mrs. Lincoln, with the words "that in this little box is the heart of France."

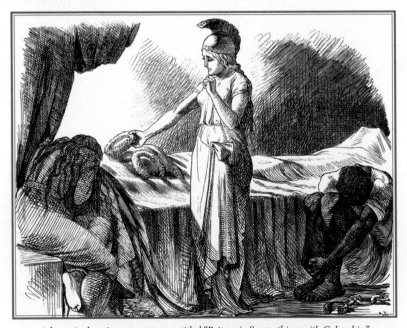

A hauntingly poignant cartoon, entitled "Britannia Sympathises with Columbia," from the popular British magazine Punch *shows a helmeted Britannia laying a wreath on Lincoln's prone form, while two onlookers are bowed with grief.*

> "OH, IF ONLY LINCOLN HAD LIVED! ALAS THAT THE GOOD PRESIDENT IS DEAD! WE HAVE LEARNED TO MEASURE THE GREATNESS OF OUR LOSS BY WHAT HE LEFT BEHIND HIM."
>
> CARL SCHURZ, UNION GENERAL AND STATESMAN

inter Lincoln on a prominent hill in the center of town. Mary strenuously objected and exacted a promise that the tomb monument would be erected in the newly established Oak Ridge Cemetery, and "that no other bodies, save the President, his wife, his sons and sons' families shall ever be deposited within the enclosure."

On May 4, 1865, an unseasonably hot day, thousands followed the funeral procession to Oak Ridge. With final sermons and ceremony, Lincoln's coffin was placed in a temporary tomb and Willie's beside it. Of the family, only Robert and a cousin, John Hanks, were there to say farewell. But an estimated million people had said good-bye to Honest Old Abe on his winding path home.

Walt Whitman, who had been in Washington throughout the war and who had often seen the President in passing, mourned Lincoln deeply and devoted several poems to his death. Whitman echoed the nation's pain in his famous elegy:

"O Captain! my Captain!
   our fearful trip is done;
The ship has weather'd every rack, the prize
   we sought is won …
But O heart! heart! heart!
O the bleeding drops of red,
Where on the deck my Captain lies,
Fallen cold and dead."

AFTERWORD

ABRAHAM LINCOLN "IS A GREAT MAN. GREAT NOT AFTER THE MODELS OF THE WORLD, BUT with homely and original greatness. He will stand out to future ages in the history of these crowded and confused times." Ignatius Donnelly, Lincoln's political opponent, was right. In the years since his death, Lincoln has outgrown the confines of his own confused times to become a universal icon.

The apotheosis of Lincoln began immediately after his death, with Americans raising him to near godlike status. Thousands of books have been written on him—"more than on God," historians like to joke—and yet he remains an enigma, open to each fresh interpretation. Memorials to him have been erected, and his name is attached to streets, cities, buildings, ships, and universities worldwide. On Mount Rushmore, Lincoln's likeness stares out alongside those few other immortal Presidents. And since 1922, his massive form has overlooked the National Mall, a benediction to such historic moments as Martin Luther King, Jr.'s "I have a Dream" speech.

Lincoln's most lasting legacy is no doubt inspiration. This man of the people who saved a nation and ended human bondage has been a beacon to generations of freedom fighters and liberty lovers. Jawaharlal Nehru, who fought for India's independence and became its first prime minister, kept a bronze cast of Lincoln's hand on his desk. "It is a beautiful hand, strong and firm, yet gentle," he explained. "I look at it every day and it gives me strength." Nehru's partner in the fight for independence, Mahatma Gandhi, was also inspired by Lincoln, as was President George W. Bush, British Prime Minister Margaret Thatcher, and South Korean President Roh Moo-hyun, who wrote a book about him. In Cuba, schools and hospitals are named for Lincoln. In Tirana, Albania, the Lincoln Center invokes his principles to create new opportunities in the post-Communist world. And in Tokyo, Meisei University's Lincoln Center is devoted to documents and memorabilia about the 16th President.

Beyond the leaders and the scholars, the "common folk" too take hope from Lincoln—from his tenacity, his self-determination, his courage, even from his failures and weaknesses. They make him seem eminently human, but a human who somehow overcame his own humanness. "His genius is still too strong and too powerful for the common understanding," the great Russian novelist Leo Tolstoy once wrote, and that is still true. To Tolstoy, George Washington "was a typical American. Napoleon was a typical Frenchman, but Lincoln was a humanitarian as broad as the world."

OPPOSITE: *Lincoln's Tomb, dedicated in 1874 in Springfield, Illinois,*

About the Abraham Lincoln Presidential Library and Museum

On April 19, 2005, the Abraham Lincoln Presidential library and Museum joined the select community of institutions celebrating the lives and legacies of America's chief executives. The museum immediately captured the public's attention, attracting over 1.5 million visitors in just three years and generating a wave of positive reviews and visitor recommendations. No doubt, the reason for the museum's initial and ongoing appeal resides with the man at the center of our story. America's 16th President has long held the imagination of people everywhere in ways matched by few other men or women in history.

A story told is not always a story told well, however; it is the unique way the museum and library narrates Mr. Lincoln's story that is at the heart of our institution's popularity. Our exhibitions and educational programs remind the visitor that Lincoln failed several times before he became a self-made success. We show not just the resolute leader of the Civil War years, but also the doting father and the loving—if not always attentive—husband, the circuit-riding lawyer and the astute politician, the awkward suitor and the martyred national leader, the grieving parent and the resolute emancipator. We bring Lincoln down from his pedestal, and yet, in the process, remind visitors just how extraordinary his achievements were. In Springfield, Illinois, Lincoln the icon becomes Lincoln the man.

The museum is interactive in the best sense of the word. The exhibitions so skillfully crafted by BRC Imagination Arts appeal first to the heart. A visitor's journey begins with Lincoln's boyhood in Indiana and ends with the sad return of his body for burial in Illinois. Recreated scenes from his life skillfully intermingle with original artifacts and video and audio elements designed to elicit emotional responses. The showmanship throughout engages visitors' emotions so that we may more effectively also engage their heads. The scholarship is impeccable, based on our library's unmatched collections and research resources as well as the ongoing advice of the nation's best historians and biographers. Ultimately, the experience leaves the audience wanting more. For every question we answer, we hope to spur our visitors to want to learn even more about the life and times of Abraham Lincoln and his continued significance in the evolution of our nation.

Imitation is one of the sincerest forms of flattery. Museum professionals from all over the world regularly travel to the Abraham Lincoln Presidential Library and Museum to learn how we are able to tell Mr. Lincoln's story in such a compelling fashion. There are many reasons for our success, but one stands out above all the rest—Abraham Lincoln himself. There is no more compelling and important historical figure in our nation's history, and, indeed the world; we are fortunate to be charged with the responsibility of sharing his history.

—RICK BEARD
President & CEO
Abraham Lincoln Presidential Library Foundation
www.alplm.org

The Abraham Lincoln Presidential Library and Museum (below) is dedicated to documenting the life of the 16th American President. It contains the largest collection of pre-presidential Lincoln materials in the world.

About the Author

K. M. KOSTYAL has written several books on the Civil War era, including *Stonewall Jackson: A Life Portrait* and *Field of Battle: The Civil War Letters of Major Thomas J. Halsey,* as well as books on topics ranging from world music to Virginia's art and history to explorer Ernest Shackleton. She has spent much of her career as a magazine writer and editor, most recently for National Geographic. She lives in Alexandria, Virginia.

Acknowledgments

As strange as it may seem, I'd first like to acknowledge Abraham Lincoln. It's a well-known syndrome among biographers that they come to dislike their subjects. While I could never call myself a Lincoln biographer, the time I spent researching him for this book left me in awe of the man. Beset with so many obstacles—personal, financial, emotional, and political—he rose to the tasks before him and achieved a greatness that I think would have awed him as well, could he see it now in hindsight.

On a more current note, my deepest thanks to Thomas Schwartz, the Illinois State Historian at the Abraham Lincoln Presidential Library and Museum (ALPLM), for his unswerving patience and guidance throughout the book; to James Cornelius, Curator of the Lincoln Collection at ALPLM, also for lending his guidance and his erudition on the artifacts featured in the book; to Susan Mogerman, consultant to the Abraham Lincoln Presidential Library and Museum Foundation, for her belief in and advocacy of the book; to Robert Mazrim for sharing his deep knowledge of Lincoln's New Salem; and to Mary Ann Pohl and Jennifer Ericson at ALPLM for their assistance in my research.

To my editors, a special note of gratitude for their professionalism and support. Barbara Brownell Grogan's steady editing hand clarified and strengthened the text, and Barbara Levitt's diligence kept the project on track through to the end.

And, as always, to my husband, Buzz, for his ear and encouragement through many long days, nights, and years of writing.

Illustrations Credits

INDEX

Boldface indicates illustrations. *Italic* indicates time line entry.

ABRAHAM LINCOLN'S
EXTRAORDINARY ERA
BY K. M. KOSTYAL

PUBLISHED BY THE NATIONAL GEOGRAPHIC SOCIETY

John M. Fahey, Jr., President and Chief Executive Officer
Gilbert M. Grosvenor, Chairman of the Board
Tim T. Kelly, President, Global Media Group
John Q. Griffin, President, Publishing
Nina D. Hoffman, Executive Vice President;
   President, Book Publishing Group

PREPARED BY THE BOOK DIVISION

Kevin Mulroy, Senior Vice President and Publisher
Leah Bendavid-Val, Director of Photography Publishing
   and Illustrations
Marianne R. Koszorus, Director of Design
Barbara Brownell Grogan, Executive Editor
Elizabeth Newhouse, Director of Travel Publishing
Carl Mehler, Director of Maps

STAFF FOR THIS BOOK

Barbara Levitt, Editor
Dana Chivvis, Adrian Coakley, Illustrations Editors
Carol Farrar Norton, Art Director
Sanaa Akkach, Designer
Richard S. Wain, Production Project Manager
Robert Waymouth, Illustrations Specialist
Jennifer A. Thornton, Managing Editor
R. Gary Colbert, Production Director

Special Contributors: Stephanie Hanlon, Barbara Seeber,
Jane Sunderland, Tiffin Thompson (text)

MANUFACTURING AND QUALITY MANAGEMENT

Christopher A. Liedel, Chief Financial Officer
Phillip L. Schlosser, Vice President
Chris Brown, Technical Director
Nicole Elliott, Manager
Monika D. Lynde, Manager
Rachel Faulise, Manager

Founded in 1888, the National Geographic Society is one of the largest nonprofit scientific and educational organizations in the world. It reaches more than 285 million people worldwide each month through its official journal, *National Geographic,* and its four other magazines; the National Geographic Channel; television documentaries; radio programs; films; books; videos and DVDs; maps; and interactive media. National Geographic has funded more than 8,000 scientific research projects and supports an education program combating geographic illiteracy.

For more information, please call 1-800-NGS LINE (647-5463) or write to the following address:

National Geographic Society
1145 17th Street N.W.
Washington, D.C. 20036-4688 U.S.A.

Visit us online at www.nationalgeographic.com/books

For information about special discounts for bulk purchases, please contact National Geographic Books Special Sales: ngspecsales@ngs.org

For rights or permissions inquiries, please contact National Geographic Books Subsidiary Rights: ngbookrights@ngs.org

Library of Congress Cataloging-in-Publication Data

Kostyal, K. M., 1951-
  Abraham Lincoln's extraordinary era : the man and his times / Karen Kostyal.
    p. cm.
  Includes index.
  ISBN 978-1-4262-0328-2
1. Lincoln, Abraham, 1809-1865. 2. Lincoln, Abraham, 1809-1865--Anniversaries, etc. 3. Lincoln, Abraham, 1809-1865--Miscellanea.
4. Abraham Lincoln Presidential Library and Museum--Archives.
5. Presidents--United States--Biography. 6. Political leadership--United States--History--19th century. 7. United States--Politics and government--1845-1861. 8. United States--Politics and government--1861-1865. 9. World politics--19th century. I. Title.
  E457.K675 2009
  973.7092--dc22
  [B]   2008034796

ISBN: 978-1-4262-0328-2

Printed in U.S.A.